THE DYMAXION WORLD OF
BUCKMINSTER FULLER

THE DYMAXION WORLD OF BUCKMINSTER FULLER

Robert Marks
and
R. Buckminster Fuller

ANCHOR BOOKS
ANCHOR PRESS/DOUBLEDAY
GARDEN CITY, NEW YORK

The *Dymaxion World of Buckminster Fuller* was originally published by Southern
Illinois University Press. This slightly revised Anchor Press edition is published
by arrangement with the Southern Illinois University Press.

ANCHOR BOOKS EDITION: 1973

PREFACE

The form and the language levels of this book are fitted as closely as possible to their subject; and this subject is a protean maverick. Buckminster Fuller sees global economic patterns where others see nothing more than the tracks of migrant birds, and he finds the autograph of the universe wherever paths of energy interlace.

It is a difficult matter to interpret Bucky. He has the genius' constant onrush of dream flow and dream logic. And he is graced with the quality now known, in cybernetic circles, as *positive feedback* — mirror-multiplication of the information communicated. Each thought that Bucky expresses feeds back into his mind, there to generate families of fresher thoughts, broader in scope and more intense.

Bucky has never been easy to understand — even by those best equipped to grasp his meanings, and those who know him best and love him most. The reason is both psychological and semantic. He overloads the channels of communication. He is ever ready to give too much of himself too spontaneously, too richly, and too quickly. The simplest question evokes a torrent of insights. And these he expresses in an incisive, private argot, resplendent with word coinages, hyphenated Latinisms, and tropes.

Although his cardinal ideas have about them the skeletal simplicity we associate with the best Greek thought, they sometimes come through to the casual listener as a cascade of ambiguities. And this only because there is too much. You would not expect to take in the first six books of Euclid at a single hearing, nor without a reduction of text language to conversational level. Yet with Bucky, the equivalent of this technical richness is offered untranslated, at each meeting. His conversation, thus, is always a subtle form of flattery. It implies that he believes you are at ease in all the areas of his talk, and that you can with equal agility go "second powering," "tetrahedroning," "inwardly-outwardly-to-and-froing," or go bouncing on a four-dimensional pogo stick down the slopes of Parnassus.

This book reflects my impressions and interpretations of Bucky's life and work, and my deep affection for him — after almost 18 years of close friendship. And it is my view, biased perhaps by personal warmth, but tempered by hundreds of hours of hard talk, that there is no man in America today who makes as much sense in such a fundamental way.

R.W.M.

New York City

Buckminster Fuller — you are the most sensible man in New York, truly
sensitive. Nature gave you antennae, long-range finders you have
learned to use. I find almost all your prognosticating nearly right —
much of it dead right, and I love you for the way you prognosticate. To
address you directly will be a hell of a way of reviewing your book — I
know. I should write all around you, take you apart, and put you
together again to show — between the lines — how much bigger my own
mind is than yours and how much smarter than you I can be with it
and leave the essence of your thought untouched.

But I couldn't do it if I would and I wouldn't if I could. To say
that you have now a good style of your own in saying very important
things is only admitting something unexpected. To say you are the
most sensible man in New York isn't saying much for you — in that
pack of caged fools. And everybody who knows you knows you are
extraordinarily sensitive. . . .

Faithfully, your admirer and friend, more power to you — you
valuable 'unit.'

FRANK LLOYD WRIGHT

Taliesen
Spring Green, Wisconsin,
August 8th, 1938.

Excerpt from a review by Wright of Fuller's book, *Nine Chains to the Moon*
(Lippincott, 1938). The passage quoted was published in the *Saturday*
Review of Literature, September 17, 1938.

CONTENTS

THE DYMAXION WORLD OF BUCKMINSTER FULLER

1 *R. Buckminster Fuller*

FULLER—THE MAN
AND HIS PHILOSOPHY

To people who are sensitive to the freshness of ideas and the pressure of mental designs, Buckminster Fuller is one of the most significant men of our time. To others he is alternately frightening and incomprehensible. To almost everyone he is puzzling.

Within a span of forty years Fuller has made front-page news as an architect, engineer, inventor-designer, cartographer, and mathematician. Yet he is none of these by profession. He is a maverick with a genius for seeing the world as something more than the sum of its isolated parts.

"I did not set out to design a house that hung from a pole," he once said, "or to manufacture a new type of automobile, invent a new system of map projection, develop geodesic domes or Energetic Geometry. I started with the Universe — as an organization of regenerative principles frequently manifest as energy systems of which all our experiences, and possible experiences, are only local instances. I could have ended up with a pair of flying slippers.

This statement, a good example of Fuller's verbal shorthand, requires interpretation. It is a credo. It is an assertion, in the tradition of Pythagoras and Newton, that the universe as a whole displays certain signs of orderliness — recognizable patterns of energy relationships. These patterns can be transformed into usable forms. "Valving" is

Fuller's special term for the transformation. "Valving," he holds, "embraces the concept of generalized design whose ultimate properties are determined only by frequency and angular modulations."

Another term which recurs with hydra-headed persistency in Fuller's private linguistic world is "regenerative." The dictionary meaning of this word, more or less, is having the ability to be born again, to reproduce, or to generate anew. In Fuller's special argot, however, "regenerative" means "multiorbital, cyclic, precessionally concentric" — a definition which itself requires definition. By it he means the ability to display one form, then another, in a gamut of phases; each phase, however, like a tree ring, or a wave generated by a stone thrown into water, has its own orbit; and the various orbits progress outward or inward in concentric circles or shells. A seed is regenerative. A crystal is regenerative. Energy itself is an ever-generative patterning entity. Its forms are protean. It can appear as the breath of a hawk or coign of a cliff. It can cloak itself as radiation, as mass, as design, and as the wellspring of work. And since by fundamental law, energy can be neither created nor destroyed, its fate in the cosmic scheme is to meander through eternity in persistent, regenerative bliss.

To Fuller, what matters fundamentally with regard to both scientific method and social usefulness, is the total physico-economic picture, the Gestalt of nature — the patterns that are inherently comprehensive and universal, in contradistinction to what is local. Specific parts of a pattern, the local designs, can be derived from the general design, the comprehensive scheme. The reverse, however, is not true; in nature, society, and industrial complexes, wholes express more than the simple effect resulting from the sum of their respective parts. Fuller refers to the integrated behavior patterns as synergy, which he defines as "the behavior of a whole system unpredicted by the behavior of its components — or any subassembly of its components."

An illustration of the synergetic effect is the behavior of metallic alloys. The physical properties of several metals in combination is not implied by the properties they exhibit in isolation. A typical case is the tensile strength of chrome nickel steel. The tensile strength of chrome alone is approximately 70,000 pounds per square inch. Nickel has a tensile strength of some 80,000, iron of 60,000. The sum of their strengths is 210,000. But the actual strength of the three alloyed together is in the order of 300,000 pounds per square inch which is six times as strong as the alloy's weakest link, four times the strength of its strongest link.

Yet from general formulations, particular instances can be derived. This explains, to some extent, Fuller's approach to the existing geodesic domes. He regards no single dome of any generic importance; each is to him no more than a local application of a comprehensive system which he calls *Energetic Geometry*. This geometry is the separating out of individual cases from a comprehensive pattern. The geometry develops mathematical statements for what he calls, "the most economical relationships of points in universe and their transformation tendencies." These statements determine the stress patterns of all geodesic domes.

A comparison can be made with the Einstein equation relating energy to mass. No specifications are given for the preparation of an atomic fission reaction; but from the equation a host of conclusions can be drawn — derived data which tell very simply how much usable energy can be extracted from substance of a given mass. The general statement, in short, covers all specific instances.

In times past, most pure scientists confined themselves to the physical world and its system of exact relations. Pythagoras, despite his wanderings in mysticism, was essentially a mathematician; Newton and Einstein were mathematicians; Copernicus was an astronomer; Max Planck, a physicist. Fuller departs from this tradition in that he is equally concerned with exact and social science. He is passionately concerned with a comprehensive view of nature — of the physical world as a patterning of patternings (his term is "macro–micro–oscillocosm") whose constituent functions are fields of force, each of which compenetrates and influences other localized fields of force. But his concern is also social; it asks the persistent question: How can an expanding technology maximize the benefits to be derived from the knowledge and possible control of the energies in nature? How, in fact, can we as knowledgeable as well as social beings maximize our technological advantages?

This is the essence of Fuller's world view. It is a concern that joins the several seemingly unrelated areas in which he has worked over the past four decades.

Another dimension of this Weltanschauung is expressed by the term *Dymaxion*, a label Fuller has used to qualify the implication of his various inventions, developments, and projected ideas. This distinctive Fuller trade-mark has a function which lies somewhere between Occam's Razor — the principle which asserts that assumptions should not be multiplied unnecessarily — and de Maupertuis' so-called principle of least effort. In its simplest form, Fuller's Dymaxion concept is that rational action in a rational world, in every social and industrial operation, demands the most efficient over-all performance per units of input. A Dymaxion structure, thus, would be one whose performance yielded the greatest possible efficiency in terms of the available technology.

Yet there is another field in which Fuller follows a great tradition: the field of method. The spread of Fuller's creative work is a direct consequence of his special method of thinking.

At a time of crisis in his life Fuller set himself, like Descartes in his Dutch stove-heated compartment, to survey the whole of the human dilemma — all the obstacles that stood in the way of man's survival and in the way of man's potential development. His philosophical starting point was the totality of possible events — "universe," as he called it, defining it in terms of the way it impinges on the human mind. "Universe," Fuller held, "is the aggregate of all men's consciously apprehended and communicated experiences." The communication can be directed inward as self-communication; it can be passed on to others as social wealth. But "universe" as a whole is a concept as difficult to handle as Hegel's Absolute. Our minds can grasp what we regard as "things" and qualities of "thingness" — what Fuller prefers to call "event constellations and pattern characteristics of constellations." These are individual experiences. Their reality is guaranteed by the data of our senses.

The universe as a whole escapes us. Yet it is a necessary conclusion that if a finite number of events or experiences exist individually, they also exist collectively.

Fuller regards wholeness as a collection of events. The universe, as "the aggregate of all men's experience," is such a collection. It can be compared to an encyclopedia. We can accredit the collective integrity of an encyclopedia, although we are not able to consider all of its entries simultaneously. The universe, as Fuller envisions it, presents a spread of events that cannot be grasped simultaneously; nevertheless these events are integral parts of a functioning whole, and they were in existence prior to any of our individual acts of investigating, or sorting out, specific parts. Physical science has established that the physical universe is entirely energetic; and the first law of thermodynamics — the law of conservation of energy — attests that energy can neither be created nor lost. It follows that the totality of energy is finite.

External to this law, however, are experienced phenomena that are other than physico-energetic. These are the infinite spreads of metaphysical phenomena — the limbo of psychological events.

Fuller's definition of "universe" is an attempt to treat *all* experience as finite. In his wording: "It brings the heretofore metaphysically bush-leagued scientific activity into full membership of inherently potential accountability as integral functions of the finite whole."

The latter statement requires interpretation. Fuller regards all human experiences as energy events finite in extent. All experiments performed, books written, thoughts expressed, and structures completed, are finite energy events. Together they form a totality, a cornucopia of patterned quanta. His approach makes experience as finite as any other energy phenomenon, and encompasses, he feels, both Eddington's definition of *science* ("the attempt to set in order the facts of experience"), and Mach's definition of *physics* ("the attempt to arrange experience in the most economical order"). Fuller views his definition as operationally justified, and refers to it, at times, as "the law of conservation of experience."

The scientific and philosophical explorations Fuller undertook, in terms of this definition, were what he calls, "a natural, logical search for orderly patterning processes of complex-complementary, self-transforming, inter-self-multiplication-and-division, inter-disassociations and associations, their minimum-maximum degrees of inherent freedoms of actions, and the relative frequencies and over-all lags of such inherent event patterning."

In effect, he attempted the progressive subdivision of "universe" into a generalized mathematical schema, whose end product is a strategy of evolution radically opposed to Darwinism.

Fuller makes cumulative experience a pivotal factor in change. Experience is finite; it can be stored, studied, directed; it can be turned, with conscious effort, to human advantage. Darwinian evolution is assumed to be operative in ways independent of individual will and design. Darwinism posits chance adaptation to survival; Fuller's approach pivots on the conscious, selective use of cumulative human experience.

The progressive expansion of this idea, augmented by his "finite accounting logic," led Fuller to postulate a comprehensive, global economic strategy whose sole concerns are the advantages that can be directed toward man's survival and growth. The energy and "universe" assumptions led Fuller to an ultimate philosophy of industrialization "which,"

he maintains, "permits and implements man's conscious, though limited, participation in his own evolutionary patterning transformation."

In this Fuller can be considered to have out-Marxed Marxism. Karl Marx proposed a way of bettering society as a consequence of political change. Fuller regards politics as an outmoded activity — a naive attempt to achieve through games of words what must ultimately be derived from technology. More lives can be saved by antibiotics than by acts of Congress; more shelter can be had from alloys and polymers than from social legislation. No matter how beneficent in spirit a legislative act may be, it is useless in fact unless it is underpinned by the technology adequate to its aim. The assumption which follows is that if you possess six fish, a way can be found to divide them among five people; the difficult thing is to provide dividends from no fish.

Fuller conceives of real wealth as the total organized capacity of society to deal with "forward event controlling," that is, with future contingencies. His estimate of existing wealth, at any given moment, would consist of a specifically quantitative rating of the technological level of production and supply then in effect, the point of reference being the number of human beings who could continue to survive x number of days without dependence on additional research or addition to the existing inventory of tools and facilities. He holds that when Adam and Eve sojourned in the Garden they owned no wealth whatever. Yet had they picked even ten "forward days'" supply of fruit, wealth would have accrued. It is what man adds to the "Garden" that determines his wealth. The transforming factors are work and ingenuity; both are functions of energy.

Real wealth to Fuller is thus nothing more than the extent to which man, at a given moment, has harnessed forms of universal energy and, in the process, has developed a re-employable experience. Since energy can be neither created nor destroyed, Fuller's primary wealth constituent is non-depletable. The other constituent, re-employable experience, is augmented each time it is brought into play. Experience can only grow; like time, its quantity cannot be diminished. It follows that wealth, thus conceived, increases only and always with use. It is not derived from money; money is derived from wealth. Fuller observes, ironically, that although there is only some 40 billion-dollars' worth of gold in the entire world, three trillion dollars of real wealth have been invested, during the last half century, in the development of the airplane alone. The harnessing factor — the activity which "valves" the mass-energy of the universe to human advantage — is inventive wisdom born of intuition and experience and put to use in a global industrial complex.

Wealth is now without practical limit; all its constituents are inexhaustible, and all are on inventory, available for development and exploitation. "Science has hooked up the everyday economic plumbing to the cosmic reservoir." This was a philosophical point Fuller raised, in 1958, at a meeting with Nehru, in India. Man's survival is a technological, not a political problem. Abundance is a function of production, not protocol; and man's chances of transforming a disease-ridden, famine-threatened society into a realm of orchestrated abundance depend on his ability to set in order the facts of his experience. Such an order requires a "comprehensive, anticipatory design science."

Perhaps dedication to this cardinal idea, a *comprehensive, anticipatory design science*, is the clue to Fuller's anomalous position in the professional world. Established men tend to be suspicious of men without establishment. It is apparently a human urge to classify and label. The maverick is suspect. And Fuller, as was noted, fits no standard classification; he is identified by no familiar label. This may be partially explained by the fact that all his later years and thought have been a dedicated quest for all that is implied by the phrase, "a comprehensive, anticipatory design science." And we have as yet in society no professional category that admits a quest so all-embracing.

To sidestep the difficulty, he sometimes refers to himself as a machinist (he is a card-carrying member of the International Association of Machinists), or as a sailor (he holds the "confirmed" rank of Lieutenant U.S.N. [Resigned], with life tenure in Class 1, Fleet Reserve). Both identifications are to his liking; both, he feels, are marks of craft and competence with reference to the essential human experiences: survival, fabrication with tools, and the turning of hazards into advantages.

For years functioning engineers and key-name industrialists looked at him with friendly but condescending eyes, often putting him down as an amiable lunatic whose ideas were always stimulating and frequently good for a laughable quote. *Fortune*, in 1946, lampooned him as "a chunky, powerful little man with a build like a milk bottle, a mind that functions like a cross between a roller-top desk and a jet engine, and with one simple aim in life: to remake the world." *Time*, ten years earlier, spoke of him more charitably, as an industrial prophet noted for "arriving incoherently at logical conclusions."

Although in times past many automobile, aviation, and construction officials were proud to claim his friendship, and architects, including Frank Lloyd Wright, sometimes consulted him on technical problems, only off-beat mathematicians and mavericks sensed the seriousness and the scope of his ideas. Today Fuller holds four honorary doctorates and has lectured at most of the leading universities of the world; but in the late twenties he was heard only at off-campus college meetings and in the dim rooms where idea people develop abstractions about other abstractions. Yet even then he seldom failed to influence those who heard him; his ideas seemed always to generate conclusions which were fresh and unexpected, which had the "synergetic" quality — an intellectual singing in the sails that was more than the wind.

His economic and scientific ideas were served up as jig-saw picture fragments. Those who saw only the unarranged pieces regarded Fuller as a man dabbling in philosophical Dada. But the pieces invariably fitted together. And when assembled, they made a clear picture, with implications few observers were in a position to grasp. A case in point is Fuller's interpretation of the revolutionary world economic effects which would ultimately result from an application of Einstein's relativity theory and the formula relating energy to mass. In a book, *Nine Chains to the Moon*, written in 1935 and published by J. B. Lippincott in 1938, he devoted three chapters to Einstein, the last of which was called "E $= MC^2 =$ Mrs. Murphy's Horsepower."

Fuller argued that theory induces experiment and experiments pace science; science paces technology; technology paces industry; industry paces economics, and economics paces the everyday world. Consequently, the measurements of the speed of light and the new knowledge of energy — which together gave rise to Einstein's new theories of the universe — must, in due course, "catalyze a chain reaction ultimately altering altogether the patterning of man's everyday world."

"This stupendous fact seems apparent," he wrote. "Newton's static norm must be replaced by Einstein's dynamic norm — always operative at the speed of light. *No change*, the norm of economic conservatives, must give way. The new turn of events will force the conservative — albeit unwillingly — to adopt *constantly accelerating change* as his economic norm."

When his publishers read the book in manuscript form, they were dismayed by Fuller's presumption. To them, Einstein was Jovian and sacrosanct. His habitat was the upper reaches of rarified air — particularly that part of the atmosphere which hovered over Europe — and his work so esoteric that its significance was grasped only by twelve legendary, but qualified, European scientists. Who was Fuller to rush in and link the great man and Mrs. Murphy?

To his publishers' assertion that he had overreached himself, Fuller had a simple answer: "Why not send the typescript to Dr. Einstein and see what he says?"

The full book was posted to Princeton.

On a momentous day, three months later, Einstein came to New York from Princeton, the typescript under his arm, and arranged to see Fuller.

"I have read your interesting book," Einstein said, without ceremony. "Regarding the three chapters treating with me, the first on my philosophy, the second on my energy equation formulation — these are satisfactory to me. But, young man, regarding myself and Mrs. Murphy, you amaze me. I cannot conceive of anything I have ever done as having the slightest practical application. I have propounded my theories only for the consideration of cosmogonists and astrophysicists in their broad accounting of an energy universe."

Three years after this, Otto Hahn and his co-workers at the Kaiser Wilhelm Institute in Berlin discovered the possibility of splitting the uranium atom. And within a few years it was Einstein himself who communicated to President Franklin D. Roosevelt the awesome potential of fission. What followed was the Manhattan Project, whose developments yielded the atomic bomb — violent physical proof of the objective reality of an abstract theory.

"Einstein's out-of-this-world hypothesis," according to Fuller, "became the most momentous application of abstract theory in all history. The hypothetical equation, E equals mc², proved to be the generalized accounting of the local energies on inventory in the masses of all elements — everywhere."

He maintains that the pre-World-War-I conservatives who shuddered at a U. S. national debt of some two billion dollars ($1,191,000,000 in 1915), and considered this figure an indication of carelessness in avoiling uneconomic changes, forty-odd years later grudgingly rocketed the national debt to almost 300 billion ($276,343,000,000 in 1958). In the late 1950's, the annual debt increased at the rate of 40–50 billion a year, a progressive increment forced by the "cold war" — which, in turn, was the outcome of an acceleration in the revolutionary transformation of world technology. The question, "Who is loony now?" Fuller holds, used to mean, "Who is crazy?"

In the new accounting, Fuller holds, the question, "Who is looney now?" means "Who are the sanest, strongest men to whom the multi-billion dollar moon-shoot contracts should be awarded?"

Lecturing to a group of students at Massachusetts Institute of Technology, Fuller once outlined the scope of Energetic Geometry — showing how the basic energy patterns in nature could be expressed by families of geometric "solids" whose common metric is the tetrahedron (four-faced pyramid). On that occasion, John Ely Burchard, vice-president of M.I.T., introducing Fuller to the students, said with great solemnity, "I refrain from calling Mr. Fuller a genius because this is a term we usually reserve for foreigners."

When the lecture was repeated before a mathematics class at Columbia, Edward Kasner, who was then professor of mathematics at the university, made a single laconic comment. "My only regret about tonight," he said, "is that Euclid and Pythagoras could not have been here."

In 1934, the novelist, Christopher Morley, who had become one of Fuller's closest friends, published these words on the dedication page of his book, *Streamlines*: "For Buckminster Fuller, scientific idealist, whose innovations proceed not just from technical dexterity, but from an organic vision of life."

In reviewing such appreciation, it is not easy to account for the length of time it took for Fuller's essential ideas to gain even the semblance of public acceptance. Over a forty-year period most of his proposals, inventions, discoveries, and developments have been hailed and then shelved — so much so that almost each new creation, even those having immediate use-value, was greeted in the politer journals with a thunderous *ave atque vale*. Always there was simultaneous acclaim and dismissal. The industrial world, happy to pick up the phraseology of Madison Avenue, called him "failure prone."

Yet to Fuller there were no "failures." He was not in business. A "failure," to him, was a word invented for purposes of business accounting. Working theories, made in advance of experiment, may fail, but nature never fails. The principles of physics are integrities; they are observed regularities within a system. And all of his experiments had dealt with these regularities, these existing patternings of forces and stresses. All his models met the pragmatic test; they worked. His early Dymaxion house, his Dymaxion cars, his die-stamped bathroom, his Dymaxion map, his first Geodesic domes, were what he called "reductions to practice"; they were experimentally proven and industrially reproducible prototypes of desirable and possible constructions.

But until 1955–1956 — when industry and the Armed Services could no longer ignore the enormous technological advantages of Fuller's structures — the straight run of practical people continued to regard Fuller as a professional visionary and observed that nothing much ever seemed to have come from his prototypes. Why, they asked, did he never really exploit his successfully-demonstrated inventions and his pilot models? Why, instead of taking a solid job in industry, was he content to drag along on an income of $4,000 a year or less, and waste all his "technically accredited advantage" — the phrase is Fuller's — talking like Socrates in the market place?

But what few could realize was that Fuller's energies and discipline were centered in a single drive: to promote *the total use of total technology for total population* "at the maximum feasible rate of acceleration."

2 *Model of 10-deck 4D house with shield*

NONCONFORMITY AND
NEW ENGLAND CONSCIENCE

Fuller is temperamentally as well as intellectually a nonconformist, although he would maintain, perhaps soundly, that his apparent revolts are genuine conformities — but to broader patterns than those standardized in schools, politics, and industry. It would never occur to him to criticize the law of gravity, or to assume that the angles of a Euclidean triangle added up to more or less than 180°. But the world into which he was born appeared to him to lack this logical validity. And in such a world, like Robin Hood, his childhood hero, he has been traditionally against the impracticality of shortsighted, "practical" tradition.

An exception, perhaps, is his feeling about his ancestry. For many generations his ancestors were New England nonconformists, so much so that within the Fuller family it is conformity itself which is nonconformist.

Fuller's great, great, great, great grandfather, Lt. Thomas Fuller of the British Navy, was born on the Isle of Wight and, in 1630, came to this country on a furlough, his curiosity piqued by the Puritan excitement. In New England he was infected by the freedom fever; and there he remained. His grandson, the Rev. Timothy Fuller, Harvard Class of 1760, was a Massachusetts delegate to the Federal Constitutional Assembly. He refused to vote for ratification because the drafted Constitution did not prohibit slavery, as he felt it should.

His son, the Hon. Timothy, born in 1778, was a founder of Harvard's Hasty Pudding Club. As a penalty for his part in a student revolt, he was graduated second, instead of first, in the Harvard class of 1801.

Fuller's grandfather, the Rev. Arthur Buckminster Fuller, Harvard, Class of 1840, was an ardent abolitionist. Although he was minister of the First Unitarian Church of Boston and Chaplain of the Fifth Massachusetts Regiment, in the Civil War he led a successful Union charge across the bridge of boats at Fredricksburg, Virginia, and in this combat was shot dead. Fuller's father, Richard Buckminster Fuller, Sr., Harvard, Class of 1883, was a Boston merchant-importer, the only Fuller in eight generations who had not been either minister or lawyer.

His great-aunt, Margaret Fuller, was the famous feminist, author, editor, and conversationalist, sometimes listed in histories as the "high priestess of Transcendentalism." She was a pioneer champion of women's rights. She was a friend of Emerson's, and with him founded *The Dial*, the literary journal she edited, and which first published the work of Emerson and Thoreau. When Horace Greeley established the *New York Tribune*, she became the *Tribune's* literary editor. Her column, always centrally positioned on the paper's first page, was a catalytic American force. In it, Margaret Fuller consistently disparaged the tendency of

Americans to imitate European creative styles; she championed genius of expression wherever it was to be found. Always an individualist, she stood aloof from the cooperative social experiment of her friend, Bronson Alcott, the community organization known as Brook Farm. "Why bind oneself to a doctrine?" she asked. "A man should stand unpledged, unbound."

Richard Buckminster Fuller, Jr., was born in Milton, Mass., in 1895. He went to public school in Milton, later to Milton Academy. Ultimately he was enrolled at Harvard, representing the fifth generation of Fullers, in direct father-to-son line, to be listed in the college's rosters.

He learned at an early age that the teachers lacked satisfactory answers to all the questions he had to ask. One day, for example, the geometry teacher attempted to explain the basic definitions. She put a point on the blackboard, then rubbed it out. "A point," she said, "does not exist — it has no dimensions." She then drew a line. "A line," she continued, "is made up of points but there are no lines." Bucky looked at her wide-eyed as she defined a plane in terms of parallel lines. His eyes opened wider when she announced that no planes exist. The final blow was her presentation of the cube. "A cube," she said, "is a solid stack of square planes whose edges are equal."

"I have some questions," Fuller said, raising his hand. "How long has the cube been there? How long is it going to be there? How much does it weigh? And what is its temperature?"

For a short space Fuller was at Harvard. In the middle of his freshman year, when time came for the mid-year exam, he felt he had enough. He cut his exams, took a train to New York, looked up a girl he knew in the chorus of the current show at the Winter Garden. He also looked at the chorus line from backstage. Then with the gesture of a suave boulevardier

he said, "I would like all of you to be my guests for dinner."

He entertained lavishly at Churchill's, then one of New York's most fashionable and expensive restaurants. When the waiter presented the check, which ran into bankers' figures, Fuller signed his name with a grand flourish and said, authoritatively, "Charge this to my family's account."

When Fuller returner to Cambridge, he found that his presence at the university was somewhat less than *grata*. The following week the Fuller family made arrangements to have Bucky work as an apprentice millwright in a cotton mill at Sherbrooke, Quebec.

Bucky was contrite. He plunged deep into the world of machines and mechanics, studied well, taking what he called "a self-tutored course of engineering exploration." He emerged an enthusiastic technician.

The following year, 1914, an appeased family succeeded in having him re-admitted to Harvard. But Fuller was still an unregenerate anti-academician. After a short period he was again dismissed, this time for what was called "continued irresponsibility and lack of interest in the formal curriculum of the college." He then went to work for Armour and Company in New York, starting as a meat lugger. In two years he had become an assistant cashier. Meanwhile World War I had begun. Fuller made several attempts to enlist in the Army and was rejected because of his eyesight. In 1917, however, he found the Navy less critical; he was accepted and immediately assigned to active service. A few months later he married Anne Hewlett, the eldest daughter of James Monroe Hewlett, a well-known architect and mural painter, later a director of the American Academy at Rome.

The Navy years for Fuller were both strenuous and pivotal. They gave him a first-hand experience with problems of survival, with the uncompromising terms of the sea, the cold, and the wind; they gave him a glimpse of the technology required to keep men alive in the face of a hostile environment. The dangers, in turn, provided a challenge to his ingenuity. His first action was as commander of a crash-boat flotilla; and while on this assignment he was witness to deaths which occurred to seaplane pilots when the planes, coming in for a landing at sea, porpoised and tripped over their own pontoons, pinning the belted-in pilot, head downward, to drown. Fuller's first invention to see service was a combination mast, boom and grappling gear which, installed on his crash boats, made lightning rescue possible. Seaplanes were hoisted from the sea while their pilots were still alive.

As a reward for this contribution to the service's technology, Fuller was given a special appointment to the U. S. Naval Academy at Annapolis, where he continued his limited formal education.

Fuller found no resistance in his mind to Naval studies for the simple reason that to him ships and shipping were in direct contact with realities. A ship at sea does not survive unless it is designed to meet forces as they are; and the study of these forces was to Fuller a discipline that justified itself. ("Every ship designer knows what it means to shunt winds, tides, tension and compression to human advantage.")

When the war ended, Fuller returned to Armour and Company as assistant export manager (1919–1922). There was a brief stint as national account sales manager of the Kelley-Springfield Truck Company, which went out of business. Then, still in 1922, Fuller, with his father-in-law, James Monroe Hewlett, founded the Stockade Building System, a company manufacturing a new fibrous building block formed from a material later ac-

quired by the Celotex Company and manufactured by them as Soundex, a flat-packed fibrous acoustical wall material. Fuller's Stockade organization eventually operated five factories and constructed 240 buildings. The walls of the Field Building at the University of Illinois are made of Fuller's blocks.

"That was when I really learned the building business," he claims. "And the experience made me realize that craft building — in which each house is a pilot model for a design which never has any runs — is an art which belongs in the middle ages. The decisions in craft-built undertakings are for the most part emotional — and are based on methodical ignorance."

In 1922, the year the company was started, Fuller's first daughter, Alexandra, died at the age of four — after suffering in sequence influenza, polio, and spinal meningitis, illnesses which were epidemic during the war. Her death brought on a crisis in Fuller's life. He sank into a depression. He lost all taste for ordinary living, all interest in ordinary values. It seemed to him then, as today, that money cannot buy anything of basic importance, and that conventional success has no meaning except as a sop to vanity.

In time, however, he lost control of the management of the company. Fuller had been a minority stockholder; when Hewlett, faced with financial problems, in 1927, found it necessary to sell his stock, the buyers set up a new management. "Mr. Fuller," the management said, "we find your services no longer essential." The same year, Allegra, a second daughter, was born.

Fuller was stranded in Chicago, without income, dismayed, confused. His illusions about the logic and reasonableness of business operations were dispelled; the business men he had dealt with seemed unconcerned about the values he regarded as fundamental. "I was dismayed at the corruptibility and contradiction of the complex dogma that I had coped with," he said, "under the inspiration that a better construction system would, if industrially developed and demonstrated, thereby induce a spontaneous and simple acceptance. But what I had learned was that the advantages are dissipated in a multitude of windmill battles with contiguous inertias, ignorance, and irrelevant ambitions." He decided, however, to make a final effort to hold his ground in both place and principle. He moved with his wife and new baby to a cheap, Northwest Side Chicago tenement.

It is characteristic of Fuller, when in distress, to focus critically on his own behavior patterns, rather than on the behavior of others. To blame others for difficulties or for failures, no matter how much the blame may seem to be warranted by fact, he regards as a dissipation of creative and critical activity, a negative gesture. His own ways could be analyzed, amended, redirected; the ways of others were constants given by the environment; over these he had no direct control. In this 1927 moment he was overwhelmed by what he considered his "manifold ineptitudes." He had been blindly enthusiastic in his special credo; he had been naive in his assumption that his business associates were also shareholders in his dedication. "I looked in dismay," he said, "at my pattern of vulnerability. I had not been vicious; yet, even to myself, I appeared, in retrospect, a black, horrendous mess. I had wanted to give, not take, but I seemed to have converted the opportunities to give into negative waste."

In the tenement district where the Fullers now lived their next door neighbor was an Al Capone trigger man. When Mrs. Fuller carried trash to the incinerator, he gallantly assisted with the load, guns ever bristling from his armpit holsters. The environment symbolized Fuller's mood. This was a lower depths period; the surroundings were in harmony with desperation. Fuller weighed the thought of sending his wife and child back to New York to stay with his or her family. If he did this, he could quietly do away with himself. He felt himself close to suicide. He concluded, finally, that there was only one reason not to. "Bucky," he said to himself, "you've had many more industrial, scientific and social experiences than most of your steadier contemporaries. And if these experiences are put in order, they might be of use to others. Through them you might be able to discern and design environment controlling mechanics and structures that would provide spontaneously travelled bridges for mankind, which completely span the canyons of pain into which you have gropingly fallen. Whether you care to be or not, you are the custodian of a vital resource."

Yet Fuller was aware that ideas and conclusions have no social importance unless they are transformed into tangible entities. "I realize then," he said, "that if I were going to turn these experiences to account I must utilize them. They had to be organized, translated into forms people could see, feel, operate, and understand; they had to be realized technically. And the translation was for me a mortal affair."

CRYSTALLIZATION
OF AN IDEA:
4D BECOMES DYMAXION

Perhaps the most significant element in biography is the study of crises. These are the existential moments when a man's world falls away from him, and he is left with nothing but the agonizing environment which is himself. William James at such a moment made the reassuring discovery that the one process in the universe over which he had a slight measure of control was his own thoughts, and that by giving them direction he could, in some sense, reconstruct his world. Fuller, in his moment of crisis, also turned his mind inward. He made an inventory of his values, his equipment, the goals which were obtainable, procedures which were available.

His justification to himself for continuing to exist — the rationalization of his plight — was that he had no moral right to destroy the techno-economic resources which were contained in his personal experience; these resources belonged to society. This position was then, and is

now, a special Fuller Categorical Imperative, a universal statement of an ethical position. But to translate this into practical action was clearly another matter. The translation called for comprehensive analysis, unique methodology, and rigid self-discipline.

Toward these ends, Fuller made a hard contract with himself. He agreed to dedicate himself to a persistent search for the all-over social design factors—principles that could make possible the quantum jumps to human betterment—and to make this search his cardinal concern. He looked on himself as a development and holding company for the insights that belonged properly to society itself — including the billions of persons still improperly privileged and inadequately sheltered.

In his inventory of the factors relating to what he called the potential human emergence from general disadvantage to general advantage over physical environment, he found that the problem demand-

15

ing the highest immediate priority — and the one with which he was best equipped to deal — was that of shelter.

He developed, first, a concept of major and minor ecological patterning, that is, regularities in the relations of organisms to their physical environment. For example, birds' seasonal, world-sweeping migrations represented to Fuller a major ecological patterning; birds' nest-building and "local regenerative to-and-fro-ing," he regarded as the related minor ecological patterning. He drew parallels with the human situation, developing a concept of major and minor ecological controls in the economic life of homo sapiens. Here the world's industrial network emerged as the major control. The minor, or local, ecological control was shelter. With his usual comprehensiveness, however, Fuller conceived of shelter as virtually everything which gave man a local technical advantage in his struggle against the elements. It included not only a house, but the utilities which tended to make a house autonomous and the transportation which shuttled a man between his place of work and his place of physiological renovation.

It was then a logical necessity for him to make the jump from shelter to the constituent parts of the universe — and from these to the mathematical relations which maintain the parts in dynamic spatial equilibrium. "If man is to demonstrate any important mastery of his universe," Fuller maintained, "then all the fundamental behavior phenomena of his dynamic universe — as demonstrated in the 92 (atomic) primary team plays — must be involved directly or indirectly in the process."

His argument was this: To master the universe progressively, man must first master the synergetic principles governing the relation of parts to wholes. Sec-

ondly, he must master the principles establishing the most economical relationships systems. Finally, he must master the principles determining the "evolutionary transformation tendencies of the hierarchy of parts relationships and their family of coordinate and accommodative complementarities."

These are tightly-compressed general statements whose immediate meanings are clouded by Fuller's technical Latinisms. What they imply is that society's effective control of its environment requires, progressively:

(1) a grasping of the general system patterns of the physical world, such as that expressed in the Einstein energy-mass equation;

(2) the most economial ways of converting these system relationships to work.

The geodesic domes, which provide maximum structural strength with minimum structural materials per operative unit, are examples of such economic energy transformations.

It is Fuller's third point which provides difficulties. It contains a subtle idea whose implications are not immediately apparent: Action and interaction of events are accompanied by relative displacements and accommodations of other events. For example, when a stone is dropped into a tank of water, the stone does not penetrate the water molecules. The molecules are jostled; they "accommodate" the stone, and in the process jostle their neighboring molecules, which, in turn, jostle their own border companions. Thus waves of relayed jostling are propagated. Each relayed wave, although a composite of local actions, provides a synergetic continuity of those actions. The consequence is a pattern of events which has an integrity of its own, independent of the local accommodations (which are innocent with respect to the overall synergetic pattern). The same stone, dropped successively in pools of water, milk, and gasoline, will generate the same wave patterns. Yet the waves are essences neither of milk nor water nor gasoline; the waves are distinct and measurable pattern integrities in their own right. The invariant relationships which govern pattern integrities in nature Fuller refers to as "pure principle." The stone thrown into the tank inaugurates a complex of accommodative events operative in pure principle.

When radio or television waves pass through the walls of a house, when light waves pass through a window or a lens, there are always some comprehensively relayed local jostlings, some sets of submicroscopic eddies of force, that accommodate the push through. The complementary effect — what in conversational language is the "resistance" of the wall, window, or lens, and what Fuller calls "the precessionally shunted pattern relay" — is responsible for re-election, refraction, and filtering.

To Fuller, the end product of man's progressive striving to master the universe is society's *common wealth* in its most basic sense: "the industrially organized ability to project certain and constantly improving standards of survival by the many — *without deprivation of any.*"

Fuller observed that for the first time in history it was possible for men to set themselves methodically to the task of production for all on a scale entirely without limit, and that this massive production could be effected without any fundamentally new capital accounting — because the real costs have been discharged in advance. The underwriting has been the enormous, and as yet undocu-

mented investments of time, intellect, and disciplined effort by the pioneers in scientific principles and comprehensive technology — the men who separated out atoms, structured new molecules, and measured the cosmos. These resources he regards, collectively, as the "consciously-initiated design science operative (through its tool complex) as a synergetic wave patterning of global magnitude."

All that is keeping society from a realistic attempt to utilize total resources for total production for total population, Fuller reasoned, is a naive preoccupation with economic tactics long ago made obsolete by science. These tactics are side effects of ancient fears. They are vestiges of social memories, the vague recall of times of scarcity and isolation, of plagues and disasters, when the tragic sense of life was intertwined with the belief in the inevitability of war of all against all.

Fuller's thoughts about housing and transportation were definitive. He envisaged the contemporary living pattern as local spherical control systems, everywhere surrounded by an air ocean. The most direct route from place to place is by air, and transportation of men and buildings is possible by air. Air-lifting, he concluded, is the key to around-the-world shelter distribution.

Of importance in Fuller's thinking was the problem of transporting large units of structure. If shelter was to be given the economic advantages which derived from mass production, entire houses and apartment houses must be constructed in factories and delivered as totally assembled products, like automobiles. But with existing transportation facilities, no house can be moved more than a few miles. It is not practicable to load a house on a flatcar or a trailer and transport it through city streets, under and over bridges, and through tunnels. It is theoretically possible, to deliver a full-size, pre-assembled house by air. The air ocean has its shores everywhere, and its lanes are open. In 1926 an Italian dirigible had flown safely to the North Pole and back; the dirigible was a large rigid structure containing gas cells to float it, and was enveloped by a unitary skin with low aeronautic resistance. In 1927, the *Graf Zeppelin* was in building. Her structure was the dimensional equivalent of a 30-story skyscraper in horizontal attitude. Aeronautical delivery of housing was to Fuller as realizable as it was basic; it could make the project of mass-producing shelter feasible.

Toward this end he proposed a house exhibiting maximum strength at minimum weight per unit of structure. Unlike conventional houses, whose essential form had not altered since the time of the Egyptians and Babylonians, the Fuller house would be stressed like an airplane with compression parts and tension parts separated out. Conventional houses, built brick upon brick, or beam on column, are almost pure compression structures; yet brick and stone support no more weight today than in the day of the Walls of Jericho. The great technological advance was in tension materials like the new steel alloy cables. A logical modern house would have a structure similar to that of a wire wheel turned on its side, with the hub acting as a central, pre-fabricated compression member — an inflatable Duralumin mast. The remainder of the house would consist of walls and cable supported floor decks suspended around the mast.

Many of these ideas were contained in a book Fuller published in mimeographed form, in 1927. The title of the work was 4D; the symbol stood for the "Fourth Dimension" in relativity physics, the time-space dimension. Two hundred copies of the book were run off and bound; a subsequent edition, incorporating comment, charts, and additional material, was called 4D, *Timelock*.

THE 4D HOUSE

In April, 1928, Fuller completed the essential designs of the 4D house, and filed a patent application covering the central features.

The house was actually the world's first tangible embodiment of what one French architect hopefully designated as a "Machine-for-Living." Its purpose was avowedly not only to keep the occupants sheltered from the bite of the elements, but to reduce to a minimum the drudgery of physical existence. The central mast, in which basic utilities were factory-installed, came ready for instant use. The windowless walls were of transparent, but swiftly-shutterable, vacuum-pane glass. The house was to be dustless; the air drawn in through vents in the mast was filtered, washed, cooled or heated, then circulated. Laundry was automatically washed, dried, pressed, and conveyed to storage units. Clothes and dish closets, refrigerator and other food compartments contained revolving shelves rigged to move at the interruption of a light beam.

The entire house was designed to be relatively independent of piped-in water, thus fully operative wherever it was erected. A ten-minute atomizer bath was produced with a quart of water, which in turn would be filtered, sterilized, and recirculated. Fuller's toilets required no water. They consisted of a splashless hermetic and waterproof packaging system which mechanically packed, stored, and gross-cartoned wastes for eventual pickup for processing by chemical industries. Dusting was by compressed air and vacuum systems. Floors and doors were pneumatic and soundproof. Beds were pneumatic. There were no partitions qua partitions. The various living pattern areas were divided by Fuller's prefabricated utility units, which contained vertically- and horizontally-moving shelves and hangers, or laundry or other utility facilities. These pneumatic based and crowned utility components reached from floor to ceiling; the intervals between them were opened and closed by pneumatically positioned and inflated drawer curtains.

To Fuller, partitions in a house are negative elements, symbolic of an economy of scarcity. They are what he calls "a make-do, like socialism." When there is not enough space to go around, both provide an arbitrary subdivision of inadequacy. But competent design can always provide adequacy. In the 4D house, the occupants were given ample space, and the logical arrangement of the equipment automatically developed the privacy appropriate to psychological grace.

Fuller holds privacy to be a condition that can be violated only through the sensorial spectrum. Sight, hearing, touch, and smell ranges, however, are readily controlled within economic limits. At an open-air tea party you cannot hear, touch, smell a group in conversation on the other side of the lawn. Optical privacy is readily had with inexpensive opaque membranes.

It is a cardinal assumption of Fuller's that all design should be muted at zero as with a musical instrument. A violin or a piano is not itself a form of music, nor is it a container of music; it is a device for articulation. A house has a corresponding function. The harmonic potentials for design should be articulated by those who live in the house; what is significant is the personality of the dweller, not the dwelling. Yet the range of harmonic capabilities of the house should be comprehensive with respect to the spontaneous articulation of all the senses of the dweller. In this the esthetics of a house has a broader sensorial spectrum than the esthetics of an orchestra whose instrumental harmonies have only auditory charm. The total sensorial spectrum is characterized by a variety of expressive frequencies. Where musical tempi are expressions at a relatively high frequency, both in man-made music and in the sound patternings of nature, the visual and olfactory patternings of nature have slower rhythms. The white of winter, the variety of the summer's greens and the reds of autumn, even the lilac scent held for two weeks in May — these are low-frequency, long wave expressions in contrast to the rustlings of leaves, the song notes of birds, or the high-frequency hiss of the surf. And in all of these areas of sensation a house must be sympathetically resonant.

The 4D dwelling was designed to provide what Fuller conceived as "high-standard functioning, unconsciously compatible with man's unconsciously coordinated internal mechanisms and chemistries." The design, he held, must implement, but not impose. "There must be no lion's claw feet on the instruments, nor frozen rococo music to impede the regenerative evolutionary preoccupations of the ever-emergent new life. It was the ever-new life, with its incredible and as yet little understood complex of faculties, sensibilities, and intuitive initiations, to which the 4D dwelling was dedicated."

What was economically sensational about the planned 4D house was the cost to the consumer. Based on the price scale then current in the automobile industry,

Fuller estimated that if such a house, completely equipped, could be mass-produced, it could be marketed at 25¢ per pound (in terms of the 1928 dollar). Fords and Chevrolets at that time were selling at 22¢ per pound. (Today Fords and Chevrolets, completely equipped, sell for 80¢ per pound.) Fuller's 4D house dwelling machine of 1928, optimally equipped, weighed a total of 6000 pounds. At 25¢ per pound, this meant a 1928 retail price of $1,500. On a 1960 basis of 80¢ per pound for approximately the same brand of "metallurgical pound cake," the 4D house, mass-produced and distributed by the automotive industry, would sell for approximately $4,800 — installed and ready for occupancy anywhere in the United States.

It should be emphasized that this price would be possible only through the use of mass production techniques. However, at present there are more than 100,000 house producers in the United States whose total output averages only 500,000 craft-built houses per year (or five units per builder). The biggest craft builders are turning out 5000 houses a year. Yet in the auto industry even an output of 5000 units by one of the six prime producers is regarded as a small *day's* run.

Because of its price and the ease with which it could be air-transported and erected, the 4D house, in Fuller's eye, was a relatively dynamic commodity. Because the houses would be provided as incidental instruments (like telephones) by a service industry, they could be installed anywhere in the world, freeing their users from shackles to any one locality, "ergo, making possible world citizenry." The houses could not only be installed and removed in minutes, by the service industry, but their progressive obsolescence would be methodically digested by the service companies by progressive substitution of improved types, with every new installation.

It was Fuller's belief that his projected shelter utility companies would necessarily operate with the economic philosophy which has characterized the telephone utility policies, namely, that systematic replacement of obsolete equipment with more effective equipment is a dynamic economy which results in constantly increasing dividends. Thus an industrial complex serving more and more people, in more and more places, with increasing efficiency, performs what is fundamentally a wealth-multiplying operation. The benefits accrue to all, consumers, management, stockholders, suppliers, and subcontractors. And since the benefits keep feeding back into the system, such techno-economic patterns are infinitely regenerative.

In keeping with his total-dedication-to-comprehensive-design principles, Fuller, in May, 1928, offered to assign full proprietary rights in the 4D house patents to the American Institute of Architects, whose vice-president, at that time, was Fuller's father-in-law, James Monroe Hewlett. The offer was not accepted; but at the annual meeting, in which it was taken under consideration, the Institute passed a resolution: "Be it resolved that the American Institute of Architects establish itself on record as inherently opposed to any peas-in-a-pod-like reproducible designs."

Four years later, Archibald MacLeish took up the cudgel for Fuller in a *Fortune* article called "The Industry Industry Missed." He pointed out that the human problem today is not more *house* for the money, but more housing for the money. It is not enough to have old houses, at old prices, in new envelopes. The problem is at bottom a problem of fundamental design — and this Fuller alone had faced.

"Mr. Fuller's design," he wrote, "has an importance altogether apart from the probability or improbability of its general acceptance. It may well be the prototype of a new domestic architecture. And at the very least it will destroy the great architectural dogma that a house is what our great-grandfathers called a house, and that the architects' sole opportunity is to modify what already exists."

4D BECOMES DYMAXION

The term Dymaxion, now so decidedly a Fuller trade-mark, was coined in 1929; and, ironically, not by Fuller. The Marshall Field department store, in Chicago, that year had to introduce for sale its first stock of "modern" furniture purchased in Europe after the Paris Exposition of 1926. Casting about for a setting which would dramatize the advance design of the furniture, the Marshall Field promotion experts came across the 4D house, which had been featured in the *Chicago Evening Post* by C. J. Bulliet, then editor of the art news section. The 4D house existed only as a model; but psychologically astute promoters at Marshall Field reasoned that such a model, prominently displayed, advertised, and lectured about in a hall next to the room with the so-called "advanced design" furniture, would make the "modern" furniture appear conservative — new, but not too new. It has always been a trustworthy sales practice to walk forward backward.

The promotional minds of the Marshall Field organization decided that for maximum publicity effectiveness Fuller's "house of the future" required a name more acceptable than "4D," which seemed to suggest not so much the "fourth dimension" as a grade in public school or, perhaps, living quarters on the fourth floor of an ordinary apartment house.

Waldo Warren, an advertising specialist identified to the organization as a "wordsmith," was assigned to Fuller for the specific purpose of forging a more seductive name. Warren listened as Fuller outlined the philosophy embodied in this prototype house. He took note of the key sentences and boiled these down to key words. From the significant syllables of these words, he manufactured a series of synthetic words each of four syllables. Each word combined the meanings of a pair of others. Fuller was asked by Warren to eliminate from each pair the word he found most offensive. The surviving combination was "Dymaxion," a fusion of syllables related directly and indirectly to "dynamism," "maximum," and "ions." Fuller maintains he did not choose this word and that "it just emerged." Marshall Field copyrighted "Dymaxion" in Fuller's name.

Fuller did not, in 1927, regard the 4D Dymaxion house as a project then ready for industrial production and distribution. The design called for materials of standards higher than those then available: high-strength, heat-treated aluminum alloys; rustless steel cables with a tensile strength in excess of 200,000 pounds to the square inch; structurally stable transparent plastics in large-scale functions; photo-electric eyes; relay-operated door openers. "I simply stated what had to be done," he claimed, "and what I knew could be done. And by taking an inventory of my experience, I could predict within good proximity what would be available — and when. I could see that it would be a minimum of 25 years before the gamut of industrial capabilities and evolutionary education of man — as well as political and economic emergency necessities — would permit the emergence of the necessary physical paraphernalia of this comprehensive anticipatory design science undertaking."

Posing against a vision the existential facts of social change, Fuller delivered a lecture to himself. "If I were an absolute dictator," he said, "I might be able to inaugurate the full-scale industrialization tool-up of earth-girdling, air-deliverable dwelling service with the investment of one billion 1928 dollars. However, such a billion-dollar, stitch-in-time investment is utterly unrealizable at this time. In spite of the fact that the goal and path to it are clearly visible, the sad reality is that society will probably saddle itself with trillions of dollars of pay-as-you-go, trial-and-error, evolutionary expenditures. If I am not willing to live through a quarter century of tantalizing, frustrating, completely insecure development, I had best drop the whole matter at once — and get myself a good job as a 'thing' salesman."

The developments followed, more or less as Fuller predicted. In 1927, seeking photo-electric cells and relay-actuated devices, he wrote to his brother, Wolcott, an engineer with the General Electric Company, asking for technical cooperation. Wolcott wrote back: "Bucky, I love you dearly. But can't you make it easier for your relatives and friends by not including preposterous ideas."

The following year Fuller received this telegram from Wolcott:

YOU CAN OPEN YOUR DOOR BY WAVING YOUR HAND AFTER ALL STOP . WE HAVE DEVELOPED PHOTO-ELECTRIC CELL AND RELAY STOP SEVENTY TWO DOLLARS FOR THE SET.

Fuller met the same kind of reaction when, in 1927, he talked with engineers at the Aluminum Corporation of America. He showed them drawings of the proposed 4D structures in which he specified aluminum alloys as yet unrealized, but alloys that it seemed to him reasonable to expect in the quite-near future.

One engineer laughed. "Young man," he said, "you don't seem to realize that we don't use aluminum in buildings. It is used only in percolators, pots, ashtrays, and souvenirs."

Fuller saw no joke. "Don't you have any alloy stocks in your laboratory — alloys that are heat treatable for my experimental purposes?"

"Look," said the engineer, resentful of Fuller's persistence. "We have two kinds of aluminum, soft, and softer. Which do you want?"

Five years later, in 1932, the first heat-treated aluminum alloys became available; and the development marked the realistic beginning of the large-scale airplane industry.

Shortly before the opening of the Chicago World's Fair, young Dawes, the son of Charles Dawes, of Dawes Plan fame, approached Fuller with the suggestion that the Dymaxion house be made a feature of the Chicago World's Fair; young Dawes was one of the Fair's promotion executives.

"I would not be willing to display just a mock-up of the house," Fuller said to him. "But I would be willing to develop a true prototype—one fully engineered and ready to go into production."

"How much will it cost?" Dawes asked.

"I will have to re-check my figures," Fuller said, "and let you know."

The interim five years since his cost estimates of 1927 had seen the realization of many technical developments, including the heat-treated alloys of aluminum whose development he had anticipated, and which arrived industrially on schedule. The implication followed that the research and development yet to be completed could now be covered by a figure considerably less than his original "stitch-in-time" billion dollars. After recalculating his costs, Fuller again met with Dawes. "The basic cost today," he said, "is a hundred million dollars."

Certain that he was dealing with a lunatic, Dawes turned and left the room. He was aggrieved. All he asked for was a house; Fuller offered him an industry.

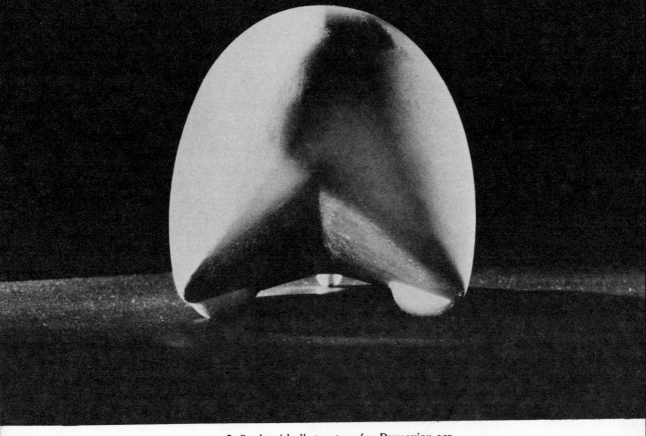

3 *Study of hull structure for Dymaxion car*

DYMAXION
TRANSPORT UNITS

When, in 1927, Fuller had arrived at a working concept of his light-weight, wire wheel structured 4D houses and had discovered the feasibility of delivering them by air to remote places, where their semi-autonomous facilities made a high standard of living possible at negligible land occupancy cost, he turned to the problem of transportation. If a house is to be significantly autonomous, it must not be dependent on roads, railways, even airplane landing strips. A dwelling which could function with maximum effectiveness, wherever it was placed, required a family transport unit that would have the selective maneuverability of birds. It should be able to come in and go out by air, land and take off from a spot; in addition, it should be capable of taxiing on land or water.

Late in 1927 he turned his attention to this transport phase of his comprehensive plan. For a long time, in fact, since his Navy crashboat days, Fuller had been turning over in his mind the possibility of an omni-directional transport that could hover in the air, or could be directionally controlled by the jet blasts from gas turbines. The basic idea was locomotion on twin jet stilts, each directionally oriented and throttled as a discrete unit.

The airplane shares with the sea gull the ability to create a low pressure area above its wings. The dynamic effect of this partial vacuum is "lift"; gulls and planes in flight are sucked skyward. The lift provides the primary support for gliding. Ducks, however, are anatomically unfitted for such aerial roller coasting; their wings are too small to generate a pressure difference sufficient to "suck-suspend" the duck body in mid-air, and to permit it to enjoy the gull's kind of lazy free-wheeling in the updraft of an atmospheric thermal.

The duck, however, has proprietary rights to another aerodynamic facility: the jet. With each thrust of his wings, the duck generates a momentary vacuum sky-hook above each wing; simultaneously, under each wing, a powerful air jet is extruded between the wing and the body. These thrusts compound to form, in effect, continuous columns of air. Although the tiny sky-hooks above the wings provide an intermittent series of advantages — similar in function to a series of gymnasium rings — the duck's main propulsion advantage comes from the thrust of the columns. These compressional jets function like a vaulter's pole. The duck rises from the water by making a rapid forward dash with his webbed feet, then vaulting skyward on his own jet-stream stilts.

If, while a pole vaulter were at the peak of his jump, Fuller reasoned, we could hand him another pole, somewhat shorter, but whose base lay forward in the line of motion, the vaulter could continue his

26

aerial jaunt. And if this procedure could be continued, each time with the pole somewhat shorter than the preceding, the vaulter could continue to plummet forward, downhill, exploiting gravity to accomplish a horizontal leap far in excess of any available to an ordinary broad jumper. Assume, now, that the man could be streamlined. If such a man took the proper headlong attitude, with respect to air resistance, the amount of up-push required to keep him plummeting forward should be no more than that supplied by his leg muscles to give him his initial altitude.

A duck in flight, like other short-wing, high-speed birds, can readily be seen to make its intermittent altitude gains and forward gains in the manner of this hypothetical pole vaulter. When coming in for a landing, the duck merely orients its twin "throttleable" air-jet stilts to a forward position, then allows their air cushion cones to "melt down" to a comfortable landing velocity. If the rate at which a duck's successive uplift vaulting strokes is sufficiently accelerated, the "vaults" exceed visible pulsation frequency and appear as a continuous translation of vertical advantage to forwardly controlled flight. Similarly, the high velocity of molecular explosions appears superficially continuous in the jet.

With the aeronautics of the duck as a prototype principle, Fuller, in 1927, invented what he called his "4D twin, angularly-orientable, individually throttleable, jet-stilt, controlled-plummeting transport." Explaining the invention at that time to his little daughter, Allegra, he described it as the "zoomobile" which could hop off the road at will, fly about, then, as deftly as a bird, settle back into a place in traffic.

In January, 1933, just before the launching of the New Deal, a friend of Fuller's offered to put up money to en-

able Fuller to test out some of the 4D Dymaxion ideas.

"I will only take the money," Fuller said, "under one condition: if I want to use all of it to buy ice cream cones, that will be that, and there will be no questions asked."

The money was given without restrictions.

Deflation, at the depth of the Depression, had reached a point where Bowery restaurants offered a meal for one cent. Fuller found himself, on bank moratorium day, with several thousand crisp greenbacks in his pocket. The relative buying power of this money, at a time when no one else could obtain cash, gave him momentarily the authority of a millionnaire. Yet these few thousand dollars were totally inadequate, even under the existing panic sales conditions, to finance the development of a true Dymaxion House prototype (which his recent estimate for young Dawes had shown to require a hundred million hard dollars). Nor could they be used to develop the jet-stilt 4D transport; alloys were not yet available that would withstand the intense heats of combustion generated by the firing of liquid oxygen — which Fuller then regarded as the most effective propulsion fuel.

Yet Fuller realized that in 1933 the inventory of available automotive, marine, and aircraft components made possible some significant preliminary investigations, particularly the practical testing of the ground taxiing capabilities of this unprecedented vehicle whose anatomy was to be like that of some mythological beast, reminiscent of bird, fish, and reptile. This polymorphous transport was certain to involve a cluster of unknown behaviors. The most hazardous of the events faced by both air and sea vehicles are those in wnich the vehicles make contact with land. While suspended in the fluid media, the stressing forces applied to these vessels are distributed, hydraulically and pneumatically, in an even manner. When the vessels are brought in contact with land, however, the forces often take the form of hard impacts, concentrated on one particular part of the over-all structure.

Many questions were posed. How would the vehicle behave when buffeted by heavy cross winds from directions other than that in which it was intended, and aeronautically designed, to go? When landing cross wind, would it ground loop to head into the wind, as do light planes? If so, what could be done about it? How would the car perform on clear ice? How would it behave when taxied over rough country fields?

Determined to find empirical answers to these questions, Fuller rented the Dynamometer Building of the then recently defunct Locomobile Company's factory, in Bridgeport, Conn., a city where the Depression had left idle many skilled mechanics and engineers. He engaged a crew of 27 to work under the engineering direction of Starling Burgess, a world-famous naval architect and aeronautical engineer. A careful screening of more than 1,000 job applicants provided Fuller with a cosmopolitan team of exceptional workmen, including Polish sheet metal experts, Italian machine tool men, Scandinavian woodcraftsmen, and former Rolls-Royce coachmakers. He then set out to design and construct the first Dymaxion car.

Although this car, which was demonstrated to the public, July 12, 1933, was intended to be only a road test stage of the projected omni-directional transport, it exhibited a number of significant automotive design innovations — among them front-wheel drive; rear engine and rear steering operation; aluminum-bodied, chrome-molybdenum aircraft steel chassis; ⅛th-inch aircraft shatterproof glass. Mudguards were eliminated. The entire road occupation area was included in the usable interior space. The car featured air nostrils, air-conditioning, and rear view periscopes for both front and back seats. Among other things, it introduced to the automotive field the virtues of complete aeronautical streamlining of fuselage, including belly, within whose fish form all the running gear, with the exception of the lower half of the three wheels and the air scoop, were enclosed. Th two front, differential-coupled wheels were the car's tractors. The rear wheel was the rudder. As with the pulled (rather than pushed) wheelbarrow, the ruddering tail wheel was lifted over, rather than shoved into the traveled terrain.

Fuller was aware that the body design of the 1932 automobile embodied only a negligible advance over that of the old horse-drawn buggies whose lumbering pace never made air resistance an attenuating factor. The air resistance of a vehicle increases at the rate of a second power progression. Speed increases as a first power progression. Thus, doubling speed increases air resistance four times. At speeds up to 30 miles per hour, aeronautical resistance is not an important consideration. At accelerations from zero to 30 miles per hour, tire distortion and mechanical friction are the only significant energy loads. At 60 miles per hour and beyond, however, the greater part of a vehicle's power is devoted to the rugged tasks of shoving the air apart and westling with the vacuum drag in the vehicle's wake.

By giving the Dymaxion car the type of streamlining today found in airplanes, Fuller was able to obtain a speed of 120 m.p.h., using for power an ordinary stock Ford V-8 engine. He thus obtained from a 90 h.p. engine the quality of performance which, in an ordinary 1933 sedan, it was estimated, would have required an engine of over 300 horsepower. In an all-in-motion universe, Fuller observed, all the interactive phenomena always move in the directions of least resistance. Man can by design decrease the resistances in preferred directions. The omni-medium transport must provide minimum resistance conformally, organically, and texturally, that is, minimum frontal cross-section, minimum drag, and minimum internal and external mechanical friction. A body penetrating a liquid, gaseous, or solid medium must open up the medium ahead of its penetration.

A penetrating body with rounded shoulders develops a rotation in the boundary layer molecules or atoms of the penetrated medium. These eddying rotations act like little spools winding up the penetrated medium in ever tighter bundles, which tense forwardly to supply their winding requirement, thus exhausting the penetrating medium ahead of the penetrating body. The blunt cigar nose in front of a teardrop silhouette creates a partial vacuum, conical in shape, that flares out in front of the teardrop when the vehicle is in fast motion. The consequence is a sucking forward of the vehicle. However, a long, cone-shaped partial vacuum is also created in the wake of the vehicle; and unless something is done to offset its effects, this cone will negate the pull forward. The model solution to rearward suction is seen in the structure of fish: the conic tail of the streamlined fish form is designed to conform exactly to the space created by the inherent lag in the rate of closure of the penetrated medium. The rate of closing depends on the relative viscosity and inertia of the penetrated medium.

The function of man-designed streamlining is to maximize nose pull and minimize tail drag. The tails of fishes slip, wiggle, and cancel out the drag in the fishes' wake. With no rearward drag, and a vacuum on their nose, sometimes increased by head enlargement, fishes and birds make high capital of their nose pull. Skilled light airplane and glider pilots exploit the combined wing top and nose lift of their craft at efficient design speed, maximizing forward pull.

The greater the proportion of a vehicle's weight above the springs to its weight below the springs, the less is the inertia of the sprung mass disturbed by the motions of the components below the springs. Railroad and automobile designers, in times prior to the Dymaxion, improved the riding quality of their cars by the easy but inefficient expedient of adding weight to the sprung part of the combination. Fuller's approach was that of the builder of a light plane. He saw that riding comfort could be increased while the total sprung weight was decreased. The solution was to reduce the unsprung proportion to zero.

Fuller maximized the car's springing in a sequence of steps. First, he softened the tires so that the air within the tires became the initial set of springs. He then introduced a series of secondary springs and frames.

The first frame, hinge-supported by the front wheels, carried the engine and drive shaft. Frame No. 2 was hinge-and-spring-connected to Frame No. 1, but was supported by the steerable tail wheel. The body, in turn, had its own independent frame which was sprung directly from the front axle, with a balancing spring connected back, abreast the engine, to Frame No. 1. The consequence of this multi-hinged, multi-spring arrangement was that the Dymaxion car could zoom across open fields with the agility of a light plane, yet provide a ride as smooth as any cruise on a highway. Over rough terrain the lower frames moved in hinged harmony, the body frame maintained independent inertial poise.

The steerable tail wheel gave the Dymaxion exceptional maneuverability. Although the 19½ foot car was four feet longer than the 1933 Ford sedan, it could park in a curb area a foot shorter than the space required for the Ford sedan by heading directly into the curb, then tailing in sidewise. It could turn in its own length.

One day, when he had the car filled with *New Yorker* and *Fortune* editors (the car could carry ten persons in addition to the driver), Fuller made a sharp turn from 57th Street into Fifth Avenue.

A traffic officer signalled for him to stop. "What the hell is this?" the cop asked.

Fuller opened his window. Then, while patiently explaining to the cop what the Dymaxion was about, he slowly rotated the car in a complete circle around him. The astonished officer demanded a repeat performance.

This was noontime in New York in the era before stoplights; a policeman was on duty at each intersection. The cop at 56th Street witnessed the performance at 57th, and demanded a demonstration for his own pleasure. The 55th Street cop was not to be undone by his colleague a block above. Fuller was called on to perform by every cop on duty, from 57th Street to Washington Square. That day it required a full hour to nose this high speed transport a single midtown mile.

The Dymaxion was a traffic stopper in New York streets. Once, when parked outside the New York Stock Exchange, it blocked all traffic flow in the financial district, and Fuller was asked by the New York Police Department, as a special favor, not to drive the car below Canal Street.

The officials of the 1934 New York Automobile Show invited Fuller to exhibit the car at the show in Grand Central Palace. At the last minute the invitation was withdrawn, supposedly at the request of the Chrysler Corporation. Chrysler had bought the central command show space to dramatize the introduction of the Chrysler Air Flow car. And here was a maximum "air flow" car, to be exhibited by a non-manufacturer — and to be exhibited free.

General Ryan, then police chief of New York City, invited Fuller to park the Dymaxion in the street, directly in front of the entrance to Grand Central Palace. The day of the grand opening, Fuller drove up, parked, and again stopped traffic — and stole the show.

In the period between 1932 and 1934, Fuller produced three Dymaxion cars, all experimental models whose purpose was to test features related to an eventual omni-directional transport; in this sense they were all prototypes. The first car was sold to Captain "Al" (Alford F.) Williams, then holder of the world's speed record for seaplanes and manager of the aviation department of the Gulf Refining Company. Williams called the car "aviation's greatest contribution to the auto industry" — and drove it across the country in a nationwide campaign to promote the sale of aircraft fuel.

A second car was built on order from a group of English automobile enthusiasts. They commissioned Col. William Francis Forbes-Sempill, an English aviation expert, to come to this country and test the performance of car No. 1. Col. Forbes-Sempill crossed the ocean on the *Graf Zeppelin*, which on this trip went on to Chicago, because of the Chicago World's Fair. Capt. Williams sent the Dymaxion to Chicago from Pittsburgh, driven by a racing driver named Turner, to be placed at Forbes-Sempill's disposal. And when Forbes-Sempill was ready to leave, arrangements were made to have him driven in the Dymaxion to the Chicago airport, from there to be flown to Akron, where the *Graf Zeppelin* had been moored, after touching down at Chicago. En route, the Dymaxion was rammed by another car. Both cars overturned, but the driver of the Dymaxion car was killed, and Forbes-Sempill severely injured — virtually at the entrance to the World's Fair.

When reporters arrived on the scene, the other car, which belonged to a Chicago South Park Commissioner, had been removed. The newspapers featured only the news about the Dymaxion; the headlines were unfavorable without exception. One read: "Two Zep-Riders Killed as Freak Car Crashes"; another: "Three-Wheeled Car Kills Driver." The *New York Times* reported that, "the machine skidded, turned turtle and rolled over several times. Police say it apparently struck a 'wave' in the road." No mention was made of the other car.

At the coroner's inquest, postponed until 30 days later (because of Forbes-Sempill's injuries), it was established that the accident was the result of a collision of two cars racing each other and weaving through traffic at 70 miles an hour. By the time this fact had become record, the smashup had lost its news value. The earlier reporting was never amended in the press.

Both Williams and Fuller, after carefully inspecting the Dymaxion's functioning parts and reconstructing the sequence of events, were convinced that the Dymaxion car itself had no design or structural fault which had a bearing on the accident. The car was repaired, and Williams subsequently sold it to the director of the automotive division of the U. S. Bureau of Standards. Ten years later it was destroyed in a fire in the Bureau's Washington garage.

Car No. 2 was completed in January, 1934. Because of the unfavorable publicity, however, it was no longer wanted by the English group. Some time later, when Fuller was entirely out of money, he sold it to a group of his Bridgeport mechanics. Car No. 3 was bought by Leopold Stokowski and his wife, Evangeline Johnson, and placed on exhibition in Chicago during the second year of the World's Fair. It was eventually sold and resold many times, and for some years disappeared from the news. In 1946 the car turned up in Wichita, Kansas, when it was bought by the local Cadillac distributor. It is rumored to be still in existence, stored in a private garage in Wichita.

At the request of Henry Kaiser, in 1943, Fuller redesigned the Dymaxion, making use of the newer products of automotive technology. According to the design which was never built, the new version was powered by three separate air-cooled "outboard" type (opposed cylinder) engines, each coupled to its own wheel by a variable fluid drive. Each of the engine-drivewheel assemblies was detachable. In case of engine trouble, or when an overhaul was desired, the entire assembly was replaced by a spare. The engines themselves were run always at the optimum speed; the speed of the car was controlled by varying the quantity of fluid in the coupling.

This engine coupling provided maximum torque with minimum engine size. The engines were of low horsepower — 15 to 25. And since only one engine was required to maintain cruising speed, once starting inertia was overcome, the car would average 40 to 50 miles per gallon of gas. When additional power was required for climbing hills or rapid acceleration, the second and third engines cut in automatically.

The projected Kaiser Dymaxion was designed to be steered at cruising speeds by the front wheels. The rear wheel steering, intended as an auxiliary to be used for acute turns, was brought into play by a crank handle set in the regular steering wheel. When all wheels were turned in the same direction, the car could move sidewise like a crab into its parking place. When the tail-wheel was turned in a direction opposite to that of the front wheels, the entire car could be rotated in its place like a Lazy Susan. Structured on an aluminum frame, the new Dymaxion's weight was to be 620 pounds. Five passengers could sit abreast on the single front seat. The tail-wheel was mounted on an extensible boom. At high speed, the boom extended to give the car greater wheel base, and a smoother ride. When the car decelerated, the boom retracted automatically.

DYMAXION TO
ENERGETIC STRUCTURES

In 1936, with the last of the three Dymaxion cars completed, Fuller was out of funds. He went to work for the Phelps-Dodge Corporation to assist in setting up a department of research and product development. His first significant operation there was to design a new type of non-ferrous, metal-to-metal brake drum. Made of solid bronze, and fitted with hard rubber inserts, this drum and shoe conducted away the heat generated in braking at a rate impossible in steel components. It thus eliminated brake "grab" and "fade," and halved the necessary deceleration time of existing brake assemblies. The Fuller bronze brake established the metallurgical principle of the disk brakes now used on the wheels of heavy bombers. Another invention of this period was Fuller's successful oxy-acetylene, melted-tin-ore centrifuge. This was used to process "hard head," a form of tin ore that would not yield to other economical methods of refining.

THE DIE-STAMPED BATHROOM

The most dramatic development, however, was the Dymaxion bathroom, complete with all fixtures and facilities, designed for mass production by die-stamping. Like most of Fuller's inventions, it was designed for the first Dymaxion 4D house of 1927. In 1930 he had produced its first full-scale prototype for the American Radiator Company's Pierce Foundation. However, the prototype was never shown to the public because, in Fuller's words, "The manufacturer was convinced that the plumbers' union would refuse to install the bathrooms."

But in 1936, Fuller's designs now realized by Phelps-Dodge made is possible to manufacture entire bathrooms at little more than the cost of an automobile sedan body. Like refrigerators or washing machines, these bathrooms could be installed in any house in the space of minutes. Once the prefabricated manifold of intake, vent and waste pipes and the electric harness terminals were connected, the bathrooms were ready for operation. It should be emphasized that these were not marginal sanitary utilities, but luxury bathrooms, equipped with all usual facilities and some new ones, such as air-conditioning. A dozen prototypes were produced and successfully installed and, at this writing, more than half of them are still in use — as sound as on the day they left the Phelps-Dodge laboratory.

The Dymaxion bathroom consisted of a tub-shower compartment and a lavatory-toilet compartment. The complete unit was composed of four basic pieces, each of which was formed by sheet material by stamping and was light enough to be easily lifted and carried by two men. To assemble the bathroom the four basic pieces were simply connected by bolting. The whole interior appeared to be one homogeneous surface in which all of the sharp angles and corners usually found in a room were supplanted by smooth curvatures. Either of the compartments could be installed as an independent unit; when the lavatory-toilet compartment was used in this way a shower could be included, with curtains isolating the shower space from the other fixtures. The complete bathroom, including plumbing and air-conditioning, occupied a floor space five by five feet and weighed 420 pounds, approximately the same as the weight of an average cast iron porcelain finished tub.

The Dymaxion bathroom was designed by Fuller for ultimate production in plastics, when plastics had been developed to an adequate point (a state he believes has now been achieved). In the prototype bathroom shown on these pages, the bottom half of each compartment was fabricated of copper sheet and coated on the interior surface with a non-corrosive alloy of silver, tin, and antimony. The upper half of both compartments was made of aluminum sheet and was coated on the interior surface with a colored synthetic resin used in finishing automobiles. All exterior surfaces were sprayed with a mastic and asbestos material to eliminate the tinny sound that would otherwise occur when an interior surface was struck. When joined, the two compartments formed a six-inch partition which concealed the plumbing assembly and heating equpiment. A U-shaped doorway in this partition provided access to and served as a seat for the tub-shower compartment. To permit easier cleaning, the floor of the tub-shower compartment was raised nine inches; an integrally formed cork-covered step led to this compartment.

Plumbing connections were standard-ized and could be factory fitted or assembled on the job to conform to variations in local building code requirements or labor policies. Ventilation was provided by a small fan located under the lavatory; air was drawn from the nearest room and exhausted through ductwork to the outside. Heat was provided by electric resistance strip heaters applied to the hidden surface of each compartment; it was conducted to all parts of the bathroom and radiated to the occupant by the metal enclosure. Indirect lighting was provided for both compartments by a fixture built on the head of the doorway between them. Other local lighting included a standard medicine cabinet fixture and a special built-in indirect light in the bottom of the tub-shower compartment, which illuminated the water and the floor.

The first bathroom was constructed in the laboratory of the William B. Stout Engineering Corporation in Detroit. Later, an improved model was installed in the research laboratory of the Nichols Copper Company, a subsidiary of the Phelps-Dodge Corporation, for use by the research workers. A year later it was removed to Christopher Morley's Long Island house. Twelve other models were made in 1937 and 1938, and eleven of these were eventually installed in private houses where several are still in satisfactory use. One bathroom was installed in the hydraulic testing section of the Bureau of Standards laboratory, in Washington, and was found to comply with all requirements of the various U. S. building codes.

Nevertheless the Dymaxion bathroom never saw general use. Although Fuller maintains that "it is only the general inertia of the building world" which kept it out of production, a contribution to this inertia may have been the fact that one of Phelps-Dodge's largest customers, the Standard Sanitary Company, apparently still apprehensive of the plumbers' union, warned Phelps-Dodge that the Standard Sanitary-American Radiator business might suffer if they went ahead with the development of the bathroom.

"The reaction was unfortunate," Fuller said, "because the Plumbers Union, in 1936, stated officially in the union's journal, *The Ladle*, that the plumbers of the country were in enthusiastic support of the bathroom because it could be purchased on the same basis as a refrigerator to be moved with the household furniture, whereas the public which rents its living quarters never owns its bathroom fixtures. The Dymaxion bathroom would provide the nation's plumbers with some of the chattel mortgage market which is now enjoyed by the electricians."

THE DYMAXION DEPLOYMENT UNIT

Industry, as Fuller has anticipated in his "trial balance" inventory, had shown no special enthusiasm for either the Dymaxion car or the Dymaxion bathroom. The Dymaxion house was hibernating in his mind, awaiting the technological breakthrough which, according to Fuller's original reckoning, was due sometime in the 1950's, assuming an approximate 25-year lag between the inception of the basic idea and the conditions for its acceptance. Meanwhile, he occupied himself with other activities and projects. From 1938 to 1940 he was a technical consultant on the staff of *Fortune*. During the war years he was in Washington, first as Director of the Mechanical Engineering Section, Board of Economic Warfare; later as Special Assistant to the Deputy Director of the Foreign Economic Administration.

An interim development in this period was Fuller's Dymaxion Deployment Unit, a special type of emergency shelter. One day in the summer of 1940, he was driving through Missouri with his friend, the novelist. Christopher Morley. As they approached Hannibal, where Mark Twain once had his home, Fuller pointed to a row of glistening, galvanized and corrugated steel grain bins. "You see those little steel cylinders out in the wheat fields," Fuller said, pointing. "There is the most efficient engineering unit for a small prefabricated house now on inventory in the mass production phase of industry. Moreover, the grainbin provides enough room to house a small family, all at a cost of less than $1 per square foot of floor space of fireproof construction.'" This figure was 80% under construction costs in the competitive market of that time.

He explained that a cylinder encloses more space than a cube of the same wall area; with proper materials the walls are rigid, requiring no internal supports or bracing; the cylinder produces the most efficient distribution of internal heat; and its inherent streamlining cuts external heat losses to a minimum. This was Fuller's idea, but he was too short of money to do anything about it.

"I'll tell you what I'd like to do," said Morley. "I've just written a novel called *Kitty Foyle*. If 'Kitty' is a success, I'd like to let her help you produce cylindrical steel houses."

Kitty Foyle was an astounding success. And she was true to Morley's word. Bucky developed the basic plans for his "Dymaxion Development Unit," took them on a flyer to the Butler Manufacturing Company, producers of the steel grain bins which dotted the Kansas fields.

As a result the United States Army Signal Corps and Air Corps were able to have the first radar operating huts light enough to be flown and simple enough to be speedily assembled, in the most remote places. In New York, the Museum of Modern Art set up one unit as a special exhibit in its garden. Hundreds saw service in the Pacific Island and in the Persian Gulf area during the war. Hundreds, pirated from Fuller's designs, were in use in Saudi Arabia.

When the U. S. Government restricted the use of steel, officials in charge of supply came to the conclusion that the Dymaxion Deployment Unit — used only as a dwelling — was not of high priority.

Seventeen years later (1957), a curious incident occurred. Fuller was driving with Mrs. Fuller along the same road he had traveled with Morley. As they approached Hannibal, Fuller looked again at the same grain bins which had inspired the project. "How typical that was of Christopher," he said, "how warm, and how generous!" A moment later he turned on the car radio and heard the solemn voice of a news announcer say, "The novelist Christopher Morley died today."

In retrospect, it seems clear that the actual financial "help" Morley and "Kitty Foyle" gave was not of Fort Knox significance. It amounted to little more than the costs of air travel and hotel lodging during Fuller's initial week of talk with the Butler people. Yet to Fuller, Morley's gesture was as important and pivotal as it was generous: "He put up for me something no money can buy: a backing of creative enthusiasm, a confidence and joy in individual initiative, amusement over the paradoxes of adversity, and complete submission to the administration of what Christopher spoke of at Don Marquis' funeral as 'the Holiest Ghost we shall ever know: creative imagination.'"

THE WICHITA HOUSE

In 1944, a serious labor shortage developed in the aircraft field, the war effort's top priority industry. In Wichita, Kansas, for example, where the previous year the population had jumped from 100,000 to 200,000 because of aircraft production needs, and people were sleeping three alternate shifts to a bed, workers suddenly began quitting their jobs for work in other industries in other cities. A point was reached where the net falloff averaged 200 per day per factory. Union heads believed that the labor turnabout was caused by the fact that people felt the aircraft industry had no dependable postwar future.

Somebody in Washington remembered that Fuller had been talking about the possibility of a post-war conversion of the aircraft industry to housing.

Labor officials, including Walter Reuther, of the U.A.W., and Harvey Brown, president of the International Association of Machinists, interviewed Fuller. "What can your house contribute to the labor situation?" they asked.

"It might provide two things," Fuller answered. "It might provide an immediate solution to the looming postwar housing shortage. And it might provide permanent employment in the aircraft field because there is no basic difference between the fabricating of aluminum parts for the Dymaxion house and for the fuselages of B29s."

"If and when adequate time, money, resources, and know-how have been invested in the Dymaxion houses," Fuller continued, "they will be installable anywhere around the world with the same speed with which telephones can be installed. And with such economy of use of resources as to open up their universal availability to world's peoples." However, Fuller pointed out that the original estimate of a quarter of a century gestation period for this new industry, which began in 1927, indicated a "birthday" of 1952. "Ergo, whatever might be done in 1944 could be accredited only to the gestative functions. The time is premature for a consideration of this new industry as a commercially-exploitable undertaking."

He showed the labor men plans and figures indicating that a house weighing 6,000 pounds could be mass-produced for the cost of the comparable weight of a top-price automobile, at that time, $1 a pound. "All the component parts," he added, "could be packed in 300 cubic feet, although they will enclose 12,000 cubic feet when assembled. The house could be rented to the consumer for a basic installation fee plus a monthly charge."

Eric Peterson and Elmer Walker, vice presidents of the International Association of Machinists, both were convinced that this would interest Jack Gaty, of Beech Aircraft. "Beech," they said, "has the best labor relations in the aircraft industry. We will arrange a meeting for you at Beech Aircraft, if you will go to Wichita."

Fuller flew to Kansas.

"I'll make a deal with you," Gaty said. "I will let you have space in the Beech Aircraft plants, give you access to tools, use of the Beech Aircraft purchasing department, all on a nominal space rental basis. I will loan you top-ability engineers and mechanics on a per diem basis. That is, you will be able to inaugurate activity in a going aircraft plant saving any capital investment. You will pay for your own materials, telephones, and so on."

In the face of the high priority rating of the aircraft industry, this was a fabulous offer.

Fuller resigned his government post, moved to Wichita, developed drawings and specifications for the new Dymaxion house. Meanwhile, he was invited, on many occasions, to speak to the various aircraft labor union locals of the Wichita region. The results were immediately visible in the employment picture. The weekly net gains in employment abruptly replaced the net losses in all the aircraft plants of the region. (It was the consensus of the War Production Board, War Manpower Commission, the Air Force, and the aircraft labor unions, that this reversal of the labor situation in Wichita was directly attributable to the introduction of Fuller's house project to the aircraft industry.) To guarantee the continuance of this employment trend, the Air Force issued an order for two houses for immediate use in the Pacific campaign. The War Production Board and War Manpower Commission moved the project into the highest weapons priority category for materials and men. What the project could use in either materials or men was negligible in view of the fundamental gains.

(Time seemed to justify this decision. The employment gains in the aircraft industry in the Wichita region continued up to the surrender of Japan.)

When the first Wichita house finally was opened to the public, many were struck by its spaciousness and air of luxury. The domed ceiling rose to a 16-foot center. A Plexiglass window flowed around the full 108-foot circumference of the structure. Accordion doors provided necessary privacy. Here were breathing room, sweeping lines, extended horizons. Beechcraft's estimate of the mass production cost of the structural, mechanical components of the house was approximately $1,800. This seemed to indicate that, after additions for freight, seller's profit, and installation costs, the house might be made available to the consumer at around $6,500 — about the price of a Cadillac.

Those who visited the house in Wichita seemed to have been swept up in an epidemic of enthusiasm. An editor of *Fortune* reported, "Paradoxically, it is because he didn't fool around with compromises that Fuller's house has such an impact on whoever sees it. Because it is so completely radical there is no basis for comparison with the traditional dwelling. . . . In the living room one sees considerable exposed aluminum; the thin cables supporting the floor pass in front of the Plexiglass windows, which are riveted together. In Fuller's house this all seems so appropriate that it rarely causes comment. The circular form, which arouses such doubts as first, looks quite unremarkable from inside and rather unpleasant. Most unexpected of all, perhaps, is the general impression of luxury."

It was also reported that reactions were so generally favorable that the Beechcraft labor locals conducted a survey to ferret out objections. When the wives of 28 Wichita workmen were queried, their reactions were: (1) "It's beautiful!" (2) "I could clean it in half an hour." (3) "I want to buy it." (Twenty-six out of 28 gave this response.)

Suddenly the war ended. The labor shortage was no longer acute. The housing shortage became divorced from the labor problem. And ten million dollars for mass production tool-up was still to be raised if the Dymaxion house was to be put on the assembly line.

The Beechcraft people, who had never volunteered to underwrite the production of the Dymaxion house, returned their attention to the private aircraft production which they pioneered. The conflicting plans of post-war factions among backers of the house led to a stalemate, and all development plans were dropped. Fuller was left with the memories of his efforts and his enthusiasm. He was also left with a determination never again to put his projects in the lap of a promotion whose life or death was determined by the speculative instincts of others.

4 *Energetic-Synergetic models*

ENERGETIC-SYNERGETIC GEOMETRY

In his Milton, Massachusetts, schooldays, Fuller had been a critical but enthusiastic geometer. Yet it occurred to him, even then, that fallacies were introduced into the demonstrations when the teachers, following traditions more or less general in schools, assumed that points, lines, planes, and solids could be thought of as existing, when actually their existence was as fanciful as the hoofprints of unicorns. Fuller has always embraced abstract principles with ardor; but his principles have abstractions or general statements of operations that can be verified through experience. He has been an excessively practical Pythagorean.

To pretend that non-existents existed, and then to memorize the rules governing their non-existing existence, seemed to Fuller, in time, to be an endless game of blindman's bluff; all the players were flushed with transcendental joy at the prospect of not knowing where they were.

Yet there was a translation of geometric principles that could satisfy the demands of the most rugged empiricist. Force existed; its pull was a line; its effect could be plotted and measured. Forces (as energy vectors) displayed themselves in patterns; there were regularities to their behavior. The lengths of the vectors were proportionate to the product of their masses and their velocities. The derivations of vectors were measurable angles. And because these vectors always embodied velocity, they must also, by the principles of thermodynamics, embody time and heat.

Also, it seemed to Fuller that men had invented mathematical coordinate systems and several independent theories concerning nature, such as chemistry, physics, and biology. And with these arbitrary coordinate systems and independent theories they set about to trap and measure Nature. When the measurements appeared to be irrational in respect to these arbitrary coordinate systems, then men rationalized that Nature was perverse, diffuse, and indiscreet, and was characterized by irrational constants such as π (3.14159 . . . +).

Fuller reasoned that a good possibility existed that Nature herself had a comprehensive, incisive, coordinate mensuration system which might even be entirely rational. He noted that chemical elements combined in rational increments only; for example, hydrogen and oxygen as H_2O, but never $H_\pi O$. He thought it possible that Nature had no separate departments of chemistry and physics. He felt that by adequate observation of nature, without recourse to any particular modular frames, and without any elementary theory, nature's whole complexes could be charted and appraised, and that such charting, or orderly inventorying, might yield generalized behavior patterns governing all nature's transformations and accommodations. Beginning in 1917, Fuller attempted to organize into a logical system, the energy patterns he observed or discovered. The consequence has been an extensive series of propositions and demonstrations which, as a collection, he calls *Energetic-Synergetic Geometry*.

What follows is startling. Fuller saw clearly that men do not make structures out of "materials"; they make large structures out of small structures — visible module associations out of non-visible module associations. The limits of the visible spectrum did not represent the threshold of change between man-devised structures and nature-devised structures. There was, in fact, no threshold. Fuller became alert to the fact that there was a regularity of patterning linking the behavior of man-devised structures, such as bridges, buildings, frames, trusses, and the behavior of the minute or invisible structures, such as crystals, molecules, atoms. It seemed apparent to him that the patternings of force in a macrocosm were not essentially different from those in a microcosm; forces interacted in the same way, moving most economically toward equilibrium in all the forms of the universe.

If this assumption were correct, Fuller reasoned, he could isolate in one coherent mathematical system the significant rules which govern all physical structures. Energy plays no favorites. What you could or could not "see" was irrelevant.

One phase of Fuller's exploration for a geometry of energy resulted in the discovery of what he named *closest-packing of spheres*, each sphere being conceived as an idealized model of a field of energy in which all forces are in equilibrium, and whose vectors, consequently, are identical in length and in angular relationships.

Fuller learned much later that Sir William Bragg, the Nobel physicist, had — around 1924 — independently discovered the same geometrical arrangement in atomic agglomerations, and had logically given the same name, *closest-packing*, to this apparently fundamental energy phenomenon.

However, when spheres are packed together in concentric layers and as closely as possible around a center sphere, certain regularities of design appear. These regularities can be described by a comprehensive vectorial, quantum geometry. To Fuller this patterning appears to be the fundamental geometry of the universe, since it apparently accounts for the forms which interacting fields of force generate, whether in the interior of an atom, the shell of an egg, or a man-made dome. If the principles of this geometry are applied to industrial construction, the greatest possible ratios of strength to weight can be obtained.

Here are some of the peculiarities of these patterns:

If one sphere is completely surrounded by other spheres equal in size and packed as closely together as possible, exactly 12 spheres, no more, no less, make up the surrounding layer.

If a second layer, or shell, be formed around the first, 42 spheres will be required to complete the shell.

To form a third layer, or shell, 92 spheres are required. This structure, according to Fuller, suggests analogies with the 92 unique regenerative atomic systems which make up the total number of chemical elements found in nature, and with the nuclear energy pattern of uranium, the 92nd element in the atomic table. He found that if we add together the 12, 42, and 92, the numbers of spheres in the first three layers, we get the sum, 146, the number of neutrons in uranium.

Fuller assumed that every layer of a finite system has both an "interior, concave, associability potential," and an "exterior, convex, associability potential." And he observed that the outer layer of an atom system always has an additional, full number, "unemployed associability" count. It follows that an additional 92 is to be added to the 146 — the sum of numbers of spheres in the first three shells. The total is 238, the number of nucleons in uranium — whose atomic weight is 238.

Additional sphere-packed layers (shells) around one central sphere can be added *ad infinitum*. Each layer, however, is a complete and symmetrical enclosure of tangentially-packed spheres.

The total number of spheres in any layer (shell) can be found by multiplying the second power (square) of the number of layers by 10, and adding the number 2. (Thus the number of spheres in the third layer, 92, is 10×3^2 plus 2.)

Because the number of spheres in any layer is factored by the second power (square) of the modular subdivisions of the radius of the system formed about the nuclear sphere. Fuller saw that there existed here, in nature's closest-packed symmetric agglomerations, an agreement with the second power factor fundamental to both Einstein's energy equations and Newton's gravitational equations; in both of these the second power of the numbers of modular subdivisions of the respective radii of the systems considered govern the relative behaviors and values of the systems.

The additional two spheres of every layer — over and above the second power factoring — function as polar terminals, one at each diametric pole in each layer. These "polar" spheres provide a neutral axis of spin for every atomic system. "They are," says Fuller, "separately accountable from the second power shell potentials as convex or concave associabilities and disassociabilities, i.e., gravitation and radiation behaviors." The multiplication by 10, he discovered, was related to the number of triangular symmetries in each hemisphere of the atom. To account for the triangular

symmetries in both hemispheres, this number is doubled.

THE "DYMAXION" OR "VECTOR EQUILIBRIUM"

Spheres packed together as closely as possible around a center sphere do not form a super-sphere, as would be expected. They form a polyhedron bounded by 14 faces. Six of these faces are squares, eight are triangles.

Fuller's name for this 14-faced geometric "solid," which is always formed when spheres are closest-packed around a center sphere, is the *Vector Equilibrium*, because the value of its radial vectors is exactly the same as that of its circumferential vectors. In terms of dynamics, the outward radial thrust, in this figure, is exactly balanced by the restraining, chordal force, hence the figure is an equilibrium of vectors.

Words that are technically meaningful often have no pictorial virtues and convey no image. It may be useful to restate the properties of the Vector Equilibrium: All the sides of this figure are of equal length, and this length is the same as the distance of any of its vertexes to the center of the figure. For this reason the Vector Equilibrium represents an equilibrium of the lines of force radiating from its center, and those binding inward around its periphery — barrelhooping. Since directional lines of force are indicated as "vectors," it follows that the Vector Equilibrium represents precisely what its terms indicate — an omnidirectional equilibrium of forces. The magnitude of its explosive potentials is exactly matched by the strength of its external, cohering bonds. If its forces are reversed, the magnitude of its contractive shrinkage is exactly matched by its external compressive archwork's refusal to shrink.

Fuller once called this equilibrium-pattern figure the "Dymaxion." He later concluded that it was a gesture of conceit to apply "Dymaxion," a term that had become for him a kind of personal brand name, to a recognized figure in non-vectorial geometry and sometimes listed in crystallographic geometry as the "cubo-octahedron." He then substituted the descriptive term, based on the figure's force properties.

However, another point of fact is to be noted. The Vector Equilibrium is the figure formed by closest packing of spheres *around a central sphere*. It is a model representing equilibrium of forces under such given conditions. But what happens if there is no center sphere?

Fuller discovered this significant point: If spheres are close packed, and the center sphere is removed or compressed, the remaining spheres close in to form a 20-sided "solid," the icosahedron.

From this it follows that a Vector Equilibrium can be translated into an icosahedron and vice versa. They are close relatives. Each has twelve vertexes, and the same number of surface-defining spheres. And each is a model of symmetrical regularities. Each, in fact, has a place in a family of relationships which is capable of cycling through a sequence of phases, hence is what Fuller calls "regenerative." Fuller demonstrated this family of relationships of regular (equal-sided) geometric figures with a construction he called a *jitterbug*. The jitterbug was simply a Vector Equilibrium constructed with flexible joints. When supported, it was a perfect Vector Equilibrium consisting of eight triangles and six squares. When released, however, it contracted symmetrically, going through a series of phases. It became, first, an icosahedron, then an octahedron. Ultimately it became a tetrahedron.

Thus it follows that the Vector Equilibrium, icosahedron, octahedron, and tetrahedron are simply different phases of the same configuration of forces.

But whereas, at the Vector Equilib-

rium stage, the tendencies of the system to "cohere" or to "explode" were in exact balance, at the icosahedronal, octahedronal, and tetrahedronal stages, the "cohering" circumferential vectors developed a progressively higher structural stability advantage over the interiorly shunted "explosive" radial vectors. Conversely, expansive transformations of the Vector Equilibrium developed configurations of structural instability in which the "explosive" radial vectors were greater than the circumferential, finite, cohering vectors.

It was no surprise to Fuller when the trans-uranium elements were developed, some time later, and it was found that these elements disintegrated within split seconds. Fuller describes the trans-uraniums as trans-Vector-Equilibrium configurations — that is, atomic arrangements in which the radial vectors (the "explosive" force lines) exceed the circumferential restraints.

The steps in Fuller's logic that led from closest-packing of spheres to Vector Equilibrium, and from Vector Equilibrium to Geodesic domes, are not easy to follow. Nevertheless they represent a brilliant demonstration of deductive reasoning, rich in unexpected observations and conclusions. It is not possible to oversimplify the reasoning without sacrificing the precision and neatness of the derivations.

This is the sequence of arguments:

The closest-packing of spheres generates the figure of the Vector Equilibrium. When the Vector Equilibrium is partially contracted, it rotates sectionally, to form an icosahedron (a figure with 20 faces, all equilateral triangles).

Each vertex of the icosahedron is surrounded by five equilateral triangles. The icosahedron has 12 such vertexes, and each vertex is assumed to represent a sphere, that is, a spherical field of force.

If the process of contraction, or compression, is continued, the icosahedron is transformed into another geometric pattern. Each of the six pairs of the 12 external spheres will be so compressed that one sphere of each pair will swallow the other. There will then be only six spheres left, all arranged in symmetrical triangular faces. The comprehensive pattern which is thus formed is the octahedron (a figure with eight faces and six vertexes).

There are four equilateral triangles around each vertex of the octahedron.

If the contraction is continued further, the same surface rotations occur, and two of the pairs of external spheres accommodate the contracting force by the geometric cannibalism we have already witnessed: one sphere in each of these pairs "swallows" the other. What remains are the four spheres (vertexes) of the tetrahedron (a figure with four faces and four vertexes) in their closest-packing arrangement.

Three equilateral triangles surround each vertex of the tetrahedron system.

We come now to the conception of a *system.* Fuller defines a system as a patterning of force that returns upon itself in all directions—that is, a closed configuration of vectors. Insofar as a system loops back on itself, its dimensions are limited; hence the system is finite. It has an inside and an outside, what Fuller calls "withinness" and "withoutness." Every system consequently divides the universe into two parts: that which is within the system, that which is external. A plane (as defined by Euclid) can not constitute a system, because a plane is conceived to be a surface without limit. It extends on and on, to infinity, never returning on itself, never developing inwardness or outwardness.

It is characteristic of a system, as Fuller conceives it, that the angles around its vertexes must be concave or convex with respect to the position from which they

are viewed — concave if looked at from the interior space, convex when viewed from outside.

It is significant, however, that the angles surrounding a vertex can not add up to exactly 360°. For it is a condition of a system that it be finite, which is to say that it should curve back on itself from all directions. If the angles around any vertex added up to 360°, they would initiate an infinite plane. And since a plane has infinite extension, and does not close back on itself, this condition violates the requirement of finiteness — the essential property of a system.

The triangle is the geometric plane figure which has maximum rigidity, accomplished with least effort because, as Fuller shows, the vector (line) opposite any angle of any triangle is always operating at and between the ends of the levers which are the sides of the angle, thus providing maximum advantage over its own angular stability with minimum effort. Fuller therefore concluded that omni-triangulated, omni-symmetric systems require the least energy effort to effect and regenerate their own structural stability.

Fuller holds, further, that in any network, high energy charges refuse to take the long way round to their opposite pole. They tend to push though the separating space, striving to "short." Thus energy will automatically triangulate via a diagonal of a square, or via the triangulating diagonals of any other polygon to which the force is applied. Triangular systems represent the shortest, most economical energy networks. Fuller, consequently, took the triangle as the basic unit of energy configurations, whether occurring as free energy or as structure, and concerned himself with the derivative or cumulative systems that were, in essence, vectorial networks of equilateral triangles, or symmetrically-balanced sub-triangulations of these triangles.

The icosahedron (20 sides), octahedron (8 sides), and tetrahedron (4 sides) are the only omni-triangulated, symmetric systems. And all three, as we have seen, are "phases" of the Vector Equilibrium. Yet each is "locked up" — that is, it is stable; it does not of itself collapse further, or expand further, to become one of the other phases.

Each of the triangles in any of these systems can be subdivided into smaller triangles.

Symmetrical triangular systems provide the most economical energy flow, or structural, systems. Yet symmetrical triangular systems may be subdivided into sub-sets — asymmetrical triangles, each oriented to one of the three major symmetrical axes. The three sets of similar asymmetricals repeat themselves in orderly sequence around each major triangle's center of gravity. The sum total of these asymmetricals constitute synergetic symmetry of subdivision of the major symmetrical triangles. Fuller discovered a hierarchy of "most economic" networks with respect to symmetrical and asymmetrical energetic omni-triangulation of systems.

The three equilateral triangular systems, icosahedron, octahedron, and tetrahedron, and the subdivisions of their respective triangles, can be projected outwardly upon a spherical surface. The consequence is a spherical system — a spherical icosahedron, octahedron, or tetrahedron.

The great circle chords, rather than the great circle arcs, between the vertexes of these spherical systems generate a structural system of maximum economy because chords are shorter than arcs. These three chorded, symmetric, omni-triangulated systems, subdivided to any desired extent of synergetically symmetric frequency of subtriangulation, comprise the limit set of systems of least effort providing maximum resistance to external or internal forces, both concentrated and distributed.

These systems, when developed, are Fuller's *Geodesic* structures. In modern geometry, an arc of a great circle is called a "geodesic." In physics and mathematics, more is implied. Fuller speaks of *geodesics* as a physico-mathematical concept of "macro-macro energy cosmos structuring." The concept, sometimes attributed to Heinrich Hertz, was redefined by Riemann, and again redefined by Einstein. Its axioms are non-Euclidean. Fuller's own definition is this: "Geodesics are the most economical momentary relationships between separate events." To shoot a flying duck, a man does not aim at the duck, but where the duck is going to be. If the bullet hit the duck, its trajectory was a geodesic.

In geodesic systems, the higher the frequency of the triangular subdivisions, the less vulnerable is a whole system to destruction. In systems constructed with many modular subdivisions, impinging forces are swiftly distributed in the region of the impingement, and are inhibited by the succession of rings which tense around any point of pressure in the symmetrically and totally triangulated network.

(In June, 1959, Dr. A. Klug and Dr. J. T. Finck, of Birbeck College, London, wrote to Fuller enclosing published reports of their discovery of the icosa-geodesic structuring of the polio virus. In conversations with Fuller in London, in July, that year, they intimated that it is probable that all spherical viruses comprise geodesic arrangements of proteins in systems similar to Fuller's frequency modulated geodesic structures.)

Since the Vector Equilibrium, or any other finite system, could be broken down into a basic number of tetrahedra, Fuller considered the tetrahedron to be the lowest common structural denominator of nature. His hypothesis was reinforced when Linus Pauling's Nobel laureate treatise documented the discovery of the basic omni-tetrahedronal constellations characterizing not only all of organic chemistry, but also all of the combining patterns of metallic atoms as disclosed, thus far, by x-ray diffraction analysis.

An interesting confirmation of some of Fuller's assumptions of the relation of Energetic Geometry to atomic structures was given, in 1958, by John J. Grebe, Director of Nuclear and Basic Research, Dow Chemical Company, in a paper, "A Periodic Table for Fundamental Particles," delivered before the New York Academy of Sciences.

The mass of the various grouped subatomic particles, Grebe stated, "is highly reminiscent of a relation pointed out some years ago by R. B. Fuller in a report explaining the problem of building into a structure the maximum strength and rigidity with the minimum material. Fuller's solution involves the equivalent of tripods or balloons placed in closely packed cubic pattern. . . . These models could represent the structure of the so-called elemental particles mathematically, although not necessarily physically — too little is known to say that. However, it does seem as if these successive layers are significant in the properties — particularly the slow neutron cross sections — of isotopes, from the smallest nuclear masses to those of the twenty-sixth shell, and including both lead and bismuth." (Annals of the New York Academy of Sciences, Vol. 76, Sept. 15, 1958, pp. 5–6.)

THE MATHEMATICAL BREAKTHROUGH

One of Fuller's most interesting mathematical breakthroughs was the discovery that in an isotropic vector matrix (a network in which all points are equidistant from each other, hence all vectors are the same length) the existing points (which are also the centers of gravity of closest-packed spheres of identical size) are connected in such a manner as to produce a symmetrical transforming series of concentric geometrical enclosures or shells around either one central point or one central void. These enclosures can be visualized as spheres within spheres, much as the universe is envisaged in Dante's *Divine Comedy*.

Each layer discloses a pattern of points so arranged that when the points are interconnected by shortest lines, the area of the shell will be subdivided into "lots," each of which is a triangle.

The positions of the points in the layers (shells) are entirely congruent with all the centers of gravity of all the spheres of a uniform unit size which can be closest-packed around either a common center sphere or a common symmetric void.

Fuller discovered that in such symmetrical vector systems, the number of points in every layer, minus 2 (the two points that, for every layer, function as the diametric poles of the layer — "North" and "South") is the number of edge modules of the outer layer (shells) of the system raised to the second power, multiplied by one of the first four prime numbers (1, 2, 3, or 5), and again multiplied by 2:

(*No. pts. — 2 polar pts.*)
= (*No. outer layer edge modules*)^2 $\times$ (1, 2, 3, or 5) $\times$ 2

or

No. pts. = 2 + [2 $\times$ (1, 2, 3, or 5) $\times$ (*No. outer layer edge modules*)^2]

Fuller sometimes compares the frequency number of a system to the number of blades in a propeller. A given quantity of bronze can be patterned as one propeller with two large blades, or one propeller with 1,000 small blades.

Frequency, in short, is the measure of extreme modular subdivision development of a finite system.

When the term "frequency" is used in physics, its meaning is taken in just such a sense. Since energy can be neither created nor destroyed, every local event in the universe involves a local energy investment articulated at some specific frequency. The frequency number is the relative number of repeat oscillations which occur until the unit energy assigned to that event patterning is exhausted.

This, according to Fuller, is the schematic logic of quantum wave mechanics.

We have seen earlier how the closest-packing of spheres (around a center sphere) generates the contours of the figure Fuller calls the Vector Equilibrium, and how the Vector Equilibrium, when collapsed, goes through phases which form the contours of other symmetrical figures.

There are other "solids," i.e., external symmetric patterns other than the Vector Equilibrium, which are also comprised of the same pattern of closest-packed sphere layers as is the Vector Equilibrium. However, these other superficially different systems all represent symmetric contractions or truncations of the Vector Equilibrium, or additions to the Vector Equilibrium. But only "four primary systems," or "contours of symmetry," can be developed by closest-packing of spheres in concentric layers.

The exterior contours of these are the equi-edged:

1. Tetrahedron
2. Octahedron
3. Cube
4. Vector Equilibrium

In each case, the number of modular subdivisions of the outer layer's edge is regarded as the frequency of the system. (The icosahedron is excluded from this list because a concentric system of icosahedron layers cannot be formed by closest packing. All central coring must be removed or shrunken before an external icosahedron shell can be formed.)

1. Tetrahedron
If the superficial (external) pattern of the closest-packed spheres is the tetrahedron (4 sides), the number of exterior spheres (or points) will be:

$$2 + (2 \times 1) \times (\textit{No. outer layer edge modules})^2$$

2. Octahedron
If the superficial pattern of the closest-packed spheres (points) is octahedronal (8 sides), the number of spheres in the outer layer will be:

$$2 + (2 \times 2) \times (\textit{No. outer layer edge modules})^2$$

3. Cube
If the superficial pattern is a cube (6 sides), the outer layer spheres will number:

$$2 + (2 \times 3) \times (\textit{No. outer layer edge modules})^2$$

4. Vector Equilibrium
If the superficial pattern is a Vector Equilibrium (14 sides), the number of spheres in the outer layer will be:

$$2 + (2 \times 5) \times (\textit{No. outer layer edge modules})^2$$

In all four of the above "primary systems" the $2 + 2 \times \nu^2$ is constant and the only variables are the multiplication of the second 2 by one of the first four prime numbers 1, 2, 3, 5.

THE GENERAL STATEMENT OF
POINT SYSTEM RELATIONSHIPS

The number of spheres (or points) in any other symmetric arrangement of closest-packed spheres will always be one of the four first prime number formulas, as listed above. The only independent variable is the system frequency. All of the many symmetric forms, such as the dodecahedron (12 sides) and the tricontahedron (30 sides), will always prove to be one of the above formulas multiplied x-number of times by one of the original four primes. No new prime numbers are introduced.

This is to say that all omni-triangulated symmetric point systems are explicable in terms of the first four primes. This is a mathematical discovery that is significantly and uniquely Fuller's.

The general statement, in algebraic notation is:

$$P = 2 + (2 \times \overset{1 \to 5}{N}) \times (F)^2$$

or, in words, "the number of points in the outer layer (shell) of any symmetrical system is 2 plus 2 times a given prime number from 1 to 5 multiplied by the system's edge frequency to the second power."

Engineers are accustomed to think in terms of areas. Stresses on buildings are discussed in terms of the area of the surface which is involved. And surface area is computed in terms of the second power of some metric such as the radius of a sphere.

Fuller, however, observed that the function of area, or "surface," of a system is accounted for by his formula for points. He then reasoned that inasmuch as this is the equation for the number of points in the outer layer of any symmetric energy system, the phenomenon of "second powering" of the exterior of the symmetric system is to be uniquely identified with the number of existing points, not with the superficial area. The strength of a structural shell is determinable only by the energy relationships existing between the points which con-

figure the shell, not by the imaginary entity called "surface." A surface is in essence nothing more than the exterior set of a swarm of points.

Fuller also observed that "solidity," the cumulative sum of *all* the points in *all* of a system's layers, is a third power of the layer frequency, corrected for the same four prime number constants.

(The corrections consist of the addition of polar points, multiplication by 2, and multiplication again by the constant for the collection: 1, if the collection is tetrahedronal in its overall confirmation; 2, if the collection is octahedronal; 3, if cubical; 5, if a Vector Equilibrium.)

Since every symmetric system contains a neutral axis, with polar points, it follows that Fuller identifies "third powering" specifically with a symmetric swarm of points around and in addition to a neutral axial line of points. Yet another factor is involved. To find the total number of points collectively in all a system's layers, it is necessary to multiply the third power of the frequency by one of the first four prime numbers (times 2). Consequently, these collections disclose a fourth power characteristic of the number of points in the symmetric swarm — four dimensionality of total point population with reference to the frequency of the system.

A number of additional and fundamental mathematical discoveries resulted from Fuller's special energy accounting system. He found, for example, that the number of triangular faces (facets) which occur in any omni-triangulated system is always twice the number of non-polar points, that is, of the total number of all the points, except two. It follows from this that the number of triangular faces of such systems is always even.

He found that the number of circumferential lines, or "surface" edges, of these omni-triangulated symmetric systems is always three times the number of nonpolar points (all points minus 2). These constant relations of triangular facets and edges with respect to non-polar points was unknown to topology until Fuller discovered the peculiar fact that the additive *twoness* of systems was to be identified with the system's poles, and had introduced into the concept of symmetrical systems the energy economy requirement of omni-triangulation.

Another significant discovery of Fuller's was that although with respect to every non-polar point in such systems there are three lines, or edges, networking the surface, there are also always three lines (which can be regarded either as tetragonal edges, or vectors) connecting the point by omni-triangulation either to the next inwardly or outwardly concentric omni-triangulated point layer.

It follows from this that every non-polar point in the energy universe monopolizes an inherent inventory of six energy lines.

Of even more significance is the fact that each of these six energy lines, impinging on every non-polarized point ("focal event") in the universe, has a unique and symmetrical continuation beyond that point. The continuation of the lines can be regarded as negative vectors. The six positive and six negative vectors are symmetrically arrayed around the point. Consequently every point in the universe is inherently the center of a local and unique Vector Equilibrium domain, containing its 12 vertexes as the corresponding centers of 12 closest-packed spheres around a nuclear sphere.

Again, Fuller found that the geometrical voids between the symmetrically swarming closest-packed points take on well-known geometric configurations when the points are interconnected by lines representing the most economical relationships between the points. Because the points are omni-equidistant from one another, and because the lines represent the most economical relationships, there results an omni-directional omni-triangulation, by "omni-equilength" lines. This interlacing of the points discloses hierarchies of tetrahedra, octahedra, cubes, and Vector Equilibriums. At certain layer frequency levels the many polyhedra discovered by the Greeks and later geometers occur. It is to be noted, however, that all the complex polyhedra are derivatives of the first four prime number polyhedra: tetrahedron, octahedron, cube, and Vector Equilibrium.

The volumes of all polyhedra can be accounted for in terms of tetrahedra. Fuller chose the tetrahedron as a basic volumetric unit, pointing out that the identity of unit with tetrahedron permits volumetric accounting in Nature's most economical manner. The omni-angular accommodation around one point, for example, can nest only eight cubes. In this omni-angular accommodation around one point, however, it is possible to nest the exact equivalent of 20 tetrahedra.

Further, the tetrahedron is contained in the other first prime number polyhedra as multiples of simple whole numbers. Thus, by Fuller's tetrahedral metric, the volumes of the first four prime polyhedra are as follows:

tetrahedron 1
cube 3
octahedron 4
Vector Equilibrium 20

Because these metric values are rational (values that can be expressed as a ratio of a whole number), all the derivative, complex, symmetrical polyhedra geometries in Fuller's system — when expressed "tetrahedronally" rather than "cubically" — are rational. Nowhere in Fuller's geometry is it necessary to introduce irrational numbers, such as π (3.14159 . . . +).

Because the tetrahedron uses only one-third as much basic energy quanta as do cubes to account for all energy transformations, Fuller asserts, tetrahedrons are three times more economical than cubes. In structural systems, the tetrahedron uniquely articulates the prime number 1, and is therefore logically to be identified as the most economic quantation unit in universal energy accounting.

Because all energy event experimentation has shown systematic and most-economic behavior patterning, and because all most-economic pattern systems, asymmetric as well as symmetric, are resolvable into symmetric components, Fuller believes that his comprehensive point system relationship discovery provides a rational accounting of all energy patterning of "universe."

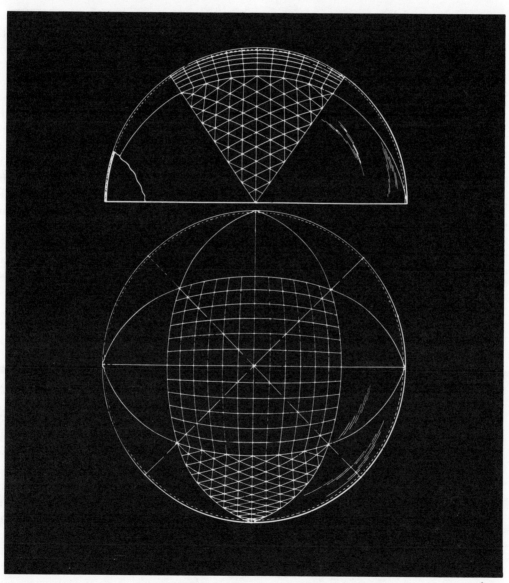

5 *U.S. patent drawing for Dymaxion map*

CARTOGRAPHY

Oddly enough, the first news-making application of Fuller's Energetic Geometry was the invention of a new type of map, the first in the history of cartography to show the whole surface of the earth in a single view with approximately imperceptible distortion of the relative shapes and sizes of the land and sea masses.

The Dymaxion map was not a shadow projection, as are other global maps, but a topological transfer of a high frequency form of Fuller's totally-triangulated systems from the surface of a sphere to the equivalent triangular spaces on the faces of a polyhedron. Unpeeling this "solid," and laying flat its unit skin, produced the continuous flat surface which is the map.

The standard map projection systems obtain true proportions in certain zones of the projection, paying for this sectional truthfulness of scale by exaggerated distortions elsewhere. Fuller's topological transfer of the earth's geographical data was accomplished with uniform distribution of the error throughout the entire planar surface. This uniform distribution reduces its magnitude at any one locality to a negligible amount.

The Dymaxion map was first published, March 22, 1943, in *Life*; as a cartographic innovation it was the first projection system to be granted a U. S. patent (No. 2,393,676; Jan. 29, 1946).

In his patent application, Fuller pointed out that all flat surface maps are compromises. The projection system of Mercator assumes that the flat surface on which the globe is to be projected comes in contact with the globe only at the equator; hence distortion increases progressively northward and southward, to the poles. If the projection system assumes the flat surface is in contact with the globe at either pole, distortion increases as the projection moves toward and beyond the equator. Other types of projection introduce compromises. A little distortion here is counter-balanced by a large distortion there; the consequence is an asymmetrical goulash of distortions.

The geometric principles underlying the Dymaxion map are the same as those used to develop the basic pattern of Fuller's domes.

The domes are based on the fact that a regular geometric "solid" (such as an icosahedron) can be projected outwardly on to the surface of a sphere (thus an ordinary icosahedron generates a spherical icosahedron).

To produce Fuller's Dymaxion map, we reverse this process. We start with a sphere, on whose surface a spherical icosahedron has been drawn. Next, we subtriangulate the icosahedron's 20 triangular faces with symmetric, three-way, great circle grids of a chosen frequency. Then we transfer this figure's configuration of points to the faces of an ordinary (non-spherical) icosahedron which has been symmetrically subtriangulated in frequency of modular subdivision corresponding to the frequency of the spherical icosahedron's subdivisions.

(The current version of the Dymaxion map consists of a transfer of points from a sphere to an icosahedron; the earlier version was a transfer to the Vector Equilibrium. The same principles apply in either case.)

The Dymaxion map has two significant virtues which distinguish it from all other maps. The first, as has been noted, is that it provides global information with negligible distortion of magnitudes. This fact may be of no importance to a man driving his car from New York City to Stamford, Conn. It is of extraordinary importance, however, to the navigational planning of global flights, and to strategists planning the course of an intercontinental ballistic missile.

The second is that it is the only flat-surface plot of the earth which presents all the true geographic scale areas in a single, comprehensive picture without any breaks in any of the continental contours, or any visible distortion of the relative shapes or sizes of these whole land masses. Thus, on the Dymaxion map, it is possible to view the whole earth's surface comprehensively as one great continental archipelago lying within a one world ocean. Consequently many geographic facts, not usually observed, become dramatically apparent. An example of this is the visual emergence of what Fuller has called the "Dymaxion Equator" — a great circle running from Cape Canaveral, Florida, across the United States, through Cape Mendocino, California, then going completely around the world, passing over 21,000 miles of open water without traversing any continent other than North

America. A guided missile fired from Cape Canaveral along this trajectory would not violate the air space of any alien power.

Another feature of this "equator" is that its north pole lies at fifty east longitude (from Greenwich) and fifty north latitude (from the equator). This "fifty fifty" point occurs at the foot of the Ural Mountains in Russia, where the Soviets maintain their missile launching station. This is the pole of a hemisphere which contains 93% of the world's population. The "south" pole of the Dymaxion equator lies in the watery wastes where there is virtually no population.

Because automatically guided aircraft or missiles usually fly most profitably great circle courses, or shortest spherical distances, the plotting of such courses can be effected accurately on a global scale, Fuller argues, when the points of reference are fixed in a world-encircling, triangular great circle grid survey.

WORLD ENERGY MAP

It is characteristic of Fuller to feed on his own creations, and to apply them to seemingly unrelated fields with surprising results.

Thus far we have seen how he moved conceptually from close-packed spheres to the Dymaxion, from the Dymaxion to the division of a supersphere into equal-edged parts; and how this led to the notion of a topological projection of points on the surface of the globe (with a uniform boundary scale) to the faces of the Vector Equilibrium, and how the unpeeling of these faces produced the Dymaxion map. But Fuller did not stop at this point. He asked himself how he could use this map for an improved presentation of the air-ocean world town plan which he had developed in 1927 and whose reference data he had shown in an earlier map.

The 1927 map could portray only half the world at a time. But now he could show the whole of the earth's surface in a single frame. Furthermore, the new map supplied a scale picture without any visible distortion so that a graphic display of vital statistics would be reliable in scale.

The primary question Fuller asked himself was: What is happening to the total population of the earth in terms of the technological advantages that might be made available? To answer this question it was necessary to reduce the idea of technological advantage to some measurable unit. Just as the French sociologist, Émile Durkheim, groped for a specific measure of human unhappiness and found it in the concrete statistics of suicide, Fuller reached for a measure of the social benefit available in advancing technical knowledge. He found his answer in the number of what he called "energy slaves" available per capita in a given section of the world.

This was the argument which led to his definition of the universal robot: One man can do approximately 150,000 foot-pounds of work in one 8-hour day, in addition to the energy spent from his metabolic income in "working" his own body. (This was a mean Fuller computed from U. S., German, and Swiss army data. A foot-pound of work equals the amount of energy required to lift one pound one foot vertically.) This additional work might be called his "net advantage" in dealing with the environment. The potential net advantage to be gained by each person each year, working 8 hours 250 days per year is 37½ million foot-pounds.

In engineering, the term "efficiency" means the ratio of foot-pounds of work realized to the foot-pounds of energy consumed by a given mechanical system. This ratio is usually stated as a percentage. The highest possible efficiency to be realized from a 1959 automobile is 18%. The low efficiency is a result of the designed in frictions of such mechanisms as banjo gears and reciprocating engines. The most modern coal-burning, steam-generating, public utility electric power plants operate at a little better than 40% efficiency. Hydroelectric power generation sometimes tops 90%. Most automobiles, as used and abused, are less than 7% efficient. House heating systems are less than 2%.

Fuller calculated, in 1950, that, in the gamut of the ill-used, ill-designed mechanical gadgetry of our mechanical civilization, it would be unreasonable to expect man to have an over-all operating efficiency of more than 4% with respect to the total energy, from all sources, consumed by him. In the United States, at any one moment during a 24-hour period, there is an average of a million cars standing in front of red lights with their motors going. In the face of Americans' love for hundreds of "horses," this means that we are paying at all times for a national stable of 200 million "horses" who are putting all their might into an invisible tap dance performed without measurable usefulness under the shining hood.

Fuller estimated, with a probable error of less than 10%, the world consumption of energy from mineral fuels (coal, oil, gas) and water power for the year 1950 as totaling 80⅙ quintillion foot-pounds (80,156,250,000,000,000,000 foot-pounds). Assuming that man's efficiency in converting his gross energy consumption into work averages an over-all 4%, the net work obtained amounted to only 3⅕ quintillion (3,206,205,000,000,000,000) foot-pounds.

Dividing this figure by 37½ million foot-pounds (each man's net annual energy output), the result is 85½ billion man-year equivalents of work done for him by machines. These man-year equivalents Fuller called "energy slaves."

85½ billion energy slaves

2¼ billion world population (1950)
= 38 energy slaves per person

Although it is probable that some day the world's energy slaves will be equally apportioned among all men, Fuller pointed to the current uneven geographic distribution. He catalogued "haves" and "have nots" among the various regions. Each inhabitant of North America, according to his computations, had some 347 energy slaves at his disposal in 1950; each Asiatic had two; each Central American had approximately none. The sociological unit, however, is frequently the family, not the individual. Despite the poor over-all efficiency of existing machinery, in 1950, every American family of five had exactly 1,735 effective energy slaves in constant attendance, not exclusively inside the house, but throughout the entire national industrial network.

Fuller then developed this information in detail and superimposed his findings on the land areas of the map, thus creating a chart sociologically as well as cartographically significant. This is the World Energy Map (first published in Fortune, in their 10th aniversary issue, February, 1940). The data indicated by coils of beads on the land areas of the map are expanded in the accompanying chart.

Energy slaves, Fuller maintains, are the natural "saviors" of society. Since the potential number of such mechanical batsmen available to humans is astronomical, man's potential control over environment is approximately unlimited. Further, such hypothetical workers, although doing only the foot-pound equivalent work of humans, are enormously more effective as industrial workers; they can work under conditions intolerable to man, in extreme heat and extreme cold; they require no sleep; they can produce items accurate to within one-millionth of an inch (skilled men can do layout work no finer than one-hundredth of an inch); see at distance magnifications a million times that of man's vision; and can voice their messages at a speed of 186,000 miles per second.

Energy slaves are the genii of industrialization. In 1810, there were a million families in America. And, sad to relate, there were then a million human slaves in this country, an average of one human slave to each family. Although many families were not the direct owners of human slaves, they lived in an economic network in which they were the indirect beneficiaries of the slaves' labor. The difference between the America of 1810 and of 1960 is not one whose democratic achievements can in any way be attributed to political democracy, Fuller holds. The difference is a consequence of the scientific design competence that made obsolete the 12-hour-of-work-per-day human slave who toiled for each family, and replaced him with a corps of 1,735 24-hour-of-work-per-day inanimate energy slaves.

Fuller asserts that the only difference between the Russia of 1917 and of 1960 is the introduction of the same inanimate energy slaves. Without the inanimate energy slaves, Lenin's socialism could only have arranged to have redistributed the grain crop of Imperial Russia so that instead of one man having a full bowl while five went hungry, everybody could have had a little in the bottom of his bowl once a day.

Fuller points out that the energy slaves have not "invaded," first America, then Russia, like the rains and the sunlight without the contriving of man; nor were the energy slaves invited to America and Russia by the persuasions or commands of politicians or militarists. The energy slaves had to be discovered in the realistic dreams of individuals and be design-invented into being. They could only be communicated with and brought to task by those intellectually disciplined to speak in the terms of science and technology, a language not spoken or understood by any politician (a generalization, he holds, to which Benjamin Franklin is the proving exception). It is the coming energy slaves which will bring the world its peace, if this peace ever is to be brought.

The essential problem of society is to populate the yurts and igloos of the world with energy slaves; freedom from want and freedom from fear are functions of environment control. And environment control depends on the availability of usable energy. If these statements seem visionary or suggest a mystique of mechanism, the reader may be re-introduced to a broader social perspective by a statistical fact. During January, 1949, when Fuller was collating his data, 5,000 people were reported to have died from exposure in a single city: Shanghai.

"As of 1959," said Fuller, "the problems of world peoples have been entirely entrusted to its political masters. The political masters ever and anon meet and get pushed by their respective sides into the word-punching ring called 'summit,' only to discover that they can not resolve anything by political statements simply because the world's problems are not political. The real problem is how to get three times as many energy slaves working as are now working, and to get them working for all the families of the world. This is a problem which can only be solved by competent scientific design ingenuity; and design ingenuity is a function unique to individual men. The near-est the politicos can come is to say: 'Let's not throw the energy at one another. Let's turn it into industrial power.' Ask them how, and they will have to call on experts. But even experts cannot be hired to invent. True invention has never been purchasable."

The net result of the farce of political premiership in the solution of world problems is that both sides descend from the summit suffused with negative apprehensions and state to their respective peoples that they must now undertake unprecedentedly greater precaution in dealing with the enemy's duplicity. They each authorize 40 billions of dollars annually to underwrite the scientific and technical inventiveness in their respective camps. The 40 billions is distributed through their respective militarys to their respective industrial establishments, with the demand that 40-billion-dollars' worth of invention be produced and "made operative."

The major industrial establishments then demand of their universities and subcontractors that they create the required inventions. Thirty billion dollars are spent in committee meetings and assistant researcher recombings of yesterday's scientific literature, patent files, and, above all, in magnificent building programs. Finally the authorities on each side find a dozen or so free-lance poet-inventors and pick their brains — thus harvesting their respective advances.

What is made operative is what the secret intelligence of each side thinks is worth copying in the other fellow's seemingly improved models.

There is an entirely inadvertent by-product to all this nonsense. In order to produce the two dozen inventors each year, both sides are finding more and more to-and-froing and more and more employment, strictly on the bird-flying basis that the more people employed the more the possibility that for every million employed, there might be one inventor. The inventor is about as scarce as heavy water. Millions of gallons of ordinary water have to be processed, to obtain an ounce of the desired product.

The rate at which all men will finally get on the payroll will probably match the rate at which the power-plumbing is being put on the cosmos, and the primary tools for the articulation of the energy slaves is created. And the foregoing rates will probably accelerate in inverse ratio to the brilliance displayed by the world's political leadership.

"You can't leave this problem entirely to the negatives," Fuller concludes. "Therefore the rate of acceleration of the coming of the day of total participation by all men in the total resource enjoyment at satisfaction levels higher than any as-yet-even-dreamed-of will be in direct proportion to the initiative taken by individual Joes in the competent disciplining of their scientific design intuitions. That is the invisible, realistic story."

6 *Geodesic restaurant, Woods Hole, Mass.*

GEODESIC STRUCTURES

It was indicated earlier that the Vector Equilibrium could be subdivided into tetrahedrons (four-sided pyramids) and octahedrons (eight-sided "solids"); actually it is composed of eight tetrahedrons and six half octahedrons.

A complex of Vector Equilibriums joined together form a matrix of alternating tetrahedrons and octahedrons. Such structures form what Fuller calls the Octet Truss. A frame built of tetrahedron-octahedron combinations provides an omnidirectional and equal dispersion of load pressures, with no member of the truss duplicating the function of any other. For this reason the truss has an enormous load-carrying ability; and its strength to weight ratio increases as the truss grows in size.

In 1953, at the University of Michigan, Fuller load tested an Octet Truss made of 170 slim 33″ aluminum struts, each weighing one-third of a pound. The entire truss, when riveted, weighed 65 pounds. This frame, no heavier than an ordinary canoe, supported a total load of six tons, the weight of a small army tank.

Fuller himself did not expect such a performance from the tetrahedron-octahedron combination. It was a surprise — the behavior of a whole not predicted by its parts. Describing the Octet Truss in a letter to his patent attorney, Donald W.

Robertson, Fuller wrote, almost apologetically, "I am sorry that my whole family of inventions tends, by rational acceleration, to sneak up on you and press you for attention. But isn't this the nature of invention? Invention is always a surprise."

TENSIGRITY

The Wichita Dymaxion House had been designed to be delivered across the Pacific in a single DC-4. The 1927 house was to be delivered by dirigible. The passing of two decades had been marked by such improvements in technology that shelter delivery was now possible by heavier-than-air aircraft.

After the Wichita House, Fuller concentrated on the problem of air delivery. He had never departed from his 1927 4D assumption that the air is our ultimate ocean, and that man's "mobilizing, re-circulating, design-regenerating technology" will eventually evolve into gossamer. But evolution toward gossamer depends on radical weight reduction; a spider's web can float in hurricanes only because of its high strength-to-weight ratio. For new design strategies aimed at radical weight reductions and strength intensifications, Fuller once again scanned the premises of his Energetic Geometry; he explored possibilities of intertwining the geometry with the inventory of war-developed technical advances.

In the planned 1927 4D house, Fuller had minimized weight by separating compression members from tension members. The central mast was a compression unit, around which hung a multiple-rimmed tensionally-cohered, horizontal wire-wheel house structure. Guy wires supporting the mast provided the balancing tension. In developing the Wichita house, however, he discovered that as he increased the diameter of the mast-and-guy-wire complex, the over-all mast complex weight grew less. And ultimately, at its dimension of least weight, the mast complex structure was congruent with the outside shell of the house.

When this "congruent phase" had been reached, the inner wall of the shell (the "mast" complex) would be in compression, the outer structure would be in tension. Although to the viewer there would be no visible separation of compression and tension elements, there was nevertheless a universal, comprehensive tension system in operation; this system laced the entire tructure into a single, finite, energetic embrace.

The universal comprehensive tension system could be interspersed locally with islands of compression, in the form of struts, in such a manner that the islanded compression struts would not touch one another. Yet these struts would force the tension network into outward patterning from the center of the total structural system in precisely the same way that molecules of gas inside a balloon press the balloon bag outwardly from its center.

Fuller saw that the gas molecules in balloons were not exploding in a radial pattern from the center of the system, but were bouncing around the inside circumference of the balloon, as sounds bounce around the wall of a circular

structure. But if the skin of a plastic balloon is viewed with a microscope, it is found to be full of holes. Therefore it was clear to him that an accurate description of a balloon is a "network" — but one in which the holes in the network are smaller than the molecules of gas. These molecules, coursing independently of one another like so many herrings inside a weir, impinge upon the weir net repeatedly, thus forcing it to balloon outwardly. Thus the action is not the result of a consolidated, group effort of the herrings in a shoulder-to-shoulder radial attack outwardly, in all directions, against the net, but rather of the high frequency ricocheting impingements of each herring.

This theoretical consideration of balloons and fish nets, herrings and molecules, suggested that the comprehensive tension network of his structural system could be patterned in such a manner that the individual compression struts would not touch one another, yet would hold the tension network outwardly in firm spherical patterning. That is, Fuller saw that he might be inventing a spherical building in which the bricks, or compression members, did not touch one another. Thus there would be a spherical building of bricks, in which the bricks would be interlaced with "rubber bands"; each brick would be in effect restrained from escaping from the pattern only by the rubber bands for no brick would be in direct contact with any other brick.

Fuller later concluded, after he had developed and successfully demonstrated a variety of discontinuous-compression, continuous-tension structures, that it was only the habitual tendency to think of all forms of matter in terms of brick-on-brick structuring that led to the assumption that the structure of the atom's nucleus could not be represented by a model — "even though the nuclear physicists had discovered certain geometric system pattern relationships with respect to the nuclear coherence."

Fuller called this special discontinuous-compression, continuous-tension system the *Tensegrity*.

What is startling about the conception is its pertinence to fields which ordinarily seem to be unrelated. Tensegrity supplied a generalized approach to the most economic forms of "man-occupiable" structures. And again, as nuclear physicists have suggested, it might provide in fact a true model of the atom's nuclear structure.

To understand how his compression struts could be successfully islanded from one another while thrusting the net outward, it is only necessary to think of a large number of pairs of live herrings, with the members of each pair so close to each other that the two appear as a unit. Each of these unit-couples are approximately evenly spaced away from the other couples but all of these evenly dispersed couples are within a complete spherical fishnet dropped into the ocean by a trawler (the neck of the net has closed after the herring have swum inside and the connecting line to the trawler has been inadvertently severed).

Imagine the herring pairs setting up a patterned herring dance; each member of each pair takes a position facing away from the other; then swims away from its partner, and continues in a straight line until it strikes the net — even if only with a glancing blow — thus pushing the net outward. After making a racing swimmer's turn, each herring races swiftly in a straight line back again to its mate, joins the mate momentarily, and then repeats this out-to-the-net-and-back linear darting, over and over again. Thus, we have a piscine ballet pushing the net outwardly in all directions.

Let us substitute for each pair of herrings, one round rod, whose two ends represent the two members of the couple; and arrange a pattern of these rods, acting as chords within a sphere, pushing at an acute angle in the opposite directions against the net in such a manner that the sum total of chordal patterns provides an omni-triangulated grid wherein the point of impingement of one rod is congruent with the mid arc of the chorded action of the next rod. It will be seen that such triangulated outward-pushing can be independently accomplished by the positive and negative chordal impingements on the net; yet the chords' ends will not be in continuous array.

This Tensegrity network principle could also be demonstrated in a linear manner — as Fuller, enlightened by a linear Tensegrity discovery of his student colleague, Kenneth Snelson, showed by developing a series of Tensegrity masts. From 1949 to 1952 his Tensegrity masts were exhibited on the campuses of many universities, including the Massachusetts Institute of Technology, the University of Oregon, the University of Michigan, and North Carolina State College.

The Tensegrity principle in its spherical omni-triangulation intensifies the structural integrity of Fuller's Geodesic structures.

It can be seen that Fuller's Tensegrity geodesics, like fishnets or balloons, could result in highly flexible surfaces. When it is desirable to have a Geodesic integrity with a non-mushy exterior, Fuller provides concentric Tensegrity spheres, one of lesser radius than the other, and the inner one of one modular frequency less than the outer. He interlaces the inner and outer spheres respective omni-triangulated point patterns. Each of the inner points connects outward to three of the outer points; and each of the outer points, as a result, is found to be interconnected to three inner points. The resulting intertriangulating of the concentric Tensegrity spheres provides an Octet Truss.

The Octet Truss, in this spherical arrangement, will be seen to be the same finite omni-triangulated patterning of Fuller's energetic-synergetic geometry, closest-packing Vector Equilibrium layers of any modular radius and frequency.

Compression columns have a limit slenderness ratio (the ratio of column length to cross-section diameter). If this ratio is exceeded, the column (strut) will buckle. (The slenderness ratio of a column of ordinary steel is approximately 33 to 1.) On the other hand, tension cables have no inherent limit ratio of section diameter to length. The "pulling strength" of a cable is the same in lengths of two feet or two miles. Thus it can be said that compression is limited and tension unlimited in relative slenderness ratio magnitudes, and their respective structural applications.

It followed from this that structures developed according to Tensegrity principles, with discontinuous compression, continuous tension, have no size limit. Theoretically it is possible to dome the entire earth in a Tensegrity envelope. Unlike other structures, Tensegrity domes increase in strength by a factor greater than that governing their growth in dimensions; the larger they are made, the stronger they become. It is only at the toy-size level that their strength-area relation does not show up to dramatic advantage.

Even at this writing, Fuller has plans developed for structures now feasible which could dome in all of lower Manhattan, or the site of an entire town. Such a dome, erected in the Antarctic, would give colonizers a temperate environment long before actual living and industrial facilities were installed.

GEODESIC STRUCTURES

The vertexes of the geometric figures which form Fuller's "systems" are points which determine great circles on the surface of a sphere. In modern geometry, as we have seen, any arc of a great circle is called a "geodesic."

When Fuller began to construct domes that were essentially networks of spherical triangles formed by the intercrossing great circles, he called these structures "Geodesic."

The three sides of a spherical triangle are formed by three great circles. A complete over-all network of great circles can be defined as a "grid"; since to form triangles a grid must have lines extending in three directions, Fuller regarded the Geodesic dome as a three-way grid of great circles.

It is not practical to catalog the thousand or more Geodesic domes constructed between 1948 and 1959 by Fuller, his associates, his companies, his licensee corporations, and his university students. It suffices to note that once the Geodesic idea got going it began — as Eugene Field once predicted of Chicago — to make culture hum.

In 1952 the Ford Motor Company became the first industrial organization to be licensed under Fuller's patents. Under this license they had constructed the 93-foot aluminum and plastic dome over the Dearborn Rotunda Building. Fuller considers the Ford Geodesic Dome as the fulfillment of his 1927 prediction of a quarter-century gestation period for his

Dymaxion enterprise. The dome arrived on schedule. Fuller refers to his first customer as "Mr. Industry himself."

Of great importance were the Geodesic radomes Fuller began producing in 1955 for the frozen tundra and icy hills of the U. S. Air Force's DEW (Distant Early Warning) line — the 3,000 mile strip of radar installations which clings to the northern rim of Alaska and Canada. Because of the violent and uncertain weather along the Arctic Circle, the Air Force required a structure that could be flown knocked-down to site, and then set up in the 20-hour margin of predictable good weather. The installation, when completed, was required to withstand a 210-mile-per-hour wind, and to be fabricated from materials which would be invisible to the radar's microwave beam. A radar beam is reflected by metal.

Fuller responded with domes 55 feet in diameter, made of fiberglass plastic. Standing 40 feet high, these domes in 1954 were the largest plastic structures that had ever been built. They were assembled on delivery, not in 20 but 14 hours; and they withstood static load testing for wind velocities in excess of 220 miles per hour.

By the time the Air Force radomes were constructed across the DEW line, the Marines had about 300 Fuller domes in use, some in the Antarctic, some around the equator. Fuller's 4D "anticipatory" realism of 1927 had at last begun to orbit; his structures, delivered in the air ocean, had spiralled the earth.

Another innovation was Fuller's paper dome; two such domes, manufactured by the Container Corporation of America, were sent, on invitation, to Italy — to be shown at Milan's international design exhibition, the Tenth Triennale, in 1954. The domes were awarded the Triennale's *Gran Premio*, the highest prize given to any participating country. The award was ironic since the United States had no official entry at the Triennale; Fuller's exhibit was a consequence of his exuberance, his dedicated belief in Dymaxion-Geodesic values, and the fact that he was able to muster enough support to lob his structures across the Atlantic.

In Fuller's opinion, however, the paper Geodesic domes were anticipatory rather than actual; they bear the same relation to the corrugated paper available today as the 4D house bore to the soft aluminum which was the only aluminum available in 1927. Even in 1954 Kraft paper having exceptional "wet tensile strength" had been developed — "wet strength" meaning the ability of the paper to retain its structural quality when saturated. But in 1954 corrugated paper board with good wet compressive strength had not yet been developed. When wet, corrugated paper board folded up like an accordion. To avoid the collapse of the Triennale and other paperboard domes, Fuller covered them with vinyl "bathing caps," aluminum foil, and other water impervious materials. He has delayed, however, any production enterprise in this area. High wet compression strength papers have already been demonstrated successfully in the laboratory, but they are not yet industrially available. When they become so, Fuller proposes to license the paperboard domes for mass production.

Large paper manufacturing mills have the capacity to produce 3000 domes per day, each dome with a floor area of 1000 square feet. Fuller estimates that domes of this type could be retailed in the $500 price range, that is, at approximately 50¢ per square foot. A concrete floor would cost about $200. The autonomous "mechanical package" for the domes — sanitary facilities, cooking and heating units — could be rolled in under such a dome for another $2000 purchase price or rented on a trail-it-yourself basis for a dollar per day. The conclusion Fuller draws is that with this type of structure, people, in time, may be able to enjoy high standard dwelling advantages at costs readily met out of a single year's income.

The U. S. Department of Commerce decided to set up a Geodesic dome as its Pavilion in the 1956 International Trade Fair, at Kabul, Afghanistan. What followed was perhaps an historical speed record for engineering planning, manufacture, and construction. The project contract was signed May 23rd. Seven days later all designs, calculations, engineering plans had been completed. By the end of June, the entire dome had been manufactured and packaged, ready for air shipment to Kabul in the company of a single engineer. The dome was light enough and compact enough to be flown from America to Afghanistan in one DC-4 plane. It was designed to be erected anywhere, by workmen speaking any language, who were in no way trained or briefed for the operation. Directed only by one Geodesic engineer, the Afghans fastened blue-ended dome parts to other parts whose ends were blue. Red ends were matched to red ends. And forty-eight hours after the arrival of the air shipment, the Afghans found that they had erected a great dome. A stranger, ambling innocently into Kabul, might reasonably have concluded that the Afghans were the most skilled craftsmen.

The Kabul dome, like Fuller's Air Force radomes, established another historical "first"; it was, in 1956, the world's largest Geodesic structure, 100 feet in diameter, 35 feet high at the center, it provided a clear-span, entirely uninterrupted floor area of approximately 8,000 square feet. The dome frame was formed by 480 aluminum tubes, three inches in diameter. The frame weighed 9,200 pounds; the nylon skin, 1,300 pounds.

A signal feature of the dome's "informational" value, at Kabul, was the fact that the dome attracted far greater attention, and attendance than all other exhibits including the Russian and the Chinese Communist. Both groups had spent months and many times the cost of the U. S. exhibit, in the preparation of their special pavilions.

Capitalizing on this success, the United States government arranged to have Geodesic domes set up at other international trade fairs. The Department of Commerce had now become interested in the kudos value of Geodesic domes. The Geodesics, it was argued, dramatized American ingenuity, vision, and technological dynamism; as structures to house American trade exhibits they would be tangible symbols of progress. Fuller's three-way grids were better propaganda than double-meaning speeches broadcast to regions in which radios were scarce. Domes as large as the Kabul dome, and larger, were flown from country to country, girdling the globe; and many of these also set attendance records. Within a short space, Fuller's domes were seen in Poznan, Casablanca, Tunis, Salonika, Istanbul, Madras, Delhi, Bombay, Rangoon, Bangkok, Tokyo, and Osaka.

The breakthrough to large-scale industrial marketing of the Geodesic idea began in the latter part of 1956. Donald Richter, a former student and associate of Fuller's, had gone to work for Henry J. Kaiser. Like many of Fuller's students, Richter had become an avid constructor of Geodesic models and had installed one miniscule dome in his office. Kaiser strode through the office one day and saw the model. "What's this?" Kaiser asked, with reasonable interest. Richter explained; and the consequence of this seemingly accidental event was that Kaiser's metal-fabricating customers geared up to mass-produce quarter-million-dollar domes.

The Geodesic "building construction," as it is called in the patent application, was covered fully by a U. S. patent (No. 2,682,235) issued to Fuller in June, 1954; and from this time on, all users of the system were required to be licensed by Fuller. Kaiser Aluminum became one of the early licensees. The initial Kaiser project was an aluminum-skinned, 145-foot-diameter auditorium for Henry Kaiser's Hawaiian Village, in Honolulu. The project construction men were startled by the speed with which the Geodesic dome went up. For Kaiser the speed had almost a shock effect. He wanted to see the dome rise; and the day the workmen started on the structure he hopped a plane from San Francisco, intending to be on hand during the first week's construction. By the time his plane reached Honolulu, however, the dome was finished. As a dramatic fillip, the Kaiser promotion men arranged to have it formally opened the same night, when it housed an audience of 1,832 and a symphony orchestra.

By the end of 1958, Kaiser Aluminum's fabricator customers had produced eight domes, including one used as a theatre in Fort Worth, Texas, one as a bank in Oklahoma City. The Kaiser organization assumed that there was a probable market for at least one dome to every American town large enough to use a community center. The domes are now available in a number of sizes, at prices ranging from $50,000 to $190,000, exclusive of foundation and interior detail. The most publicized Kaiser-erected Fuller dome of 1959, however, was the Geodesic dome housing the United States exhibit at the World's Fair in Moscow. It was on seeing this dome that Nikita Khrushchev exclaimed, "I would like to have J. Buckingham Fuller come to Russia and teach our engineers."

The largest clear-span enclosure ever to be erected anywhere in the world is the steel-skinned Geodesic structure Fuller's own company, Synergetics, Inc., designed for the Union Tank Car Company, and which was completed and put into operation at Baton Rouge, La., in October, 1958. This dome is about 23 times the volumetric size of the dome on St. Peter's Church in Rome. It has a total clear span (i.e., without posts or obstructions of any kind) of 384 feet; it rises 128 feet at the center. The relation of dimensions to weight and to cost is extraordinary: the dome has a floor area of 115,558 square feet and encloses 15,000,000 cubic feet, yet its total weight is only 1,200 tons. In simple units, this is two ounces of structural weight for every cubic foot the dome encloses. Total cost was less than $10 per square foot.

A similar dome, planned of the same dimensions was under construction in Wood River, Illinois, by Union Tank Car Company's Graver Tank Division, and was to be completed by December, 1959.

The Union Tank Car projects were born when the company was scouting for some economic way to construct a railroad car rebuilding and reconditioning plant large enough to accommodate trainloads of cars at a time. It was important to have an enormous span of clear space to permit shuttling of engines and the swing of cars around a central turntable.

Union Tank is now a licensee of Fuller's, and, through its Graver Tank and Manufacturing Company Division, is offering all-steel Geodesic domes at a probable cost of $10 per square foot, or less, in competition with the Kaiser aluminum domes.

At the close of 1959, there were more than a hundred licensees operating under Fuller's cumulative array of patents. He now has patent coverage in many foreign countries, and a number of foreign licensees. And his experiences in past operations have led him to a personal philosophy of patents. In the craft equation, he holds, the patrons have the design initiative. Professional architects and engineers are retained, and rewarded for services rendered, only at the express command of the patron initiator. In the industrial equation, by contrast, a "comprehensive, anticipatory, design scientist" not only takes the initiative in development, but holds it — years in advance of any awareness on the part of industry, the government, or the public, that there is such an initiative to be taken and held.

In the industrial equation, as Fuller views it, the designer never renders his service under patronage command. Because of the complexity of industry, and of the economic accounting by industry and the government, the only possible control the individual designer can exercise over the economic inhibition by society of the technical advantages he anticipates on behalf of society, is through the patent. The patent safeguards the designer's right to protect the future from the inertias of the past. Society, like the guppy, devours its offspring. "Future comprehensive designers," says Fuller, "will have to be masters of patent law as well as their other fundamental disciplines — if they are going to be able to preserve the regenerative advantage innate in the individual."

Of the hundred Fuller industrial licensees, the largest, at this writing, is North American Aviation — a company whose total gross is on the billion dollar level. North American, in 1959, constructed a 250-foot-diameter aluminum Geodesic dome for the American Society for Metals, the official organization of metallurgical scientists. This dome, at the headquarters of the metals society, in Cleveland, was designed by John Kelly, and is a delicate, open structure functioning as a gossamer net arching over the society's buildings, gardens, and pools. Kelly looks on this dome as a forthright statement of the advances made in the alloying sciences, and as a realization of Fuller's concept of advancing technology's "over-all trend to invisibility."

Advancing technology, Fuller reasons, crossed the threshold to invisibility in World War I, advancing from wire communications to wireless, from tracked transportation to trackless. Technology's alloying evolution developed invisible solutions to problems of strength; and these invisible solutions indirectly, in 40 years, have shrunken the world to a one-town community. The real Magic Carpet is an alloy web.

SIGNIFICANCE OF THE
GEODESIC BREAKTHROUGH

For most of the three decades, following 1927 and the days of 4D, the Dymaxion house, and the Dymaxion car, architectural and national news magazines made frequent reference to Fuller as "failure prone." Condescending accolades were heaped on his ideas, but the assumption was that nothing would come of them; nothing, it was held, came of the house, the car, the bathroom, and the host of other early prototype developments. Today the picture is quite different. Fuller has suddenly become the conservative industrialists' ideal of the pioneer scientist. Pictures of his latest projects appear regularly on the front cover of the magazines which symbolize the tycoon press, and both business and the Armed Services have deluged him with construction projects.

To keep pace with the demands for his ideas, his technological knowledge, and his computations, and to keep in order his rapidly expanding bookkeeping chores, Fuller organized several corporations wholly owned by him, which channel the licenses for the use of his patents. Geodesics, Inc., handles all government and Armed Services developments; Synergetics, Inc., deals with design and research for all private industrial operations; Plydome, Inc., is one of Fuller's private research and development companies.

There are several explanations for the sudden change-about in the world's attitude toward Fuller. Long ago Fuller observed that conservatism is part of the normal social process, and that — according to the timetable then in effect — about 25 years were required to bring about general acceptance of an important new idea. Fuller waited out his quarter-century. The praise which is now generally heaped on his head can be attributed in part to another factor: industry, which recently awoke to the vision of the great economies and profit possibilities of Geodesic structures, has tried to side-step Fuller's patent and found the evasion impossible. Fuller has a hammer-lock hold on the construction principles.

Fuller attributes his sudden success to the fact that technological developments have caught up with him. His early designs were "anticipatory," not actual; they required materials which were to come but which were not then in existence, particularly the extremely strong light alloys, and strong, transparent, weather-resistant plastics. "All you need now is the knowledge of what you want to do — the billion dollars' worth of anticipatorily scheduled research has been done," he claims, referring to the estimate he made

of the cost of producing the true prototype Dymaxion house in 1927. "But society did it the easy and slow way, which partially accounts for the 300 billion dollar national debt."

He regards domes as basic environment valves, differentiating human ecological patterns from all other patterns, microcosm from macrocosm, yet permitting a controlled interchange of energy (including heat and light) between the two separated pattern regions. As an environment valve, the Geodesic dome is not limited in size; its span can be anything from a few yards to a few miles; it can envelop living quarters, gardens, lawns, acres, or cities. As an environment valve it can make possible cities of temperate climate domed over in the Arctic, the Antarctic, or at the bottom of the sea. It can shelter the lawns, gardens, and grounds in the midst of which a house is customarily established, thus causing the conventional house to become, if not obsolete, at least increasingly superfluous. To erect an expensive house, with rugged foundations and solid walls, under a highly efficient and relatively inexpensive environment valve would be equivalent to wearing a mink coat in an apartment with central heating.

Geodesic domes of sufficient size, covered with a transparent plastic skin, tend to become invisible; the permitted extreme slenderness of supporting struts enable them to escape detection when the radius of the sphere increases beyond a certain limit. The domes can be geared to rise from the ground, or to hug the earth, at the instance of control devices operating pneumatic or hydraulic jacks. Air vents and light-regulating louvres can be introduced at will. Winter heat can be effected locally, with radiant coils coupled to heat-exchange pumps. Privacy and space division, even room and room divisions, can be established in a variety of ways without requiring an architectural imitation of an Italian palazzo, a Norman villa, or the peristyle of a Greek temple. Some alternate possibilities are suggested in the latter part of the book.

Yet Fuller puts no undue emphasis on his domes. They are steps in a progression, not an end in themselves. What is important to him in the domes is their Pythagorean overtones — the fact that they are tangible, measurable illustrations of laws fundamental to the nature of the universe, of the spread and temper of energy patterns. He finds a measure of satisfaction in that the domes perform according to the predictions of Energetic Geometry, and that they function as evolving forms in a comprehensive design science.

The possibility of the good life for any man depends on the possibility of realizing it for all men; Fuller holds to this credo today as intensely as in 1927, when he organized the first decisive postulates of his synergetic cosmology and its consequent philosophy. And the full life, which encompasses the elements without which neither freedom nor higher social expressions are possible, is a function of society's ability to turn the energies of the universe to human advantage.

All we have to work with, in our span of life, is the energy system of the universe — the system which determines the dynamic structuring of the 92 elements found in nature, and the secondary, tertiary and sequitor phase structures (molecules, crystals, alloys, shelters, vehicles) into which these elemental dynamic patternings can be formed. The universe is what is given to us in experience; it is to be found as an integrated whole, not an assortment of parts. It is a Gestalt.

The problem of science, more particularly of a "comprehensive design science," is to separate out local eddies from the universe as it is experienced, directly or conceptually; to isolate specific instances of the behavior patterns of a general, cosmic energy system, and to turn these to human use. "I am not a creator," Fuller once said. "I am a swimmer and a dismisser of irrelevancies. Everything we need to work with is around us, although most of it is initially confusing. To find order in what we experience we must first inventory the total experiences, then temporarily set aside all irrelevancies. I do not invent my thoughts. I merely separate out some local patterns from a confusing whole. The act is a dismissal of pressures. Flight was the discovery of the lift — not the push."

At the birth of the twentieth century, the architect Louis Sullivan observed that production steel, which men were insinuating within the stone faces of buildings, was permitting "stone" buildings to assume shapes grotesquely alien to the nature of stone. Sullivan, in Fuller's view, pioneered a revolution of integrity. He sought to make honest and unashamed statements in materials that expressed society's new industrial capabilities. He inspired corps of esthetic disciples and emulators. Yet in the stampede of subsequent design exploitation, both his integrity of conception and his philosophic message were lost. The exploiters sidestepped the essence of Sullivan's phrase, "Form follows function." They made the words read "The ends justify the means," ergo, "Do business at any price."

In spite of Sullivan's recognition of the industrial equation — whose myriad patterns are invisible — the building arts, until now, have been pre-empted by the non-industrial, non-priority, catch-as-catch-can crafts. And in this streamlined chaos, architects have become as increasingly marginal as journeymen, tinkers, and drivers of hansom cabs. Like patients who diagnose their own ailments and sketch for the surgeon the operation they want, clients design their own buildings, and then demand of the architect his blueprints for action. The creative architect is hamstrung. Not only do his clients tell him what kind of building they want, and how much it should cost, but community codes, building laws, and bank mortgage biases have become instruments to the tyranny. Architects have left to them little more than the privilege of being exterior-interior decorators to skeletons prefabricated by the major steel companies.

Yet Sullivan's slogan held as a justification for all the late architectural stereotypes. The more glass and shiny metal used in the decorative ensemble, the more it was claimed that form was following function. The functions were not techniques for doing more with less; the functions were shine and gleam. In contrast with this distortion of the significant virtue of form in the building field, where form is conceived only as obvious structure, the industrial equation, Fuller points out, was creating decisive advantages in invisible structures. The Model T Ford is a case in point. Henry Ford's apparent doggedness in continuing to produce the Model T over a period of years, concealed the fact that the Model T was improving functionally, while competitive cars were improving only in cushioning and external styling. Before Ford finished with the Model T, he had introduced 54 different alloys of steel into it. It was these alloys which gave the car its service durability and pioneered Ford's success. Ford was improving his cars more rapidly than his competitors, but the improvements were invisible. Visible form could no longer follow the subvisible functions.

Fuller, today, sees a new industrial world forming — one that is a decisive step forward in progression to "a second derivative and surprisingly satisfactory world era." It is symbolized by the Geodesic dome of the American Society for Metals; for here the notion of doing more with less, as expressed in the trend toward invisibility, is dramatized by the dome's open structure which is pure system integrity. And he takes it as a straw in the new wind that the dome was fabricated by the most powerful of the aircraft corporations.

When Sputnik rocketed successfully into orbit, Fuller maintains, it shot down the military airplane. This signal act closed the half century in which the world's larger nations put behind the airplane weapon a subsidy adding up, in capital enterprise, to more than two trillion dollars. The new controlled, unmanned missiles made the airplane, by comparison, virtually stand still in the air; as a weapon it was finished. The immediate consequence of this military reality was that the two trillion dollar air frame and air power plant industry was roughly thrown out of its kept-mistress luxury quarters. It was constrained to seek a living on its own.

To Fuller, this event was not a catastrophe, but an opportunity to begin "the fundamental reorientation of the whole vital economic patterning of man." This was the day he had foreseen, some 32 years earlier — the day when man's highest knowledge and comprehensive resources could be applied directly to his living needs, instead of being assigned exclusively to negative functions.

With the two-trillion-dollar subsidy of high technical capabilities now tentatively available for living rather than military problems, Fuller believes that this reorientation is about to become a reality. The touchstone is the aircraft industry. In 1946, North American Aviation, together with Douglas, Boeing, Grumman, and others, had looked on Fuller's Dymaxion house as a possible, if not probable, post-war field for their respective enterprises. But the Cold War's cumulative half-trillion defense budgeting — which produced a jet age — temporarily shunted the industry from the building arts. It postponed the last great slum clearance project of technology.

But Sputnik destroyed the airplane weapon. The aircraft industry, paced by North American, is in a position to inaugurate a world-circling building and building mechanics service industry which can fly whole cities into position overnight, as great fleets sail into great harbors, fundamentally in grace with a vast environment. And as the great fleets can sail on, to continue their usefulness wherever they are needed, Fuller holds, so may the environmental facilities of man be repositioned about the earth, giving him access to the dwellings of yesterday, the productive resources of tomorrow, and a vaster reach of the universe gained without political revolution or panacea.

ILLUSTRATIONS

ASTOR PLANE; STOCKADE SYSTEM

7–8 *News item from the* New York Herald, *Sept. 29, 1922, reporting one of Fuller's early aviation experiences, piloting Vincent Astor's flying boat designed by Grover Loening. This was the first monoplane flying boat. Fuller asserts that his 55 years of experience with "ships of the sea," and 42 years of experience with "ships of the air," account for his "intuitive dynamic sense," which he considers to be the "self-starter of fundamental invention and design." He feels that theoretical knowledge, no matter how profound, can never turn over the complex train of techno-scientific and economic gears, without whose reciprocal functioning inventions are ineffectual or abortive. He classifies "ships of the sea" and "ships of the air" as vessels or containers that are to be classified under the generic heading of "environment controls."*

NEW YORK HERALD, FRIDAY. SEPTEMBER 29, 1922.

Fullers in Astor's Monoseaplane
Fly to Bar Harbor in 4 3-4 Hours

Lieut. R. Buckminster Fuller of the Naval Reserve, accompanied by Mrs. Fuller, has just finished part of a vacation cruise in Vincent Astor's monoseaplane, and will return to New York to-day from Bear Island, Me., and fly to Boston. There they will attend a wedding at which Lieut. Fuller will act as usher, and then they will fly back to Glen Cove for another wedding on Sunday at 4 o'clock and one at Lawrence at 4:30. That night they will fly to New York so Lieut. Fuller can attend an ushers' dinner.

The Fullers left New York last Wednesday in Mr. Astor's flying boat. They went to Newport for two hours and then flew to Wiscasset, Me., where they spent the night. Then they made flights around Bar Harbor and at other points along the Maine coast, stopping at Bear Island in Penobscot Bay. The trip from New York to Bar Harbor was made in four and three-quarters hours actual flying time.

Mr. Astor's boat carries five passengers, is equipped with 400 horse power Liberty motors, and can make 120 miles an hour. Lieut. Fuller, who lives on Long Island, served in the Navy during the war and is now one of the most active officers of the Third Naval District, being in command of Eagle Boat No. 15, Naval Reserve.

9 *A garage wall made of Stockade Blocks still standing in Lawrence, Long Island, on the property originally owned by Fuller's father-in-law, James Monroe Hewlett, co-inventor of the Stockade System and its manufacturing processes. (1923) Stockade walls were a system of reinforced concrete frame construction. The vertical frames were 4-inch columns on 8-inch centers. The cylindrical vertical 4-inch columns were tied together horizontally at every floor height by concrete lintels above and below every door and window opening. This continuous, integral concrete framing was poured progressively into tubular and horizontal space openings provided by 4-inch holes formed in the Stockade blocks which were 16 inches long, 8 inches wide, and 4 inches high, each with its two 4-inch vertical tubular holes on 8-inch centers. The Stockade blocks consisted of fibrous material such as excelsior or straw, bonded with magnesium-oxy-chloride cement. The fibers, impregnated by the cement, were blown into molds which felted them together. The 16 × 8 × 4 blocks weighed in the neighborhood of 2 pounds each; they were so light that they could be thrown to the second floor scaffolding, so tough that they would not break if they fell. The blocks were laid up dry; no mortar joint penetrated the wall. After completing their functions as molds for the concrete frame, they remained in place to serve as bonds for mortar and plaster, and subsequently as insulators for the wall. They provided insulation equivalent to 4 inches of cork. Interior and exterior walls thus formed seldom cracked, as they were independently bonded to the fibrous base, could expand and contract independently. The blocks were non-hygroscopic, consequently moisture was not drawn through the walls. Being petrified, they would not support combustion. Between 1922 and 1927, Fuller constructed 240 buildings in which the Stockade System was used. The structural system and stockade material was eventually sold to the Celotex Corporation, and may be frequently seen today in the form of an acoustical wall and ceiling material.*

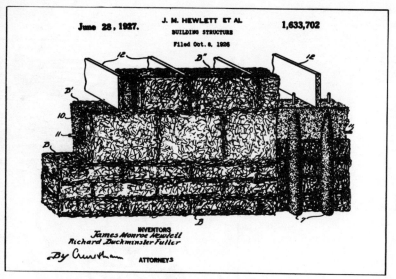

10–11   *Stockade Building System patent which was subordinate to Mr. Hewlett's basic stockade wall patent. (1923)*

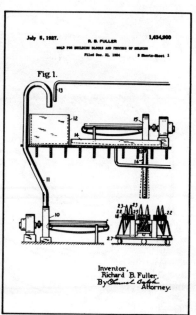

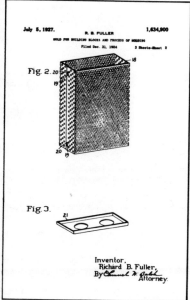

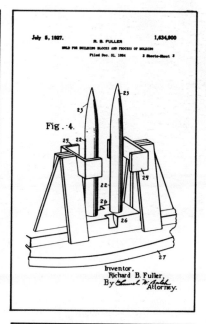

12–15   *Fuller's Stockade Block manufacturing patent, covering a wet-fibrous, pneumatic, felting forming operation, many features of which have since been adopted in the manufacture of fiberglass resin products.*

MULTIPLE-DECK
4D HOUSE;
AIR OCEAN WORLD

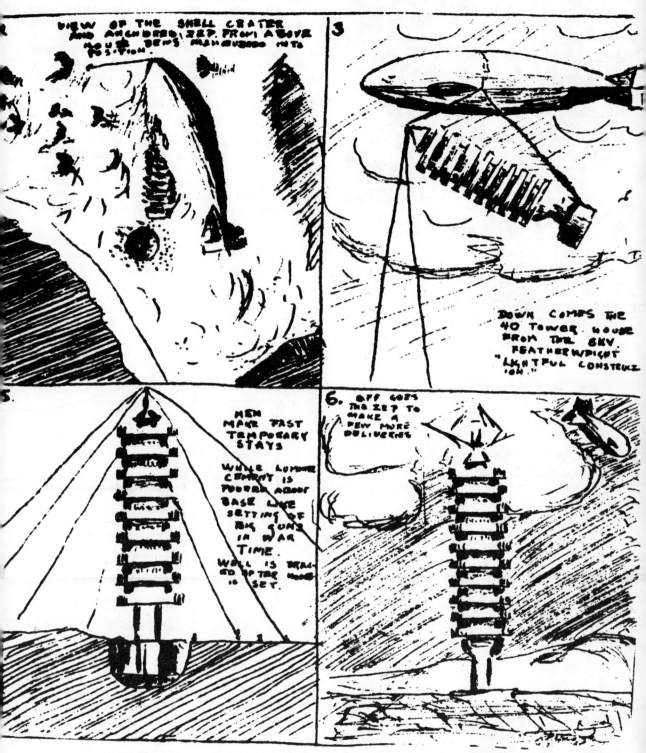

16 *Projected delivery by zeppelin of the planned 10-deck, wire-wheel, 4D tower apartment house. Fuller assumed that the dirigible, on approaching the site on which the house was to be erected, would throw out an anchor, then drop the bomb, creating by explosion the excavation to cradle the foundation. The 10-deck dwelling unit then would be lowered into the hole; the procedure, Fuller held, was "like planting a tree." The structure was to be supported by temporary stays until cement, poured about the base line, hardened. (1927)*

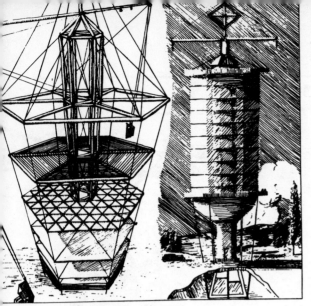

17 *Variation of 10-deck house design, 1927, showing the three-way-grid floor construction; pneumatic floor pads and their hard-shell covering; balanced boom for raising and lowering construction units and heavy pieces of furniture; tension cables; and septic tank. The hexagonal rim, to which cables are attached, is the external edge of an all-around swimming pool. At lower left, a unit bathroom (what was later to be the Dymaxion bathroom) is shown being hoisted into place. This picture by Fuller was published in the* Chicago Evening Post *in 1928.*

18 *Diagrams illustrating the effect of a streamlining shield. At left are typical air current effects: (a) a cube, (b) a cylinder, (c) an efficiently streamlined unit. The cross-hatched areas indicate the comparative size of structures which would have indentical wind resistance. At right: (d) is a model of a 10-decked 4D structure with streamlined wind shield.*

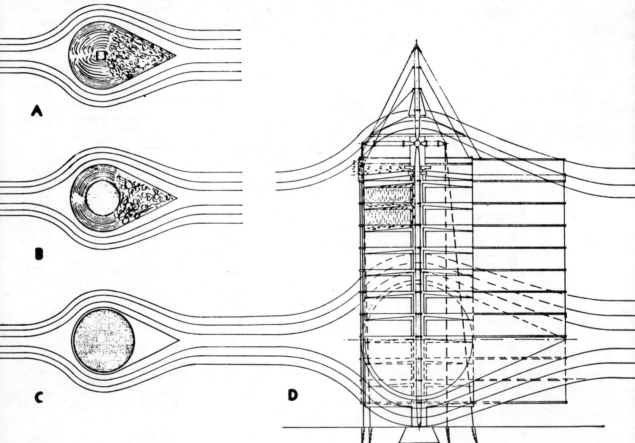

A

B

C

D

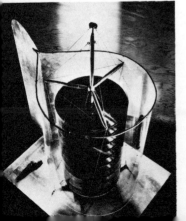

19 *The 10-deck building with streamlined shield. The heat losses of a building are proportional to the building's air drag. Fuller observed that a properly designed shield could reduce such losses to a negligible quantity. He has always been concerned with what he calls "the invisible behaviors of local environment-controlling structures." Prominent in all his environment control solutions are the invisible interior and exterior aerodynamics of structures. In the design of the 4D 10-deck building, the planned shield reduces the basic wind drag, hence reduces the necessary structural size of the building. The shield thus permitted the design of lighter structures, an essential factor in projected transportation by air. (This picture is also shown on facing page of chapter on Nonconformity and New England Conscience.)*

20 *The Air Ocean World Town Plan, 1927, showing 10-deck 4D houses, which Fuller
sometimes called "stepping stone, world airline maintenance crew environment controls,"
spotted around the earth in places where nature presented the most hostile conditions.
Installation points, inaccessible to man in 1927, included the Arctic Circle, the Alaskan
coast, Greenland, the Siberian coast, the central Sahara desert, and the upper Amazon.
Great circle air routes, which in 1927 seemed dependent on such maintenance stations,
were necessary to link the world's population centers. This drawing pre-dates by five
years any map showing great circle air routes. Fuller's original 1927 caption read:*

*26% of earth's surface is dry land. 85% of all earth's dry land shown is above equator.
The whole of the human family could stand on Bermuda. All crowded into England they
would have 750 sq. feet each. "United we stand, divided we fall" is correct mentally and
spiritually but fallacious physically or materially. Two billion new homes will be required
in 80 years.*

    *Feasibility studies showing that it was possible to have controlled environment in
inaccessible places gave Fuller what he called a "technical permit" to preview a world
integrated by air communications, hence a "one-town world." The "environment control"
structures were never built. It took the airlines many years to multiply the range of the
airplane to the point where it could "jump the inaccessible places," finally to establish
world integrating potentials. Nevertheless, the development of the Air Ocean World
Town Plan gave Fuller what he regards as a one-generation advantage in postulating an
inherently integrated world, in contrast to the traditional "remotely divided world."*

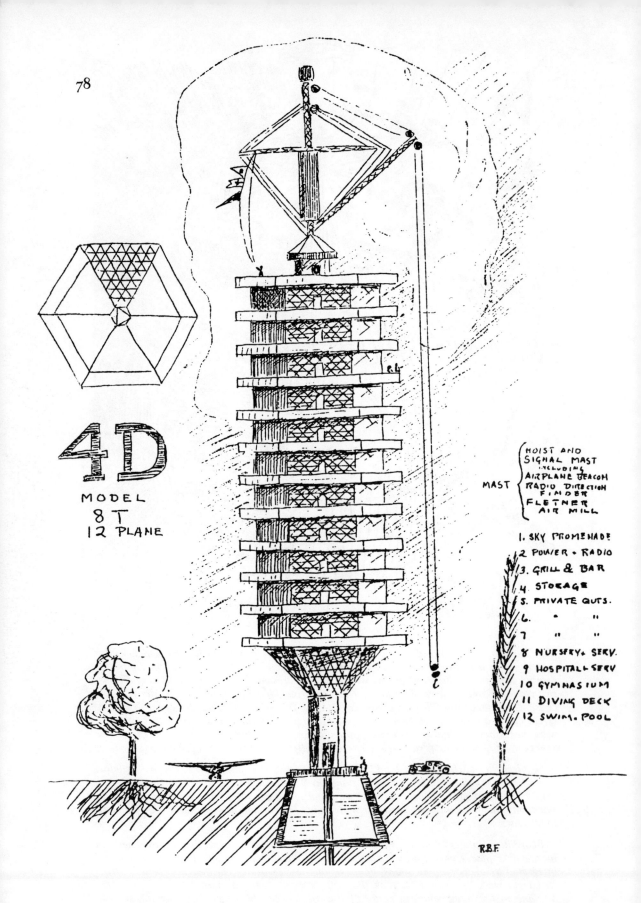

4D
MODEL
8 T
12 PLANE

MAST { HOIST AND
SIGNAL MAST
INCLUDING
AIRPLANE BEACON
RADIO DIRECTION
FINDER
FLETNER
AIR MILL

1. SKY PROMENADE
2 POWER + RADIO
3. GRILL & BAR
4. STORAGE
5. PRIVATE QTS.
6.   "   "
7.   "   "
8 NURSERY + SERV.
9 HOSPITAL+ SERV
10 GYMNASIUM
11 DIVING DECK
12 SWIM. POOL

R.B.F.

21 *Twelve-deck version of the 4D multi-story dwelling unit. Details show the hoist and signal mast, airplane beacon, Fletner air-rotor mill (wind operated power generator), sky promenade, living apartments, community facilities, diving deck, and swimming pool.*

22 *Sketch by Fuller showing the hypothetical installation of a 4D multi-story dwelling unit near the North Pole. (1927)*

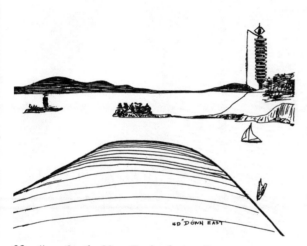

23 *". . . On the New England coast."*

25 *4D sketch by Fuller: "Entering a 4D city on the night airway express." (1927)*

24 *Interior of the overhang deck in a 4D multi-story dwelling as shown in one of Fuller's drawings on a mimeograph stencil. The cross-hatching represents triangular vacuum window plates.*

26 *Fuller's projected 100-deck office building, which was combined with a suspension bridge whose masts curbed back on themselves like the rim of a wheel from whose hub the decks were suspended.*

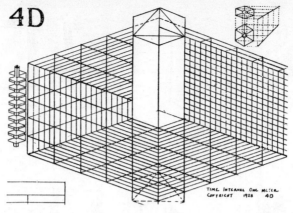

27 *Coordinate system developed by Fuller to locate positions horizontally and vertically with respect to the space encompassed by the multi-deck structures. (1927)*

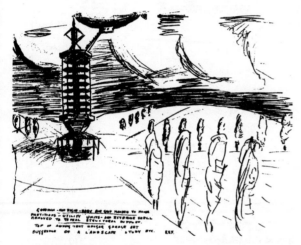

28 *One of Fuller's 1927 ideas was that the mast of the multi-deck house could be used as a dirigible mooring. Several years later, others, adopting this idea, proposed to use the tower of the Empire State Building for the same purpose.*

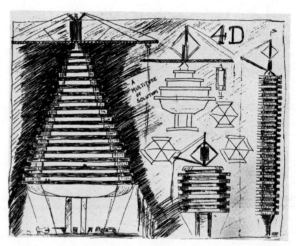

29 *Alternate forms of multi-deck 4D houses. Shown in the lower left corner is Fuller's early conception of the 4D omni-directional transport.*

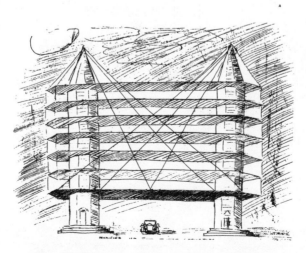

30 *Modified 4D twin tower office building.*

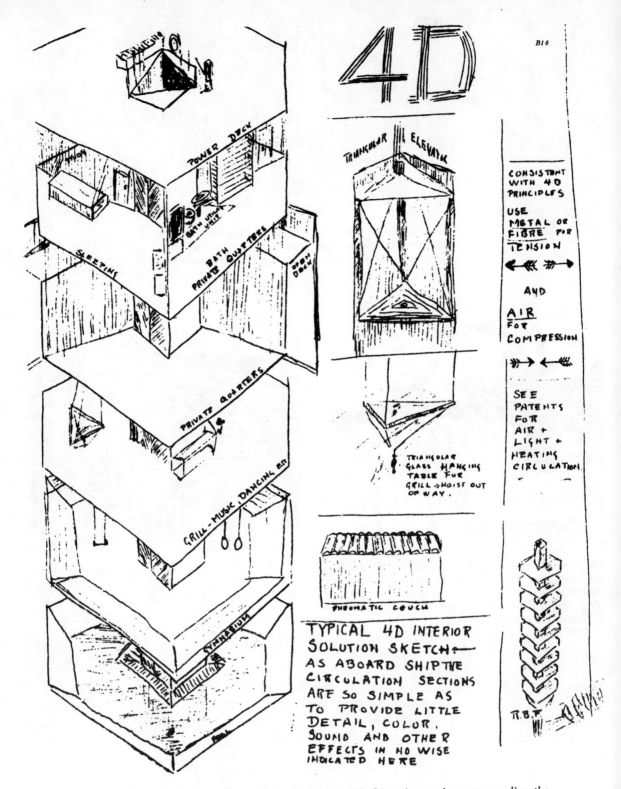

31 *Sketch by Fuller showing a cutaway view of typical interior sections surrounding the center shaft of the multi-story dwelling.*

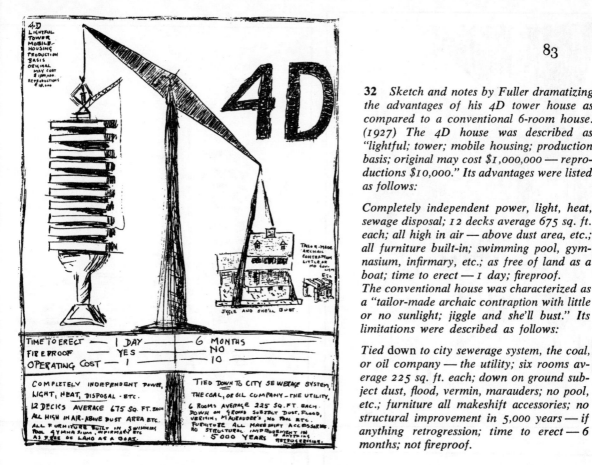

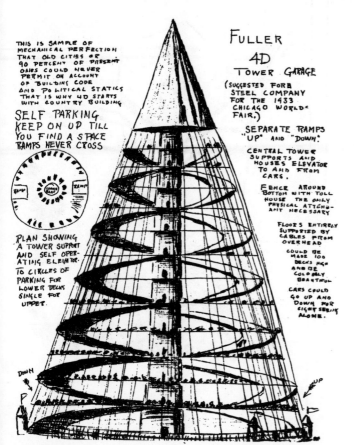

32 *Sketch and notes by Fuller dramatizing the advantages of his 4D tower house as compared to a conventional 6-room house. (1927) The 4D house was described as "lightful; tower; mobile housing; production basis; original may cost $1,000,000 — reproductions $10,000." Its advantages were listed as follows:*

Completely independent power, light, heat, sewage disposal; 12 decks average 675 sq. ft. each; all high in air — above dust area, etc.; all furniture built-in; swimming pool, gymnasium, infirmary, etc.; as free of land as a boat; time to erect — 1 day; fireproof.
The conventional house was characterized as a "tailor-made archaic contraption with little or no sunlight; jiggle and she'll bust." Its limitations were described as follows:

Tied down *to city sewerage system, the coal, or oil company — the utility; six rooms average 225 sq. ft. each; down on ground subject dust, flood, vermin, marauders; no pool, etc.; furniture all makeshift accessories; no structural improvement in 5,000 years — if anything retrogression; time to erect — 6 months; not fireproof.*

33 *Sketch by Fuller of 4D tower garage suggested as a steel company exhibit for the 1933 Chicago World's Fair. (1927) The accompanying notes read in part:*

Fuller 4D Tower Garage. Plan showing a tower support and self-operating elevator to circles of parking.

SELF PARKING — KEEP ON UP TILL YOU FIND A SPACE — RAMPS NEVER CROSS.

Separate ramps for "up" and "down." Central tower supports and houses elevator to and from cars. Fence around bottom with tollhouse — the only physical attendant necessary. Floors entirely supported by cables from overhead. Could be made 100 decks high and be colossally beautiful. Cars could go up and down for sightseeing alone.

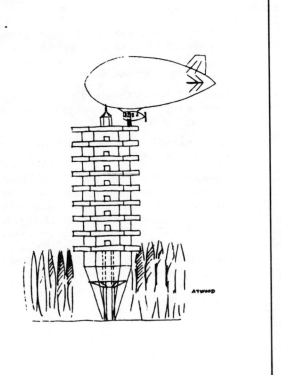

34–39 *Sketches by Fuller's drafts-men and students, 1927–28, showing various types and operations of 4D multi-deck houses. Shown in most of the sketches is the triangulated tension network which formed the shell that comprised the swimming pool as the lower component of the tower struc-ture. This triangular comprehensive tension principle is akin to the pattern used in Fuller's geodesic structures, initiated some 40 years later.*

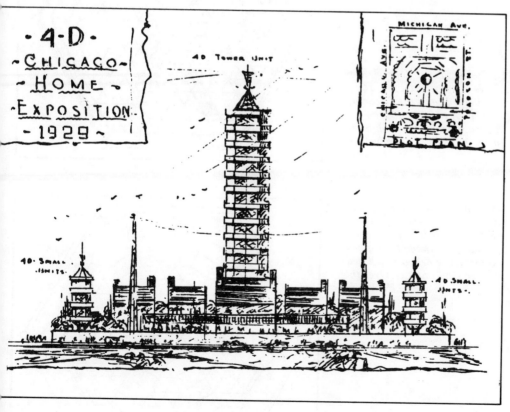

DYMAXION HOUSE

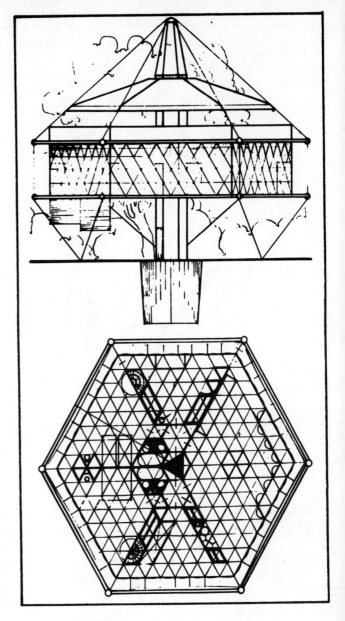

40 *Elevation and floor plan of the 4D Dymaxion House; 1928. Fuller calls this the "clean-up model" of two earlier versions, the first of which was published in the magazine,* Architecture, *in 1928.*

41 *The first Dymaxion House deck-tensioning pattern, 1927–29. Pneumatic bladders were to be laid in between the top and bottom cable network and tied-in like a bale of hay. Over this there was to be a hard shell floor.*

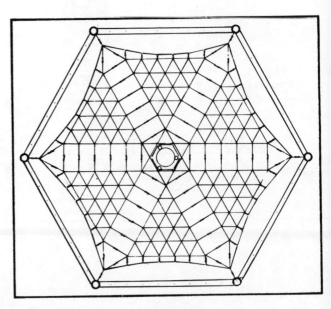

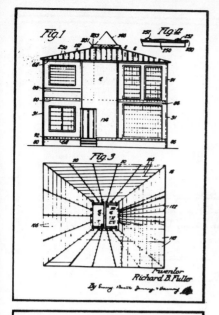

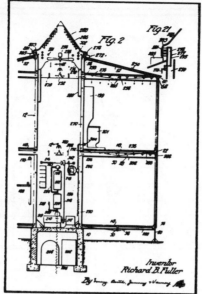

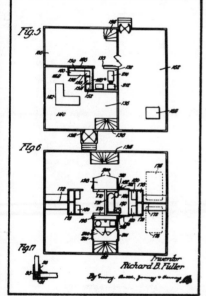

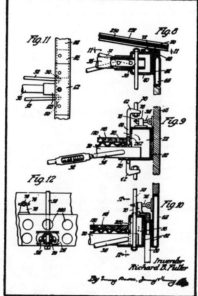

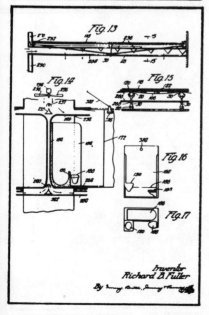

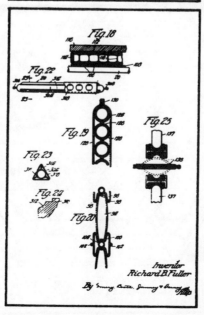

42–47 *The original 4D House patent drawings, 1927. These show the structure to be hung from a central mast, within which are located the heating, lighting, and plumbing manifolds. The heating and lighting are distributed from the mast to the surrounding rooms through the hollow ceilings in which are placed the appropriate reflectors and deflectors. Though Fuller's preferred use of his invention was in the hexagonal plan, following his attorney's advice his patent indicates that the system could also be used to provide a conventional box-like structure. The claims apply to any type of wire-wheel-like structure hung about a mast. Note in the patent drawings that (1) the foundation houses the water, septic, and fuel tanks; (2) the bathrooms and kitchen facilities do not rest on a floor, but are suspended from the upper boom; (3) all rigid supporting structures are thin aluminum tubes filled with air — true pneumatic structures; (4) the windows are vacuum flasks set in air-tight gasket locks.*

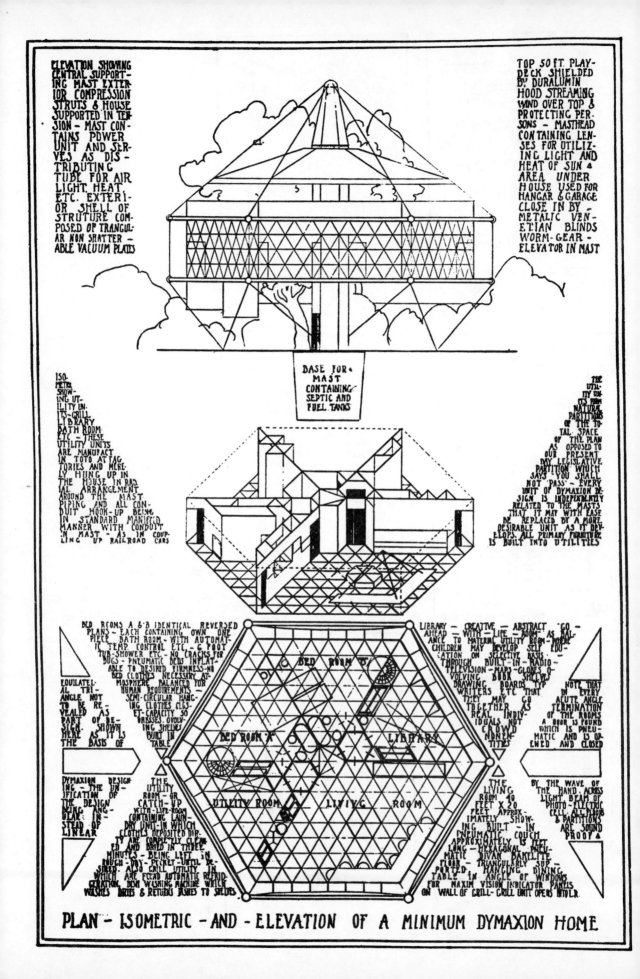

PLAN - ISOMETRIC - AND - ELEVATION OF A MINIMUM DYMAXION HOME

48 *Plan, isometric, and elevation of what Fuller, in 1927, conceived as a minimum 4D Dymaxion house. Although many of these items seem obvious and familiar today, none could be found in the architectural and home journals of 1927. Fuller's original 1927 captions, published with this picture in 1929 by the Harvard Society for Contemporary Art, read as follows:*

1. Elevation showing central supporting mast, exterior islanded compression struts, & house supported in tension. Mast contains power unit and serves as distributing tube for air, light, heat, etc. Exterior or shell of structure composed of triangular non-shatterable vacuum plates.

Top 50-ft. playdeck shielded by Duralumin hood, streaming wind over top and protecting persons. Rain drained to central down-pipe through heated mast. Masthead containing lenses for utilizing light and heat of sun. Area under house used for hangar and garage, closed in by metallic venetian blinds. Worm gear elevator in mast.

2. Isometric, showing utility units, grill, library, bathroom, etc. These utility units are manufactured in toto at factories and merely hung up in the house in radial arrangement around the mast — piping and all conduit hook-up being in standard manifold manner with conduit in mast — as in coupling up railroad cars.

The utility units form natural partitions of the total space of the plan as opposed to our present day legislative partition which says "you shall not pass." Every unit of Dymaxion design is independently related to the masts that it may with ease be replaced by a more desirable unit as it develops. All primary furniture is built into utilities.

3. Bedrooms A and B identical reversed plans, each containing its own one-piece bathroom, with automatic temperature control, etc. No cracks for bugs. Pneumatic beds inflatable to desired firmness. No bedclothes necessary. Atmosphere balanced for human requirements. Semi-circular clothes closet capacity: 50 dresses. Revolving shelves. Built-in table.

The utility room, or catch-up-with-life room, containing laundry unit in which clothes deposited directly are completely cleaned and dried in three minutes, being left in rough-dry pocket until desired. Also grill utility in which are found automatic refrigeration, dish washing machine which washes, dries and returns dishes to shelf.

Library — abstract "Go-Ahead-With-Life-Room" — as balance to material utility room — where children may develop self-education on selective basis through built-in radio-television, maps, globes, revolving book shelves, drawing boards, typewriters, etc., that they may go together as real individuals, not crowd nonentities.

The living room, 40 feet by 20 feet approximately, showing built-in pneumatic couch, approximately 15 feet long, hexagonal pneumatic divan, bakelite floor, triangularly supported hanging dining table in angle of windows for maximum vision. Indicator panels on wall of grill. Grill units open into living room.

Equilateral triangle not to be revealed as part of design. Shown here as it is the basis of Dymaxion designing — the unification of the design being angular instead of linear.

Note that in every acute angle termination of the rooms, a door is found which is pneumatic and is opened and closed by the wave of the hand across light beam of photoelectric cell. All floors and partitions are soundproof.

49–59 *Sequence pictures showing erection of the 4D Dymaxion house. Note that the structure is assembled from the top down. The house is essentially a wire wheel turned on its side, with the hub extended to become the mast. The compressional mast is islanded from the compressional "atoll" rim by the tensional web (the cables or "spokes"). This compression-tension patterning accounts for the integrity of the structure, tension providing the over-all structural coherence. (Fuller speaks of a structure, as a "regenerative pattern integrity.")*

When a wire wheel is turned on its side, another wire wheel, also on its side, can be superimposed, hub end to hub end. Fuller's 10-deck building, or a 100-deck building, could be constructed by stacking wire wheel on wire wheel. Fuller observed, however, that a stack of wheels could be "knit" together in a unit axis of hub alignments by three sets of exterior, crisscrossed, triangular tension lacings, permitting the elimination of many of the interior sets of tensional spokes within the stack. The 4D Dymaxion house consisted of two such wheels. (1927)

49 *Scale models of component parts of the 4D Dymaxion house, shown as they would appear when delivered to house site, ready for assembly.*

50 *The duralumin mast set in its foundation. Booms will be attached to the upper and lower hexagonal plates.*

51 *The wire wheel structure formed by floor beam tube held in tension by cables pulling from the mast-hub.*

52–53 *Floorplates are strung into place, tensionally laced between the hub and rim of the "wire wheel."*

54 *A hard shell placed over pneumatic bladder supports completes the floor assembly.*

55 *Utilities are swung into position, being supported by cable from the upper deck. Die-stamped bathrooms are in place, against mast. The utilities serve as space dividers; the 4D Dymaxion house required no wall partitions.*

56 *Ceiling units, connecting to mast, serve as distributors of light and air. Doors, operated by photo-electric cells, are shown at each vertex of hexagonal floor.*

57 *Transparent plastic, external wall plates have been installed and their triangular aluminum sheet camera shutter type roll curtains, and the roof deck and railings completed. The woman lying on the pneumatic bed is shown nude to dramatize the fact that within the house, temperature, humidity, and air flow are maintained at optimum levels, making clothing and bed covering unnecessary.*

58–59 *The house is completed when the Duralumin hood is suspended from the central mast. Night scenes show effect of central lighting system, located in the mast; light is reflected and diffused throughout the house.*

60 *Portrait of Fuller, 1927, with completed model of the 4D Dymaxion house. The house, as planned, was to have a total weight of 3 tons, including all equipment, and to encompass an interior floor area of 1600 square feet.*

60 *Portrait of Fuller, 1927, with completed model of the 4D Dymaxion house. The house, as planned, was to have a total weight of 3 tons, including all equipment, and to encompass an interior floor area of 1600 square feet.*

61 *The 4D Dymaxion House, with vertical section removed to show the air-breathing section of the mast top, the centrally-guttered roof deck, and the air and light distributing reflectors (between the decks and ceilings below).*

62 *View of Dymaxion house from ground level, looking up at the translucent ceiling through which the central lighting source is diffused. Fuller's early models, as well as his later full-scale prototypes, introduced color filters between the central "solar" light and heat source, and the diffusing ceilings to enable individual areas of the house to be separately flooded with light of any desired color.*

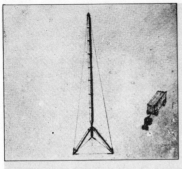
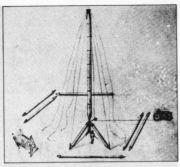
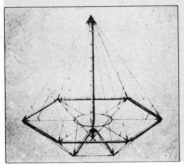
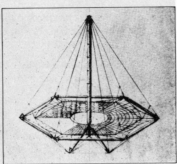
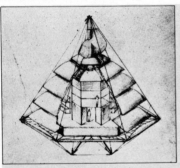

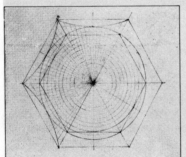
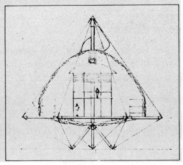

63–64 *Sketches showing the construction of the Dymaxion Mobile Dormitory around its central mast. (1931) Dormitory was a single-deck, wire-wheel structure with airfoil-type hinged skin units. Presenting these drawings in his* Shelter *magazine, Fuller suggested to the Russians that this structure would be of high advantage to them in their cooperative farm operations; it would make possible the migration of their farm workers with the seasonal patterning. The Russians informed him that the application of science and industry directly to the improvement of living standards was strictly non-priority; and that his devices would breed popular discontent with the Five Year Plan strategies which, for almost a generation, would require the reinvestment of all tooled productive capacities in the further production of machine tools. The Soviet leaders maintained, however, that after the primary Russian programs had been completed, this position would be modified; greater emphasis would then be placed on consumer goods.*

Fuller believes that this time may now be at hand. When Nikita S. Khrushchev visited the site of the American exhibit at the Moscow Fair, in May, 1959, and had his first glimpse of a Fuller geodesic dome, it was reported by the New York Times *that, "he could not resist turning back again and again to look at the huge dome made of pressed aluminum plates." Said Khrushchev: "I am thinking of authorizing Kucherenko (Vladimir A. Kucherenko, chairman of the State Committee on Building and Architecture) to do the same thing here in the Soviet Union."*

65 *Fuller has always had a catalytic effect on students. The drawings of the Dymaxion gas station shown here won the Architectural League of New York award for architectural student Simon Breines, in 1929. (Throughout the previous summer, the 4D house had been shown in the Architectural League's New York quarters.) On graduation, Breines, using Fuller's tensional-structure strategy, won second prize in the world architectural competition for designs for Russia's Palace of the Soviets. (The first prize was won by another American, for a classical style building.) Breines' solution was a large wire wheel in horizontal position. The Chicago World's Fair of 1933 Transportation Building employed the principle for the first time. Its designer, Lombiere, of Paris Beaux Arts school, consulted with Fuller on its tensional structure, but clothed it in a classically styled cylinder. The Chicago World's Fair of 1933 also saw many features of Fuller's Dymaxion house principles incorporated in its "House of Tomorrow" exhibit. Although the House of Tomorrow looked as if it were hung from a mast, it was framed from the ground up in a conventional but hidden manner. The largest building constructed on the unit wire wheel principle was the United States Pavilion at Brussels World's Fair of 1958, designed by Edward Stone.*

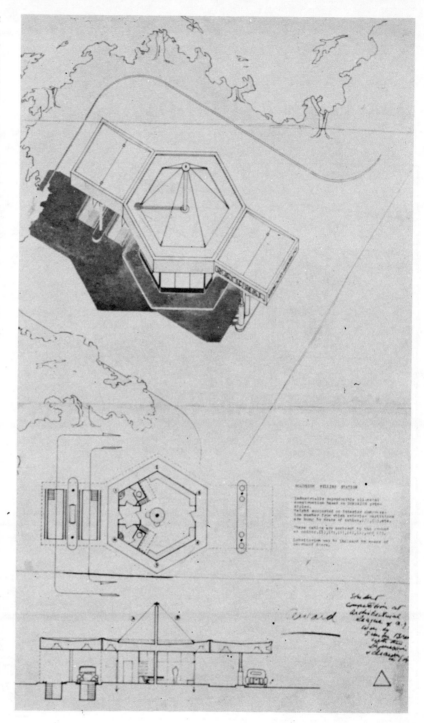

DYMAXION BATHROOM

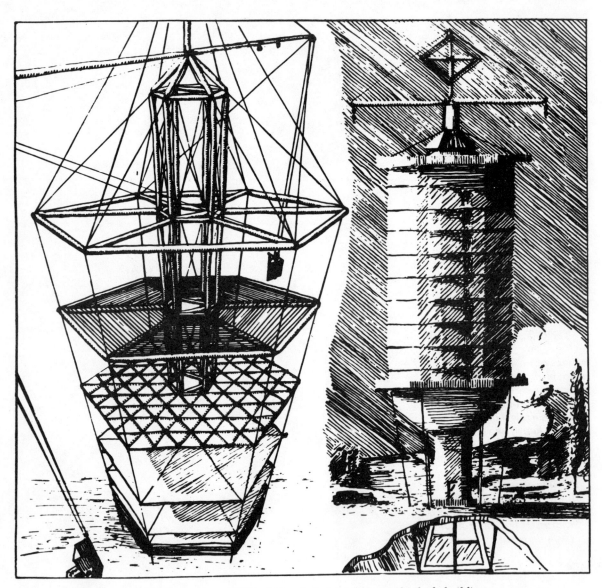

66 *Unitary bathroom shown as it would be hoisted aloft in 1927 multi-deck building.*
(This picture is also shown as 17.)

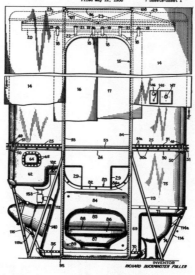

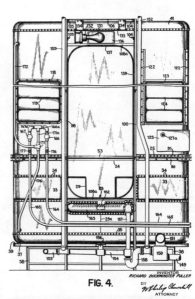

67–74 *Patent drawings showing details of the Dymaxion bathroom. (1937)*

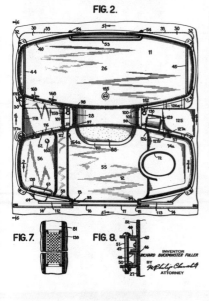

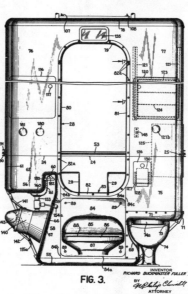

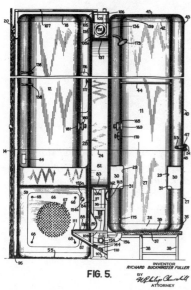

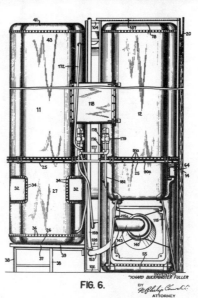

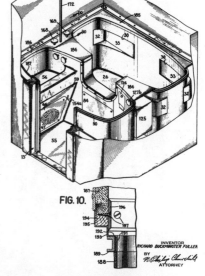

75 *The first Phelps-Dodge Dymaxion bathroom. Fuller improved on this model by making the front and back "rooms" of the bathroom in identical oval pattern, thus enormously reducing tooling costs. (1937)*

76–79 *Assembling the four main components of the Dymaxion bathroom. Each part was light enough and small enough to be carried through small doorways and up old-fashioned back stairways.*

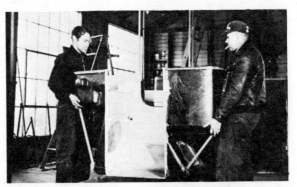

80 *Two completed Dymaxion bathrooms, showing electrical harnesses, and final control switchplate; together with air conditioning components. Each bathroom covered a floor area of 5 feet by 5 feet. In several instances two bathrooms were installed side by side as "husband and wife" units in guest and master bedrooms. (1938)*

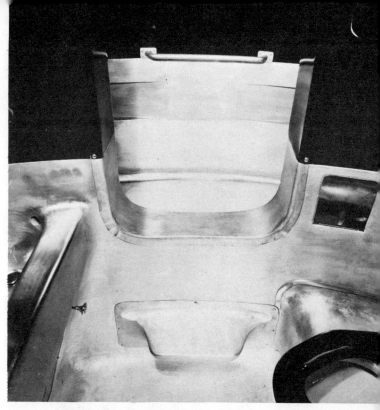

81 *View inside bathroom, showing cupboard opened in such a manner that mirror is in use even when door is open. A light was installed along base of mirror. The cabinet provided space for items as large as 5 gallon buckets. Round water control handles were of red and blue plastic. Hot and cold colorcoded water handles are now in use on bathroom fixtures in many parts of the world. Note the circular air exhaust grill on lower face of the wall, below the washstand through which steam and stale air were evacuated. The washbasin was without knobs or spigots. The waste handle for the washbasin was a black knob at knee height on the outside of the basin. The drain was actuated by a knob pushed to the right with knee.*

82 *Looking into the bathroom from the front door. Note the step for entering the bathtub and shower, at the same level as the bathtub bottom. Handles on either side of door, at entrance to tub and shower area, prevented the possibility of occupant's falling while entering or leaving tub.*

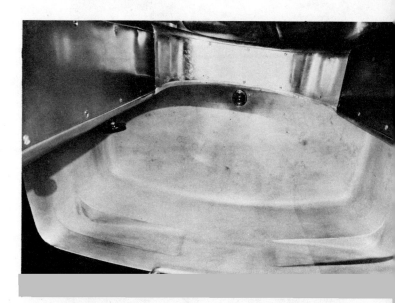

83 *View of interior of the knobless basin, showing the orifice, at lower right center, through which hot and cold, control-mixed water, spurted into the washbasin from the front toward the back of the basin. This direction of the water jet prevented water from going up the cuffs, and back-splashing. Note the overflow exhaust slots to prevent back-syphoning.*

84 *View looking down into tub section. The tub was 27 inches wide, 3 inches wider than standard tubs, and permitted the occupant's body to float freely. By placing the drain at center of the tub, Fuller was able to make the pitch of the tub floor so slight as to offset the user's tendency to slip. In addition, the tub surface was hammered to prevent slipping. Note the alcoves for sponge, soap, and arm rest at the corners of the tub; the plastic tub and shower handle on interior, at the right of the doorway; and the seat saddle at the foot of the doorway.*

85–86 *Inside and outside of Fuller's cylindrical bathroom designed for Butler Manufacturing Company in 1940. The ground-level area, as shown in the interior view, contained the shower bath, basin, and toilet seat. The water tank was above the ceiling, in the cylinder's head. The cylinder was 4 feet in diameter. The exterior view shows the bathroom attached to Fuller's 1940 Deployment Unit. The septic tanks were contained in the cylinder base below ground level.*

87 *Another version of Fuller's Dymaxion Deployment Unit manufactured by the Butler Manufacturing Company, in Kansas City. The seat, basin, and shower, with their flooring and walls, were mounted on a box chassis along with the kitchen plumbing equipment. The latter was placed on the other face of the central wall within which plumbing manifolds, electrical harnesses were installed behind readily demountable panels. (1941)*

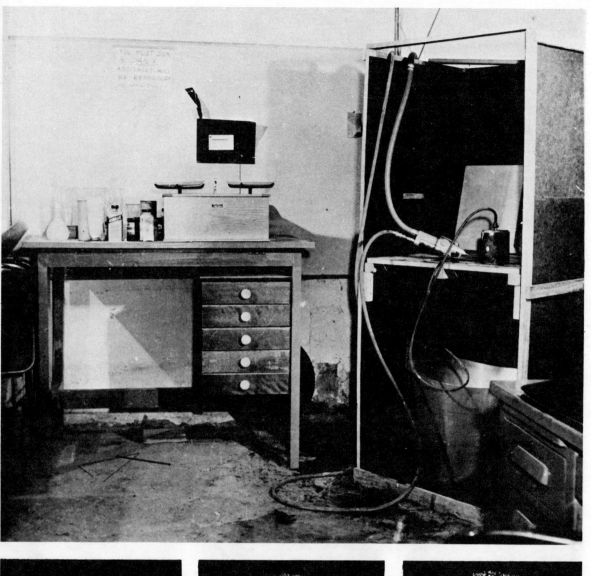

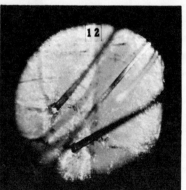
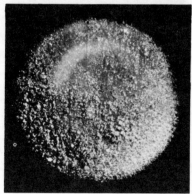
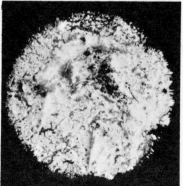

88–91 *Fuller considered the Dymaxion bathroom as an interim, mass-producible, sanitary facility; his fog gun, pictured here, afforded a new method of bathing. It combined compressed air and atomized water with triggered-in solvents. The kinetic force of the high-pressure air stream was utilized without the skin-damaging effect unavoidable in high-pressure needle-pointing of water streams. Generalizing from his Navy experience, in which engine room greases on the skin were almost unnoticeably removed by wind and fog on deck, Fuller reasoned—and later demonstrated—that the feeding of atomized water and air at high pressure on to the skin surface would accelerate the surface oxidation, and release the surface cells themselves, along with the attached dirt.*

The round pictures show magnifications of the skin surface. Two of the pictures show the dirt interspersing the "coral reeflike" structure of the pores. (1927–1948)

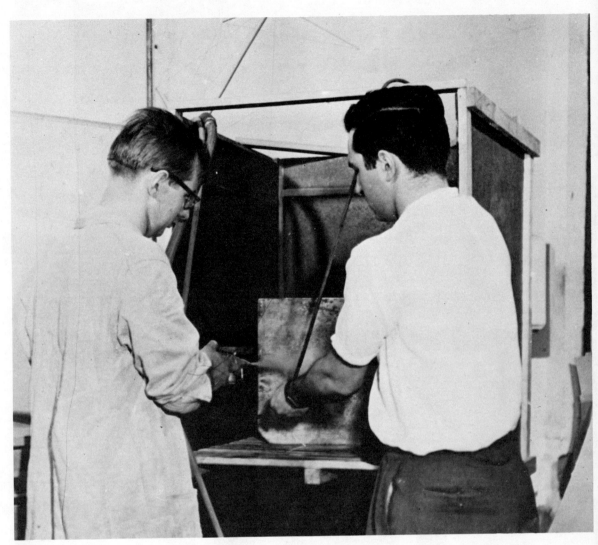

92 *Research students at the Institute of Design, Chicago, in 1948 testing the Fog Gun. (Subsequent experiments were conducted at Yale and other universities.) A one-hour massaging pressure bath used only a pint of water. If fog gun bathing were done in front of a heat lamp, all the sanitary and muscle-relaxing effects of other types of bathing could be effected without the use of any bathroom. Since there were no run-off waters, tons of plumbing and enclosing walls could be eliminated, and bathing would become as much an "in-the-bedroom" process as dressing. Fuller holds that the other functions of the bathroom may be effected by odorless, dry-packaging machinery, employing modern plastics, electronic sealing, dry-conveying systems.*

1.
THUD

2.

CLICK

SNAP

3.

THE NEWEST
prefabricated bathroom
IS ALSO NEAREST

On the 29th floor of 40 Wall St. there sits the finished model of a new plumbing fixture that might well bug the eyes of any bystanding master plumber, a fixture that to all intents and purposes constitutes a one piece bathroom. Designed by Architect Buckmister Fuller (Dymaxion House, Dymaxion Car) it accomplishes, by the simple connection of four basic parts, a complete bathroom weighing 404 pounds, with integral lavatory, toilet and bath. First known as the "Five by Five" (because that's the space it takes up), the official designation is now "The Integrated Bath".

In the research department of the Phelps Dodge Corporation it sits, ready for moderate production (100 units) in 1937. Architect Fuller has assigned his patents to the PD organization, and rumor discerns a new manufacturing and marketing subsidiary in the immediate offing. The range of uses for the unit is broad: pullmans, planes, trailers, trains, but mainly small homes. In fact, Mr. Fuller hopes this light, compact, complete bathroom will even inspire renters to install copies in their apartments, and remove them when they move. All of which lies in the realm of speculation. For the immediate future the device will probably induce fewer orders than conversations. None the less the fact remains that this prefabricated bathroom comes closer to commercial reality than any of its predecessors.

The Integrated Bathroom consists roughly of two oblong sections that form a partition where they join, which conceals the piping and other mechanical appurtenances. The sections (each

4.
PRESTO!

a monometal stamping) are each split in the middle, the top being aluminum and the bottom 272 pounds of sheet copper unmetallized and tinted by a coating of silver, tin and antimony alloy. The bottom of one section is the lavatory and toilet, of the other a flat-bottomed tub.

The toilet, though reminiscent of the old backyard one-holer, is fully sanitary. The seat lifts and remains upright by compression against the walls. Underneath is a standard form of bowl (though chrome nickel bowls are also available).

Two men can handle an installation in three hours, for all piping except a minimum amount of connection material is integral with the unit. So are electric connections, ventilation equipment, etc. Fresh air is drawn by a motor under the lavatory from the nearest room, and exhausted—wherever circumstances permit.

Miscellaneous features: A composition Venetian blind gives privacy to the bather, and, while permitting the escape of steam, prevents the escape of water. The door frame between the two sections is six inches thick, permitting use as seat. Complete cleansing of tub is easily attained. The plumbing layout was devised in collaboration with a local master plumber, copper tubing being used for water lines. Particular care was used to avoid back siphonage possibilities. Sliding doors conserve space. The metallic finish has a "hammered" appearance while at the same time being thoroughly sanitary, the inventor claims. Under surfaces of the base metal are covered with Dum-dum, a sound deadening material. An electric heating system between the two units warms the metal itself, radiating heat to occupant of bath room. Removable panels permit access to plumbing traps and connections under toilet and lavatory.

93 *Reproduction of a page from* The Ladle, *April, 1937, official publication of the New York State Association of Master Plumbers. The article documents the master plumbers' enthusiasm for Fuller's 1936 Phelps-Dodge version of his mass-reproducible unitary bathroom as a chattel mortgage appliance. Despite the plumbers' enthusiasm and large public demand, industry failed to venture in the bathroom's production and distribution.*

DYMAXION
TRANSPORT

94 *Early 4D version (1927)*
of Fuller's Omni-directional
Transport.

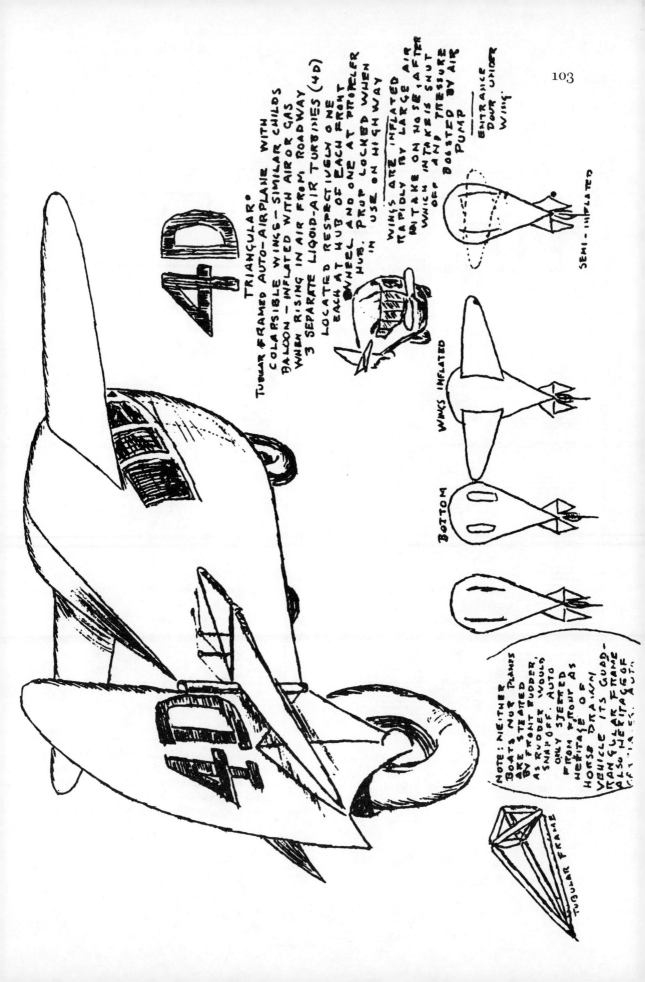

4D

TRIANGULAR

TUBULAR FRAMED AUTO-AIRPLANE WITH COLAPSIBLE WINGS—SIMILAR CHILDS BALLOON—INFLATED WITH AIR OR GAS WHEN RISING IN AIR FROM ROADWAY

3 SEPARATE LIQOID-AIR TURBINES (4D) LOCATED RESPECTIVELY ONE EACH AT HUB OF EACH FRONT WHEEL AND ONE AT PROPELER HUB. PROP LOCKED WHEN IN USE ON HIGH WAY

WINGS ARE INFLATED RAPIDLY BY LARGE AIR INTAKE ON NOSE, AFTER WHICH INTAKE IS SHUT OFF AND PRESSURE BOOSTED BY AIR PUMP

ENTRANCE DOOR UNDER WING

SEMI-INFLATED

WINGS INFLATED

BOTTOM

NOTE: NEITHER BOATS NOR PLANES ARE STEERED BY FRONT RUDDER, AS RUDDER WOULD SNAP OFF. AUTO ONLY STEERED FROM FRONT AS HERITAGE OF HORSE DRAWN VEHICLE. ITS QUAD-RAN FULLAR FRAME ALSO HERITAGE OF GET IN A CEG. AUTO

TUBULAR FRAME

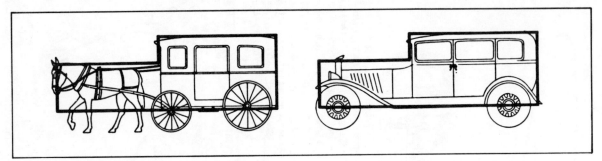

95 *The standard 1932 automobile sedan body presented almost the same contour as the unit composed of a horse and closed wagon.*

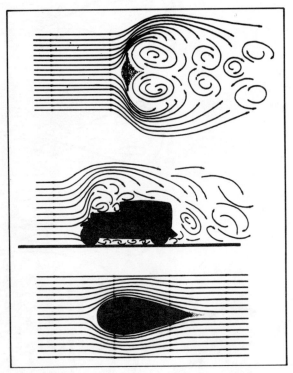

96 *Fuller's early study of air flow effects around a conventional car and one whose contour was an ideal streamline form (1930).*

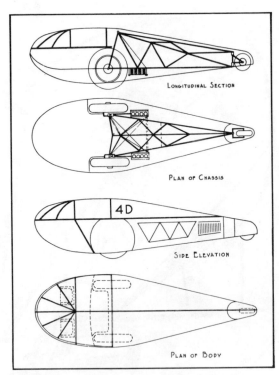

LONGITUDINAL SECTION

PLAN OF CHASSIS

4D

SIDE ELEVATION

PLAN OF BODY

97 *Study, published in Fuller's* Shelter *magazine, in 1932, of the framing, seating arrangement, traction and steering systems of the 4D Dymaxion car.*

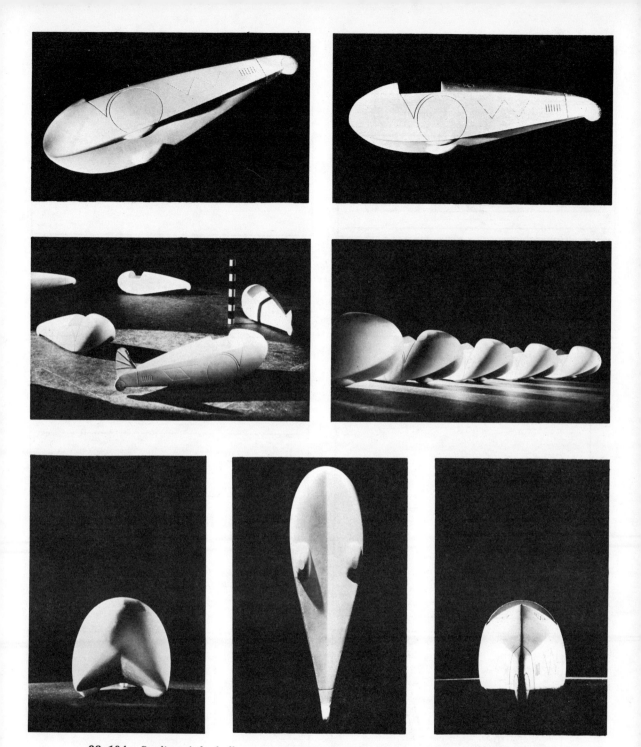

98–104 *Studies of the hull structure of the 4D Dymaxion car. The hull was to have an inverted V bottom to provide air keel at high speeds as well as to lift the tail of the transport. The consequence was to be an infinite wheel base. The faster such a car accelerated, the smoother would be its ride as in the case of the airplane. There was planned, further, a fan tail for increased rudder windage, when "planing." Under the skin of the projected transport was a pneumatic, longitudinal, guard rail. (102 is also shown on facing page of chapter on Dymaxion Transport Units.)*

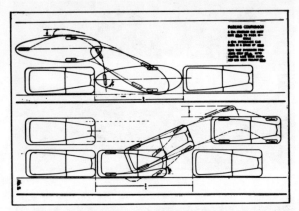

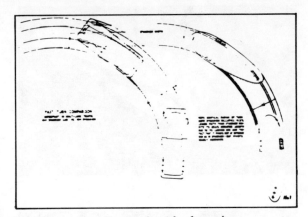

105 *Sketch showing parking path of the Dymaxion car compared with that of a standard 15-foot car. A 15-foot Ford sedan of 1932 required 21½ feet of parking space. The 19-foot Dymaxion parked in a 20-foot length.*

106 *Sketch showing the turn path contours of the Dymaxion and the standard 1932 car.*

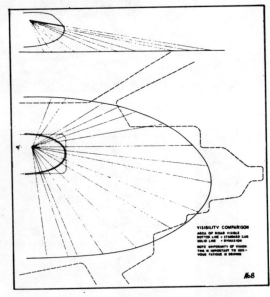

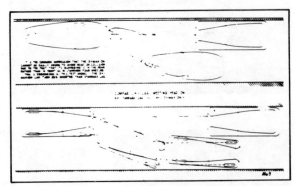

107 *Front vision comparison: the 1933 standard car and the Dymaxion.*

108 *Comparison of collision-avoiding capabilities: the Dymaxion and the 15-foot standard car.*

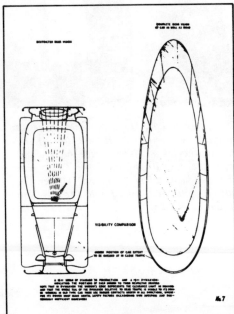

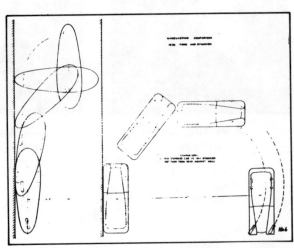

109 *Rear vision comparison: the 1933 standard sedan and the Dymaxion.*

110 *Maneuvering comparison: the 1933 Ford and the Dymaxion.*

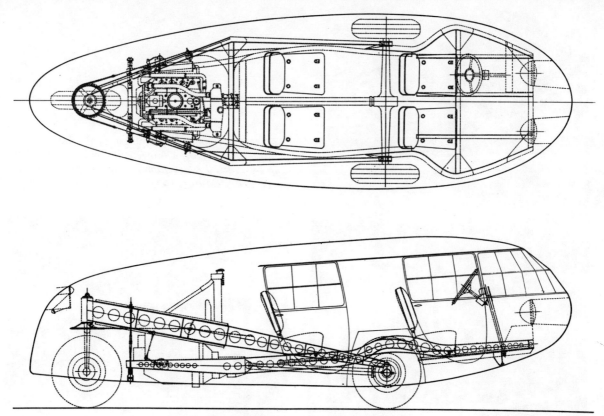

111 *Scale drawings of the Dymaxion car No. 1.*

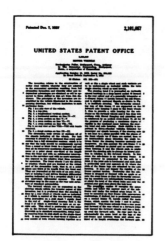

112 *The first page of the Dymaxion car patent.*

113–115 *Patent drawings showing the front, rear, side views, and main structural details of the Dymaxion car below.*

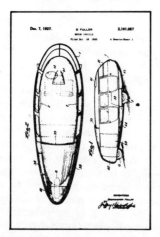 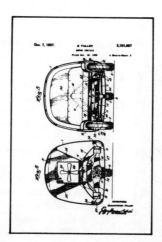 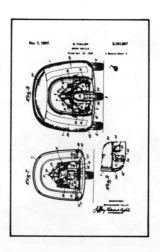

116 *The Dynamometer building of the Locomobile plant in Bridgeport, Connecticut, which was taken over by Fuller for development of the prototype Dymaxion cars. (March, 1933)*

117–119 *Interior views of the Bridgeport plant building during development of the Dymaxion cars' prototypes.*

120 *Starling Burgess, chief engineer in the Dymaxion car project. A famous naval architect, he had previously designed two successful America's cup defenders, and had also invented and flown the first successful Delta wing airplane, the Burgess-Dunn plane. During this period, Burgess was "between cup defenders," and Fuller persuaded him to serve as assistant in experiments to test "the ground taxiing qualities of the 4D omni-directional transport." Fuller shared with Burgess a conviction that "inventor-pioneers have a responsibility to society requiring that they render their publicly exposed inventions in so competent a manner as to provide means of judging the relative merits of the invention unembarrassed by shoddy, makeshift irrelevancies." (1912–14)*

121   *To obtain Burgess' services Fuller had to take on the building of a Bermuda class cruising-racing sloop which Burgess was committed to produce. The boat-building program fitted in neatly with the scheduling for the Dymaxion.*

122   *Starling Burgess seated at the wheel of first Dymaxion car, before the chassis was road tested. Fuller stands at the right.* (1933)

123   *Chassis of car No. 1 made of chrome-molybdenum aircraft steel. Notice the aircraft-type dished lightening holes in the frame members, and the forged steel rudder post, leading from the A-frame bearing to wheel hub. This structure permitted full-circle rotation of the steering wheel. Conventional steering wheels are limited to 34 degrees of steering angle.*

124   *Body construction of Car No. 1.*

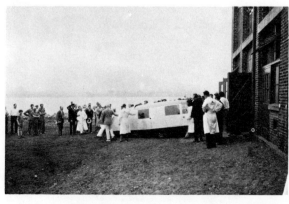

125   *The first completed Dymaxion car rolled out of the Bridgeport factory on July 12, 1933 — Fuller's thirty-eighth birthday.*

126   *Fuller and Starling Burgess with car No. 1.*

127–128 *At Bridgeport, crowds lined the private speedway of the leased Locomobile plant, to watch the first Dymaxion road tests. Extending through the roof above the driver's seat is the car's rear view periscope.*

129 *Side view of Car No. 1.*

130 *The lines of the Dymaxion are modern, even by present day standards. Here the Dymaxion is shown next to a contemporary Franklin. Mexican artist Diego Rivera is shown standing between car doors, far side of car, coat under arm.*

131 *Flyer "Al" Williams (right) and Starling Burgess with Car No. 1. Williams later bought this car.*

132 *Ralph de Palma, famous racing driver, standing beside Dymaxion. De Palma brought the first Fiat to America before World War I and participated in early Indianapolis races.*

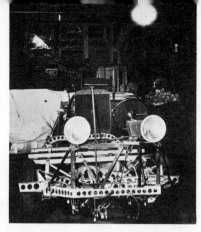

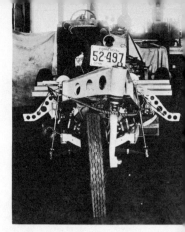

133   *Comparison of relatively heavy two-frame structure of the Dymaxion car No. 1 (right) with the delicate three-frame structure introduced (left) in car No. 2.*

134–135   *Construction details, car No. 2.*

137   *Car No. 2, complete. Headlights are recessed in body, providing "nostrils," which were intakes for air. Dry ice cooled the incoming air. (1934)*

136   *Testing the wheels of car No. 2 for strength and load distribution.*

138   *H. G. Wells, on a visit to America, in 1934, was photographed in front of the Dymaxion car. The Saturday Review of Literature published this picture on the front page, to illustrate a review by Elmer Davis of Well's latest book. Caption: "The Shape of Things to Come Confronts Mr. Wells."*

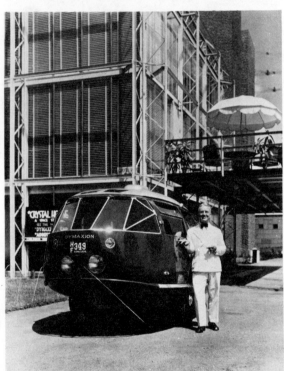

139–141 *Fuller's Dymaxion Car No. 1 had been in a collision in which the driver had been killed. The accident took place in front of the Chicago World's Fair in 1933. The other car, driven by a prominent politician, was removed from the scene before the newspaper reporters arrived on the scene. Front page headlines of Chicago, New York, and world papers carried variations of the statement: "Freak car rolls over — killing famous driver — injuring distinguished international passengers." Although the coronor's inquest 30 days later exonerated the Dymaxion car, there was no recantation of the earlier damaging news. Because Fuller was convinced that the principles of his transport were sound, and embodied technical gains over previous transport, he considered it "his responsibility to obliterate the unwarranted stigma." In 1934 he completed and sent to the Chicago World's Fair his car No. 3, pictured here. This cost him his entire family inheritance. The Chicago Fair featured it as the last episode in their pageant of American transportation, "The Wings of a Century."*

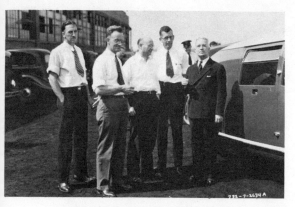

142 *Fuller with engineers of the Goodyear Corporation, at what was the zeppelin mooring field, at Akron, Ohio. The Goodyear company supplied tires for the Dymaxion on its way to the Chicago World's Fair of 1934. Bald-headed man in center is Dr. Arnstein, then chief engineer of the Goodyear Zeppelin Corporation, and for the succeeding 18 years vice-president and director of research of the Goodyear Corporation. Dr. Arnstein, possibly the world's greatest living structural mathematician and originator of the isotropic vector matrix calculus, has been for a third of a century an enthusiastic supporter of Fuller's work. His mathematics is related to Fuller's Energetic-Synergetic geometry.*

143 *Leopold Stokowski and his wife bought the Dymaxion Car No. 3 and sold it a few months later. During the next nine years the car was resold many times, and for a long span disappeared from sight. It was rediscoved, finally, in Brooklyn, in 1944, and repurchased for Fuller by his friend, J. Arch Butts, Jr., of Wichita, Kansas.*

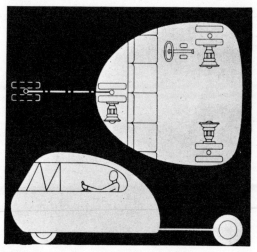

144 *Car No. 3, which was estimated to have been driven some 300,000 miles, was restored by Fuller to prime condition. It is shown here at the Wichita, Kansas, airport, in 1945, standing next to the Republic Seabee amphibian plane, which at that time Fuller owned and piloted.*

145 *Fuller's original caption read:*

With the one-half-pound-per-horse-power gas turbine coming of age, the trend is to re-explore promptly the possibilities of earth-bound vehicles. Pictured is the Dymaxion No. 4, featuring coupled-steering of all three "duo-tired" wheel assemblies. Each wheel assembly contains its own gas turbine. The fuselage is suspended by three aircraft type vertical aerol struts, and has a retractable rear wheel tail boom for lengthening wheel base at speed. It is 7 feet wide and 10 feet long (contracted) with cross-wind "fairing." It has a 7-foot driving divan, convertible into a large bed. It may "revolve into" half the parking length of present cars. The top is a convertible aluminum watermelon type. It has a faired belly with high clearance for field work, will "gun" high speed turns without skid. Weight 960 lbs.

MECHANICAL WING

146 *In 1940, Fuller designed the Mechanical Wing, a compact package intended to provide the mechanical essentials of contemporary American life in a form sufficiently mobile to be transported on an A-frame to any campsite, barn, or shell. The unit was attached to a tubular A-frame trailer, and was equipped with integral jacks mounted on castors. The Mechanical Wing consisted essentially of (1) a Dymaxion bathroom, with hermetically-sealed waste packaging and chemical disposal apparatus; (2) an energy unit, containing diesel engine, air compressor, electrical generator, and hot water heater; (3) a kitchen and laundry unit, with sink, laundry tub, electric range, refrigerator, and storage space for dishes and silver. The Fuller A-frame afterwards became popular as a trailer frame for transporting boats.*

Born 1895, Milton, Mass. Inventor machines, building products, Dymaxion house, Dymaxion car, one-piece prefabricated bathroom. Outstanding exponent of industrialization of building. Author "Nine Chains to the Moon." At present technical consultant to "Fortune."

THE MECHANICAL WING

is a compact, mobile package in which the mechanical essentials of contemporary U. S. living can be transported to the Vermont farmhouse, lakeside camp site, week-end or vacation house, or incorporated in a permanent dwelling.

It is attached to a tubular steel A-frame trailer, frame integral with axle. Attaches to car by ball joint hitch, weight sprung by car. Has integral jacks on casters for maneuvering by hand, blocking up Wing, etc. A-frame alone is useful as luggage, fuel, boat and water carrier, also as a crane for manipulating heavy objects. Note hinged-up tubular barrel chock.

Bath-dressing room unit supplied optionally with (1) water line connection where running water available, (2) combination compressed-air, water and chemical fog-gun cleansing devices, (3) hermetically sealed waste packaging and chemical disposal apparatus.

The energy unit is located between bath and kitchen. Contains diesel engine (h.p. optional), electrical generator, air compressor and tank, battery and radiator. The last uses domestic hot water to warm incoming air. The fan shown can be reversed in summer to exhaust warm air from living units.

Kitchen and laundry unit, with sink, laundry tub, electric range and refrigerator, storage space for dishes, silver and linen. Dry warm storage shelves over diesel above sink.

Side walls: waterproof, synthetic-resin-glued plywood truss. Walls and floors of the three units

(Continued on page 92)

Reprinted from THE ARCHITECTURAL FORUM, October, 1940

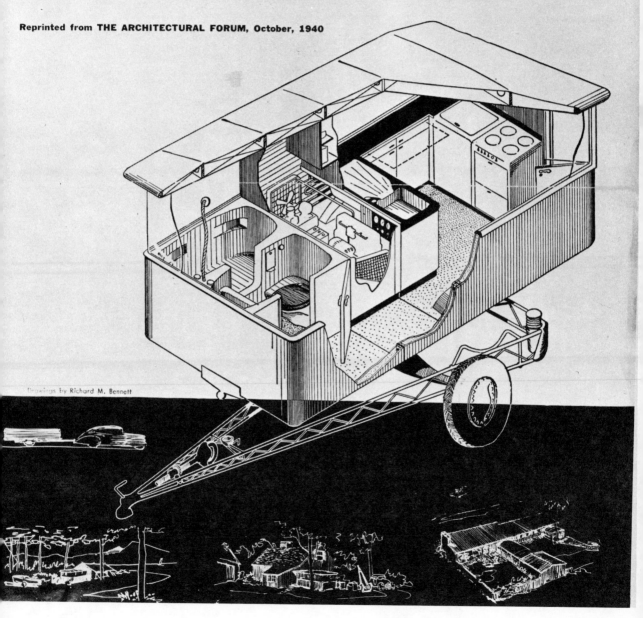

Drawings by Richard M. Bennett

DYMAXION DEPLOYMENT UNIT

147 *Converted grain bin, re-designed by Fuller as the Dymaxion Deployment Unit. (1940–41) The unit was scratched from the British wartime acquisitions program when it was discovered that all the steel that the British could ferry across the Atlantic from the United States would be needed for weapons, or other logistics higher in priority than dwelling functions. The Butler manufactured Dymaxion Deployment Unit was considered for major housing use in the United States, but again was sidetracked because of the priority of weapons steel. Almost abandoned, the Deployment Unit was suddenly accorded high priority for use on the Persian Gulf, as radar shacks and desert dormitories for American and Russian mechanics assigned to assemble, transfer, and fly-away delivery to Russia of United States fighter planes.*

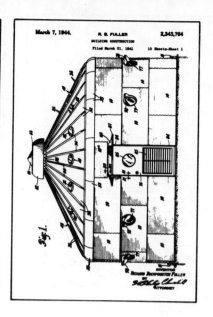

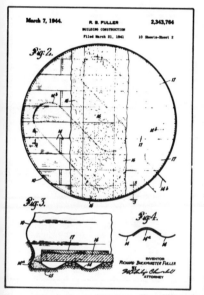

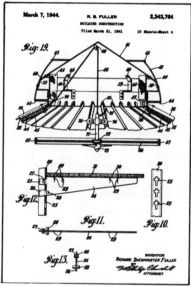

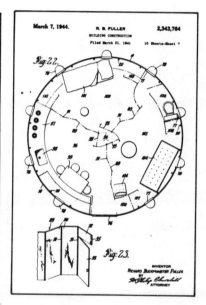

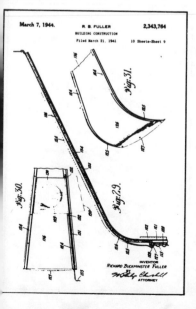

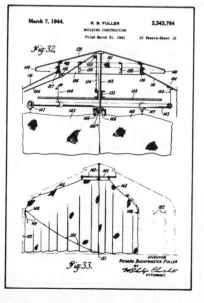

148–154 Initial pages from Fuller's patent covering prefabricated buildings, showing construction principles of the Deployment Unit.

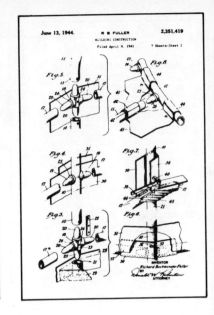

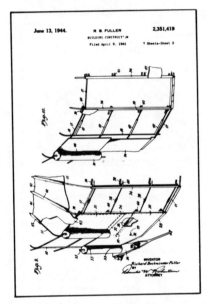

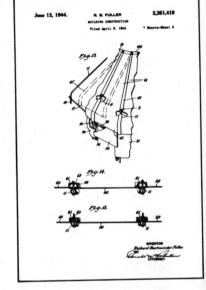

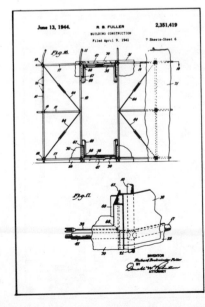

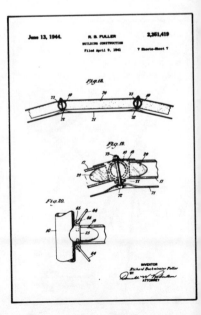

155–160 *Initial pages from Fuller's patent covering the fabrication of structures suitable for small houses; shows the construction principles of the Deployment Unit.*

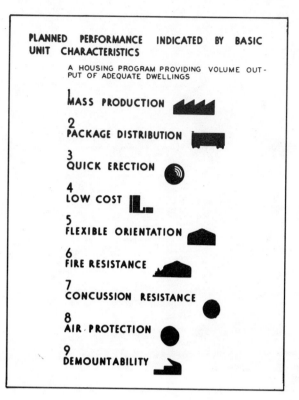

161 *Planning sheet, indicating design of D.D.U.*

162 *Sheet listing the design responsibilities of the D.D.U. In all Fuller projects, the design responsibility goes beyond the static, physical end product. The "comprehensive design responsibility" is concerned with what Fuller calls the product's "cradle-to-grave" life:*

". . . its internal and external relationships, the complementarity of the environmental control in respect to total world pattern trending, and the advantages of individuals with respect to that trending, world-around resource priorities, logical manufacturing and distributing networks, the most economic production means, the designed use of the most effective tool complexes, production flows, distributing compaction, and safeguarding of transported parts, designed transport most suitable to local and world delivery of environment controls, designed erection strategies suitable to terrains and climatic conditions, designed ease of assembly by human beings of any language or background, designed inclusion in distributed package of all tools necessary for field erection — including hand tools, scaffolds, masts, booms, and sub-assembly jigs, designed operability of structure and its mechanics, designed periodic frequency of anticipated maintenance, servicing, and parts replacement; designed removability without parts damage; designed retransportability and storage ability for further installations or upgrading rebuilds."

Tool kits were included in the D.D.U. packages. Each contain the tools typically used by carpenters, auto mechanics and householders. At the outset of World War II, Fuller insisted on including these kits in the D.D.U. shipments; Butler and government officials protested that this unheard-of practice would mean that the kits would be immediately pillaged by the men who erected the units. Fuller replied, "That's just what I expect, too." His assumption was that this pillage would be a very low cost bonus incentive to attract the installing workmen who would get the structures up in a hurry in order to be off with their booty. It worked.

163 *Small and large radius compound curvature eaves were used to convert Butler's cone-topped grain bins into dwelling units. Fuller found that the compound curvature stiffened the entire structure, and that the larger the radius of the eave, the greater the strength. 1940*

164 *Interior view of the 20-foot-diameter D.D.U. conversion of Butler grain bin, with added portholes, skylight, and ventilator.*

165 *Fuller lined the converted grain bin with wallboards, on the inner surface of which fiberglass insulation had been laminated. The wallboards were held in place by vertical channels whose entire length was stamped with keyholes; the inner ends of the long bolts that held the grain bin body sheets together were used to fasten the keyhole channels. The keyholes were later used for brackets on which shelves and any type of appliance could be mounted. The ceiling of the structure was lined with 3-inch thick fiberglass bats enclosed in fabric, providing extraordinary insulation and sound absorption.*

166 *Fuller invented a demountable, dry floor assembly to be laid directly on leveled earth, within a brick circle whose diameter was 1 foot greater than that of the D.D.U. (1941). A galvanized wire strap, encircling the brick ring, pulled the ring together much as a barrel strap pulls together the barrel staves. On top of the leveled earth (within the brick ring), Fuller laid corrugated, galvanized steel sheets, over-lapped sidewise and end-wise as shown in lower left corner of picture. Above the corrugated "snowshoes" were ½-inch felted insulating boards (Celotex), butted together, but with no fastenings. On top of the felted boards was tempered, hard-pressed Masonite, ⅛ inch thick. The Masonite pieces were placed with their main axis at 90 degrees to the Celotex pieces below in such a manner that the joints of the lower and upper layers never coincided. Because hard Masonite tends to curve outwardly along its shiny surface, Fuller turned the shiny surface upward, permitting gravity to flatten out the arch. The ends of the Masonite flooring pieces never curled upward. Thus the whole floor represented a flat assembly held together only by gravity and friction as a single disk sandwich whose top pieces were butted tightly together, yet could be lifted to allow vacuuming out of the edge cracks. Fuller has used this type of "unfastened" flooring on various terrains, and used it in South Africa in 1958. In recent years he has substituted unitary polyethylene sheets for the corrugated metal, finding that this makes an adequate moisture barrier.*

167 *The D.D.U. shown here was installed in Haynes Point Park, Washington, D. C. in April, 1941, for study by government and military housing agencies.*

At that time, the package price of the D.D.U., with the cylindrical bathroom, and the Montgomery Ward furnishings was $1250, including the kerosene ice-box and stove.

168 *The round porthole windows were glazed with acrilic plastic. The D.D.U.'s were the first structures, other than airplanes, to use this World War II, high-priority material. The skylights were screened for protection from bomb debris.*

169 *The front door was designed for use both winter and summer. Note the lower screen ventilating section, on inner side of which is button-in window.*

170 *The smoothness of the dry-laid Masonite floor, and the tightness of its seams, made for both extreme resilience and cleanliness. Note the shelves and clothes hangers installed on keyhole channels. Note also the curtain at upper right, drawn up as in a theatre's proscenium arch. Its bottom edge was weighted with tire chain so that when the curtain drawstring was released, the curtain shot into position like a grapefruit partition web, dividing the D.D.U. into pie-shaped segments. When these curtains reached common center, their edges were buttoned like Pullman-berth enclosures. The heavy tarpaulin curtaining material was fireproofed. Along with the sound absorption effect of the ceilings, it gave surprising privacy to the separated areas, in each of which were installed roll-away divan couches.*

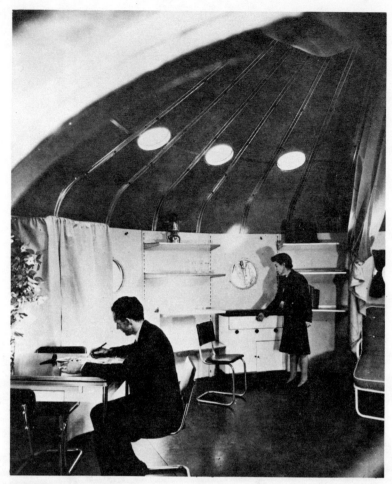

171 *Architect Walter Sanders, head of the Department of Architecture, University of Michigan, and his wife "test-dwelt" the D.D.U. in Washington, and found it completely satisfactory. (1941)*

172 *Similar to Fuller's Dymaxion 4D house, the D.D.U. was always erected from the top down. The roof parts were assembled on the ground and hoisted aloft. The body sheets were installed at a comfortable working height for workmen standing on the ground, and were hoisted in consecutive tiers. Butler's conic grain bin roofs could not be elevated in this manner because their straight line joints acted as hinges. One panel would hinge out as another hinged in, as gravity forced a hoisted conic top into a pleated-skirt. The curved joints of Fuller's compound eaves prevented such hinging. The wider the radius, the more the curvature, and the less the local effort required to maintain structural stability. (1940)*

173 *This picture represents "a milestone episode" in Fuller's experimental testing of his "comprehensive theories in environment controlling." Here the first and second tiers of body sheets have been added to the suspended roof, and hung together from a mast which protrudes through the large hole in the top of the D.D.U. — a hole which was later to accommodate a ventilator. The ring of bricks and its contained earth, together with the steel tie-downs for the D.D.U., leading to anchors buried in the earth below, are clearly visible. The picture was taken at noon, in mid-August of 1940, in Kansas City, Missouri, in the secluded test area of the Butler Manufacturing Company. Fuller had the structure hoisted in this position for the first time, awaiting the arrival of the Butler Company engineers, and the company's president, E. E. Norquist.*

The temperature was over 100° in the shade. The metal of the building was so hot that it could scarcely be touched. The Butler engineers were greatly impressed with the neatness of the demonstrated theory. Norquist, a lifelong enthusiast for structural enterprise, suggested that the group go inside. "You'd better not do that," said the engineer, "you'll burn up." Norquist, with Swedish intransigence, entered. A few seconds later, he called out: "It's air-conditioned in here."

The engineers thought he was joking, but followed him into the building. "To the amazement of all," Fuller reports, "it was truly cool — if not cold — inside. Cigarette smoke and the men's faces told them that a vigorous, cold downdraft was operating at the center. Cigarettes were lighted, and the smoke patterns studied inside and out in an attempt to comprehend the atmospheric patterning that was invisibly in operation to bring about this surprising interior coolness under a scorching sun."

What was discovered confirmed Fuller's long-held theory that energy in gases evolves unique local patternings.

He reasoned that energies could be maintained within local patterns at heat levels quite different from the heat levels of the surrounding atmospheres, just as the Gulf Stream maintains a different heat level as a unique hydraulic patterning within the comprehensive ocean pattern. If energies could be retained locally, by atmospheric patterning alone, local environment controlling for man might be accomplished even without visible walls. Visible shells, he saw, could be shaped to complement the inherent atmospheric self-shaping. Turnip-shaped shells would complement the horizontal doughnut. When a smoke ring "evolutes" at its top, it must be involuting at its bottom. If such a ring were turned upside down, it would be involuting at its top, and "evoluting" at its bottom.

Fuller's experiments disclosed that compound curvature systems provide energy's No. 1 differentializer. Energy concentrations, such as the sun (in the picture) on the convex side of the system (roof), result in the radiation from the energy concentration being diffused by the convex surface.

In this picture, the sun radiation (diffused into the atmosphere around the D.D.U.) is heating the atmosphere, causing it to expand. Hence it weighs less, and floats upward, initiating a rising thermal column around the Deployment Unit. This thermal drafts air from around the building to satisfy the upward flow, pulling the air from underneath the raised building, as well as from the surrounding area. This phenomenon, in turn, causes air from the top of the structure to be pulled downward inside the structure (through the ventilator at the top) to satisfy the partial vacuum created by the exhausting of air from under the structure. Also a cold draft spirals downward through the central core of the rising thermal and is drawn in through the top ventilator. The downward spiral of cold air inside and the energy-exchanging rising column of warm air outside together account for energy dissipations as heat. The result, predicted by Bernoulli's principle, is a natural interior cooling system. When the energy concentrations are on the outside of a convex system, they cause an interior involuting torus of the atmosphere. That is to say, the air immediately adjacent to the hot skin on the interior, rises rapidly as a miniscule boundary layer; and all the rising airs converge at the top, to be vacuum-drafted downward, thinned, and cooled in the process. When the predominant energy concentration is on the concave side of a system, the energy released causes an "evoluting" of a centrally rising, expanding, outward air flow at the top; and exterior downflowing with return to center at base of the atmospheric torus pattern, to feed again upward into the "evoluting scheme."

Fuller saw that the involuting or evoluting patterns of atmospheres could be used to provide cooling or heating efficiencies, respectively, if he would provide complementary shell shapes, proper venting controls (top and bottom), and introduce small amounts of energy into the controlled local patterning. The demonstration confirmed his 1927 assumption of "interior and exterior aerodynamics as a fundamental of the essentially invisible design problem of environmental controls."

However, despite Fuller's knowledge and exposition of the thermal column phenomenon, he finds today that dome users still tend to think of heated air only as everywhere rising. They put large ventilating fans at the zenith of their domes, and in the summer set a fan in motion to pull the air upward and outward from their domes. This simply frustrates the natural tendency of the air to flow downward and outward at the bottom of the dome. The result is that energy as heat stays impounded within the dome.

174 *In this picture, unit No. 2 of the "twin cylinder" D.D.U. is being started. The mast has been removed from No. 1, and repositioned to elevate cylinder No. 2 (1941).*

175 *The roof of No. 2 is completed and elevated. Below it is the door by which cylinder No. 2 will be close-coupled to cylinder No. 1. Immediately below the roof of cylinder No. 2 is the box chassis and partition framing of the unitary bathroom-kitchen assembly.*

176 *Cylinders Nos. 1 and 2 completed.*

177 *The adjustable translucent ventilators at the top of the D.D.U. are shown partially elevated; they could be opened 18 inches more.*

178 *Plan of the twin-cylinder D.D.U., providing a three-bedroom layout with bath and kitchen utility unit which served as a partition for one bedroom. Curtain partitions divide the larger cylinder into two bedrooms and a living room.*

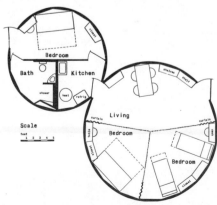

179 *Interior of Twin Deployment Unit. The large cylinder in daytime functioned as a 20-foot living-kitchen room. Note the plug-in electrical strip forming entire circle around interior of the dwelling unit at head of keyhole strips. Electrical appliances could be plugged into the strip at any point.*

180 *Bedroom in the small D.D.U. twin cylinder. The partition at left is the T-head partition on the utility unit.*

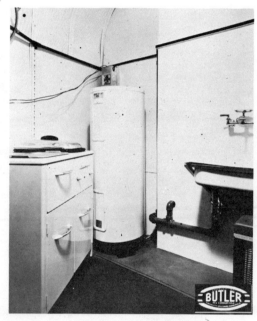

181 *Twin Dymaxion Deployment Unit being installed in the garden of the Museum of Modern Art, New York City, in the summer of 1941. Note the metal masts and their integral winching apparatus. These became standard items in the packaged unit delivered to the Armed Services.*

182 *Kitchen side of utility unit with its electric hot water tank.*

183 *Cluster of D.D.U.s installed at the head of the Persian Gulf during World War II as dormitories for aviators and mechanics assembling American pursuit planes for delivery to Russia. These units were individually air-conditioned and lighted by electrical hook-up with the generators of a ship permanently moored at the local dock.*

DYMAXION
DWELLING
MACHINE

184 *Ventilator for Dymaxion Dwelling Machine.*

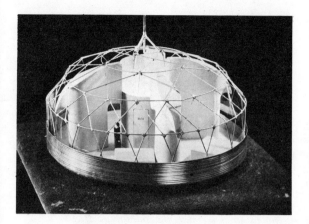 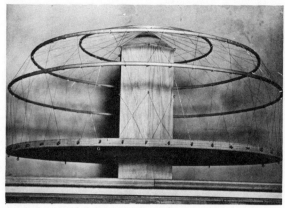

185 *An early model of the Dymaxion Dwelling Machine (Wichita House). The mechanical equipment was designed to be placed inside these aeronautically-faired space dividers. (1944)*

186 *After the external torus shape of the environment controls was established, Fuller's parallel wire-wheeled structure was developed.*

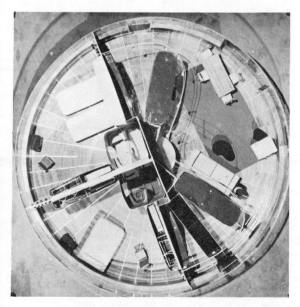 

187 *View showing the Dwelling Machine's rooms: two bedrooms, two bathrooms, kitchen, entry hall, and living room. The oval pattern of the mechanical enclosures permits a smooth, non-cornered circulation, and a diamond-shaped living room, whose long diagonal was 28 feet.*

188 *Living room area with two balconies and central stainless steel fireplace.*

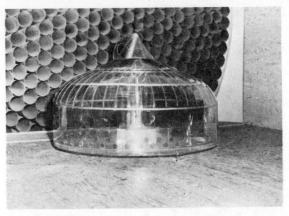

189 *An early model of the Dymaxion Dwelling Machine mounted on scales at the mouth of a Venturi wind tunnel. It was mounted to provide a surrounding aeronautical pattern similar to the pattern around a turnip-shaped gasoline storage tank on the Kansas prairie, (which had been carefully charted). Fuller was aware that air motions around structures close to the ground differ greatly from those formed around an airplane in flight. Wind motions near the ground resemble water motions at river bottoms which dig out orderly waves in the sand. Big air waves make enormous sand waves in the deserts. With these effects in mind, Fuller attempted to determine the minimum drag effects on buildings. (1944)*

190 *Close-up of the model at the mouth of the wind tunnel. The model was transparent so that colored gases introduced into air stream could make visible both the interior and exterior air patterings.*

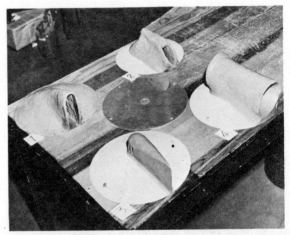

191 *Having weighed the drag on the model, at the Venturi tunnel's mouth, Fuller suspended a hard model upside down at the center of the tunnel. Wind speeds from 25 miles per hour up to those of double hurricanes, were studied. Tubular connections were made to the ventilator which is shown upside down in the picture above. The low pressure drag focus of the structure was so controlled as to occur always at the exit from the ventilator. The vacuum drag caused by air motions about the building was thus utilized to pull directly on the ventilator's exhaust.*

Because "pulled airs" may be pulled around any curves (in contrast to "pushed airs," which tend to turn back on themselves), the draft flow pattern is subject to control flows through a building from opening vents placed anywhere around the building. Thus, it was found that air could best be pulled in below the building, and made to complement the interior aerodynamics for heating or cooling purposes. Vacuum registers around the floor edges of the Dymaxion Dwelling Machine automatically sucked away dust or scraps swept close to the registers. Wind tunnel tests showed how much vacuum would occur at the ventilator exhaust at various velocities of air motions outside the building.

192 *Many types of ventilators were attached to the bottom of suspended dwelling machine models until those were found which provided minimum drag and most exhaust usefulness.*

193 *Ventilator, of a design that provided minimum drag and maximum exhaust effectiveness, is shown upside down. Its shape is similar to a cruising sailboat hull and rudder. (This picture is shown right side up as 184.)*

194 *A vacuum hose was attached to the exhaust opening of the ventilator to pull the interior atmosphere over preferred circuits. These air circuits were governed by inlet holes around the bottom of the Dwelling Machine's cylindrical shell, and by holes in its bottom at the center. By introducing colored gases below the Dwelling Machine, when the vacuum tube was pulling on the ventilator, Fuller found that air would rise through the structure's central cylinder, completely bypassing the dwelling area, and going out the zenith exhaust. Alternately, the air could be made to rise through the central cylinder, entering the top of the dwelling room area, thereafter being pulled (1) down to perimeter floor exhausts, (2) through floor ducts to a central interior column, and out and up to the main exhaust. This arrangement permitted the pulling of cold air in through ducts on a lower face of an aluminum floor heat exchanger, pulling the air upward in the mast to be heated by a central "solar" system; then out and down through the room to counter cold drafts adjacent to the window surfaces. The air would then pass into the aluminum heat exchanger floor ducts to transfer its heat loads through the duct surfaces to the incoming cold air on the other side. In this way, Fuller developed a complementary evolving torus. The upward evolving exhaust column conserved the heat within the structure in cold weather, just as the downward involuting central column, exhausting at bottom perimeter and fed by zenith intake, provided a natural cooling system in hot weather.*

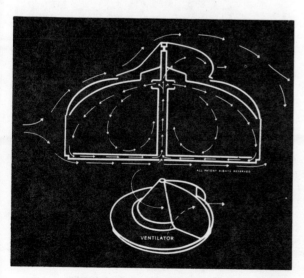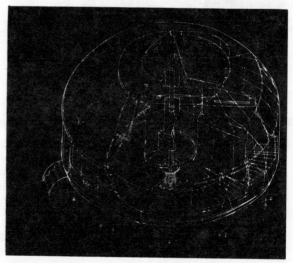

195 *Diagram showing how the external air flow, traveling its greatest distance over the top of the structure, created a vacuum drag at the ventilator, which in turn dragged the internal air flow pattern. Not shown are the two central cylinders, one smaller and concentric to the other. The incoming air was drafted upward through the large cylinder. Exhaust air pulled from the rooms was drafted upward through the smaller cylinder. Thus the incoming air was never polluted by the exhaust air, even though the exhaust air lost its heat through the metal baffle to the incoming air.*

196 *Final general assembly of the Wichita Dwelling Machine structure and mechanical complex. The drawing shows the heavy coil springs at the mast base on the ground shoe which received shock wave impacts on the structure. The total structure was tied down by vertical and diagonal tension cables fastened to anchors at the base.*

197 *View on main assembly floor of Beech Aircraft, showing the production line of twin Beech planes (far side), parallel to the production line of Dymaxion Dwelling Machine parts (left foreground). (1945)*

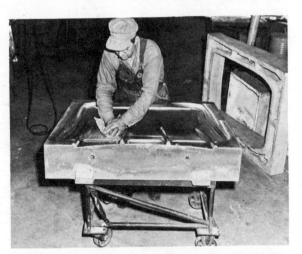

198 *Soft tool production of the Dymaxion Dwelling Machine (1945) took advantage of the unique tools developed by the aircraft industry with the implicit assumption that "change is normal"; such tools were intended to be used only for limited runs. Shown here is the male half of a Kirksite drop-hammer die. Kirksite consists chiefly of tin, whose low melting point is a factor in short-time-period tool development. First step in preparing such a tool is the construction of a clay model, from which plaster casts are made. Sand-cast models are quickly formed from the plaster casts. The solder-like Kirksite having been easily and quickly melted is poured into the sand-cast models. Kirksite dies can be dressed-down to preferred tolerances simply by sandpapering, as shown in the picture. Although the United States has no economically workable tin ore in its known geology, it has a stock of tin from Malaya, Bolivia, and Tanganyika, in the form of Kirksite dies standing in its aircraft industry storage yards, ready for re-working into new dies. The total tonnage of this tin is possibly greater than that still existing below ground in the world's far-flung tin mines. In effect, the U. S. has the largest above-ground tin mine in the world. And in this mine, the metal is continually put to good and better uses.*

199 *Male and female Kirksite dies, mounted in drop-hammer, transform an aluminum flat sheet into ventilator apron component for the Dymaxion Dwelling Machine. This component joins the ventilator cone to its 18-feet skirt. Parts were produced within 24 hours of completion of drawings.*

200 *Large press brake, transforming flat aluminum sheet into 14-foot, tapered floor beams of the Dwelling Machine, one of which is shown on table top at left.*

201 *Complete array of tapered trough floor beams installed in annular, aluminum Z-ring as floor support of Dwelling Machine.*

202 *Top surface of the floor troughs used for exhaust air conduction from the interior perimeter of the floor area through cove registers. The underside of adjoining floor beams provided the conducting chamber through which incoming cold air was led to central mast. Plywood pie-shaped floor units were superimposed on aluminum floor ribs; they were locked down by "fish-hook hat section" floor joint runner strips, which caught into a trough between the floor ribs, and provided a slide angle into which pie-shaped floor pieces, with beveled edges, were driven like wedged corks. As in the Deployment Unit, Fuller developed a complete floor without using screws, nails, or cement. Result: a completely dry, demountable, muscularly-tight system.*

203 *Underside of the aluminum floor beams, each of which weighed only 10 pounds. Shown are the ducts through which incoming cold air was led.*

204 *Only those tools unique to the aircraft industry are shown in this series. Shown is the wood die, a typical aircraft industry soft tool, used for the forming of roof ribs of the Dymaxion dwelling machine.*

205 *The wood die (lower right corner) is mounted into a hydraulically-actuated tool complex, whose operator stands at lower left in front of his electrical console control. Another workman is shown attaching one end of a 6 × 4 inch × 14 feet "hat section" strip of 24 S.T. aircraft alloy aluminum. The strip is turned upside down in the picture and looks like an aluminum gutter. Both ends of this straight piece are clinched in great hydraulic fists, called chucks, in such a way that the gutter mid-part sits in the hardwood die groove.*

206 *The wood die rises, actuated by the console controls, while the universal-jointed giant fists stretch the metal gutter piece like taffy around the wooden die's elliptical groove perimeter.*

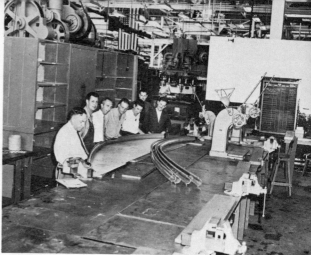

207 *The stretch press in the final forming position. The gutter piece has been stretched to conform to the elliptical die.*

208 *The 2-pound formed ribs are checked at the inspector's station for trueness of curvature.*

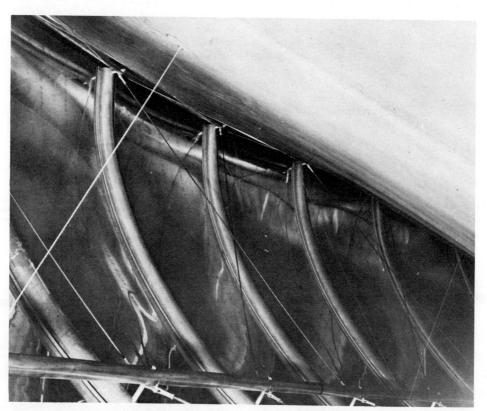

209 *View inside the domical roof of the Dymaxion Dwelling Machine with the compound-curved, 2-pound, "hat-section" ribs in place supporting the outer skin. The function of the ribs was primarily to support the roof, and any of its live loads, while at the same time acting as gutters for whatever water might leak through the joints of the aluminum sheet gores comprising the roof's skin. The closely butted edges of the roof gores occurred directly above the center of the gutter; and the gores were pulled so tightly around the ribs that any moisture coming through the joints could lead only into the gutters. These gutters led down to Neoprene gutters running around above the window height of the Dwelling Machine, internal to the structure. Any moisture or condensation inside the roof ran down to this gutter or dripped onto the fiberglass-Neoprene tent (shown in lower left hand corner) which lined the Dwelling Machine. Water coming down this skin was also led to the Neoprene gutter. All the internal gutters led through Neoprene tubes to soft rain water storage tanks. The inter-roof space could be used as a condensing machine to take the moisture out of the air in non-rainy weather.*

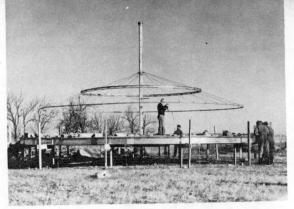

210 *Assembly of the Dymaxion Dwelling Machine began with the installation of the floor ring and radial beams, and the erection of the structure's permanent mast, mounted on a central shoe and springs. The delicate tensile, tie-down diagonals and verticals can be seen reaching from underside of floor beams, to anchor heads buried in earth. Each of the 12 anchors could resist an upward pull of 12,000 pounds. The 22-foot mast was formed by seven 3-inch stainless steel tubes clustered in closest packing. The hexagonal bundle thus formed was strapped parallel with stainless steel horizontal straps every 18 inches. The 22-foot tubes weighed a little less than 10 pounds each. The total weight of the mast, with straps, was only 72 pounds. The cactus-like, vertically fluted mast was designed and tested to carry not only the dead and live roof loads of the building, but also the weight of 120 occupants. Shown in the picture are the A-, B-, and C-rings which were the circular rims of the horizontal, wire-wheel complex. These rings have been interconnected by the high-carbon tension spokes. The B-ring, which sustained the heaviest compression thrust of the whole Dwelling Machine, was formed by tubular sections of stainless steel. None of the metals or other materials used in the Dymaxion Dwelling Machine needed to be painted or maintained. All were non-oxidizing. Dielectric gaskets were interposed between any metals which might develop electrolytic exchange, and consequent deterioration. (1945)*

211 *The 2-pound "hat section" ribs have been attached to the A-, B-, and C-rings by three bolts. Pictured is the aluminum foil sheeting being draped between the ribs; it served as a secondary radiation barrier between outer and inner skins of the Dymaxion Dwelling Machine. The workman at lower left is holding a partially coiled roof gore made from high alloy, heat-treated, aircraft aluminum, with strength characteristics approximating those of spring steel. At far left, roof gore sheet has been made fast at A- and C-rings. Two bolts catch the sheet at the C-ring, while one bolt at the A-ring pulls the gore sheet tautly around the ribs when the nut is tightened.*

212 *All the roof gores in place. Sunlight reflection shows the hyperbolic compound curvature pulled into the roof gores. Shown also is the fine tolerance of the seams between the roof gores, which let any penetrating water through to the roof gutters.*

213 *The complete roof dome becomes a rigid unity, and is shown elevated to final position and tied down to Z-floor-ring by criss-crossing stainless steel rods. The intervening hexagonal openings between rods provided generous space for doors and other traffic requirements.*

214 *View of central masthead, showing stainless steel forged cap piece of mast, into which seven 3-inch stainless steel tubes lead. The radial spokes of the dome were suspended from the forged ring and made fast with high-tension aircraft clevises. Also suspended from the forged cap were six ball-bearing sheaves (pulley blocks). Through these ball-bearing sheaves, a flexible steel aircraft cable was led in six parts, reaching upward and downward between similar sheaves attached above the mast cap. When this cable was winched in by an electric motor, it pulled the entire roof dome upward around the mast from its assembled position to its final position — with the smoothness of the curtain raising in the theatre. Shown above the masthead rings, spokes, and sheaves, are the tubular spokes of the 18-foot ventilator. The whole ventilator revolved on a Cadillac front-wheel spindle, roller thrust bearing. "Although this complex of jewelry-like, non-rustable alloy components appears to be expensive," said Fuller, "it did so much with so little (and its total poundage was so small) that Beech Aircraft was able to make firm proposals to soft-tool manufacture the Dwelling Machines at a cost of only $1800 each."*

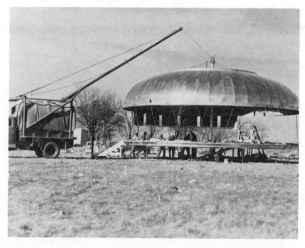

215 *The extensible boom of a special assembly truck was attached to the masthead as safety measure — when the first group assembly was intentionally erected in gale velocity winds. Experiment showed that the structure, partially-assembled, could handle its own stresses without aid of the boom anchor. In this picture, temporarily paper-coated Plexiglass window sheets have been hung below the C-ring and gutter, and the Z-section window sill has been suspended by riveting to bottom of plastic windows.*

216 *Complete 118-foot Plexiglass window has been installed. Below the window are slide-skin cylinders, designed to form two halves. The top horizontal half below the window dropped down in 12-foot curtain sections outside the lower half, providing a screened ventilating opening, 12 feet long, 18 inches high, below every two windows. All of the slide-skins could be opened simultaneously, providing an 18-inch high ventilating opening, 118 feet long, running completely around the Dwelling Machine. This screened ring was designed to implement the hot-weather, cold-down-draft natural air-conditioning of the structure. At right is shown the 18-foot ventilator and its pair of tail exhaust fins.*

217 *Ventilator hoisted by a boom to masthead-mounted spindle support. The entire ventilator could be raised by masthead mechanism to a position 3 feet above the central, top roof ring, whose 18-foot-diameter opening was screened. If a sudden low pressure area engulfed the structure as in the case of a tornado eye or a major explosion, the 18-foot ventilator would ride up its 3-foot spline, acting like the exhaust valve on a steam boiler, and effectively relieve the relatively high internal pressure.*

The marriage of the hyperbolic parabola curve fins to the conic front of the ventilator, and the broad, 28-square-foot opening tail exhaust of the ventilator, provided a structure that rotated like the broad-tailed tetrahedrons used for airport wind direction indicators, the tail form serving (as with broad-tailed bullets) to spoil flutter-causing oscillations of low pressure differences on either side of the tail surfaces. The Dymaxion Dwelling Machine ventilator always headed steadily into the wind.

218 *Final assembly of Dwelling Machine completed, showing long window sections in living room area. The bottom gutter is in place, leading to main rainwater system. The vertical cylinder, at left of hand-hold gangway, contained all component parts of Dwelling Machine. Parts were assembled around a central spindle and inserted into the cylinder for shipping. Rolling rings capped both ends of the cylinder. The total structure weighed approximately 6,000 pounds. This figure agreed with Fuller's 1927 estimate of the weight of Dymaxion House of the same dimensions that could be realized when the interim alloying research had been completed. (1945)*

219 *Total group of components of Dwelling Machine stacked before loading into cylinder. It was a fundamental responsibility of the design, as Fuller conceived it, to have all the parts compact to minimum cubage. Most parts were designed to nest together. No single part of the structure weighed more than 10 pounds. Any single part could be handled by one man with one hand, leaving his other hand free to fasten the part in its place; consequently it was never necessary for any workman to require the services of a helper.*

220 *Eight-pound scaling ladder made from two roof ribs supports a man making ventilator adjustments. Hyperbolic curvature of the roof sheets is clearly visible. At bottom and lower right are bricks and stones ready to be loaded on the living room floor to simulate the weight of 120 people clustered on one side of the building — equivalent to eccentric occupant loads under full hurricane or earthquake conditions.*

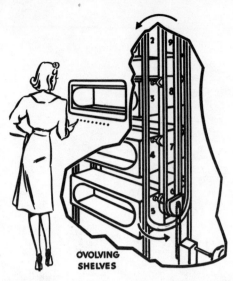

OVOLVING SHELVES

221   *The door between the bedrooms was a tensionally-supported "modernfold" door, similar in appearance to Fuller's 1927 pneumatically-inflated, vertically-fluted, side-sliding curtains. Note the Z-section aluminum window sill which developed the horizontal stiffness of the Dwelling Machine vertical wall. Double Plexiglass panes were riveted to it with 1/8 inch space between their concentric, cylindrical sheet surfaces. Fabricoid material buttoned below window.*

222   *Pater-Noster-like "ovolving" shelf-containers, mounted on a continuous chain behind the partition wall. The opening in the shelf-containers registered with a horizontal opening in partition wall, at a height convenient for adult reach-in, but too high for small children. Pressing a button at the side opening caused the shelves to rotate past the window until the desired shelf was in register. Such "ovolving" shelf storages in each of the bedrooms, provided shelf space equivalent to an 18-foot stack of shelves of the same width. Although limited to 18 feet for the Dymaxion Dwelling Machine, these shelves could be of any height (hundreds or thousands of feet), and could provide for quick reference storage of major library archives.*

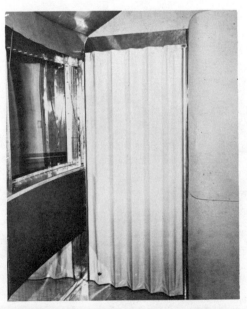

223   *Production model of "ovolving" shelves, before oval skin of the storage partition was applied. The shelf elevator mechanism was driven by an electric motor.*

224   *Fuller developed revolving, vertical clothes hangers and semicircular shoe and hat racks, all mounted on the vertical central shaft of a centrally-pivoted partition panel.*

225 *Interior view of the living room of the completed production model Wichita House, showing 37 feet of Plexiglass window in living room area. Also shown is the interior of the Fiberglass-Neoprene ceiling skin, upon whose neutrally-silvered surface, controllable color light was projected indirectly from the oval drum heads of partition units.*

226 *Musicians were impressed by the Dwelling Machine's acoustics. Marian Anderson, after singing in the Wichita House, declared she had never before heard "sound in the round" without reverberation or distortion.*

227 *Lacking the 10 million dollars necessary for tooling the Dymaxion Dwelling Machine for a 20,000-units per-year production, the development ended the Wichita experiment. Two prototypes were ordered by the Air Force and later resold to Fuller's project. They were ultimately acquired by a Kansas oil man, who combined them to form the house shown above, sans rotating ventilator. "His architectural additions and modifications in effect," said Fuller, "forever grounded this aeroplane."*

SYNERGETIC-ENERGETIC GEOMETRY

228 *An early chart of Energetic-Synergetic geometry. Fuller holds that* **synergy** *is to* **energy** *what, in the calculus,* **integration** *is to* **differentiation**. *Energetic studies of nature differentiate out or isolate unique local functionings. Synergetic studies seek to organize and comprehend the complex co-operative patterning that exists, a priori, in nature. "Synergetic geometry," says Fuller, "makes possible a childhood participation in nuclear physics as a logical and enjoyable, rather than a precocious phenomenon. However, scientific entry into the present realm of nuclear competence was accomplished with the awkward, irrational tools of energetical strategy. The development and adoption of the great computers has now relieved man of the onerous tasks characteristic of the irrational constants interlinking the many separate facts of scientific enquiry which arose from the energetic approach. Because these tasks are being carried by the computers, and men are getting along all right on their blind-flown scientific pilgrimages, there will be only slow realization of the significance of the sensorially-conceptual facility of dealing with nature that is opened up by the Synergetic geometry." (1944)*

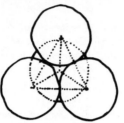

Convergently or Compressively Organised Plurality of Spherical Scualed. Exterior Ballistics 2 Visible, 2 Invisible Orbits

1 TETRAHEDRON

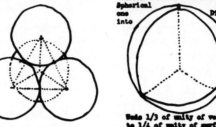

Divergently Organised Single Sphere - Interior Compression - Exterior Tension, Subdivided by Great Circles; Absolute of 2nd Orbit - Maximum Volume with Minimum Surface

Correct First Subdivision of Spherical Surface one Dimension into Four.

2 Ends 1/3 of unity of vertexes to 1/4 of unity of surface - with 6 are seg. and 4 vertexes.

EXTERIOR.

Position in Super Tetrahedron Convergent Phase of Vectors All Vertexes are Spherical Centers

3 All Angles are 60° Tetrahedron has octahedron center.

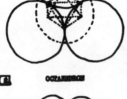

Tensive Core

4 OCTAHEDRON

5 Interlocked vectors of 3 Axes 8 Tetrahedrons

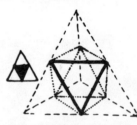

6 Center of Octahedron is Dymaxion

12 Spheres Surrounding 1, all in tangency. Outer spheres 5 contacts each. Center sphere, 12.

10 DYMAXION

6 Axes (4 Dimensions). Fully divergent Vector System with Unit tetra and octa vertex center.

16

Cube-Octave Group Within Dymaxion Center is Not a Dymaxion but an octave Reduction. Cubes do not center singly. as octave Only do so See Fig.26 collectia & 19

7

Cube corner = 6 spheres & spaces

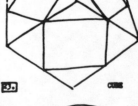

This most compact spherical agglomeration expands to infinity; new nucleus every 4 orbits.

22a

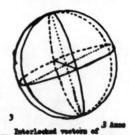

CUBE

26

8 Cube Core under Octahedron Face

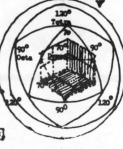

Concentric spherical triangles.
29 180° - to 60° + Great Circle is absolute triangle.

32

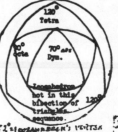

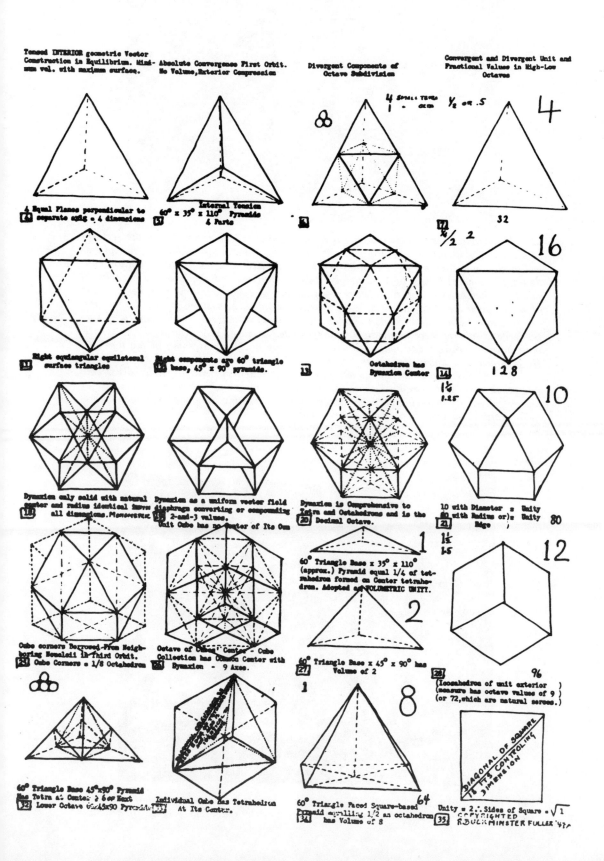

229 *Topological systems always consist of lines, vertexes, and facets. When the vertexes of systems are identified by little spheres, and those spheres are enlarged, the spheres will gradually encompass the lines between the respective vertexes. If the expansion continues, the spheres finally become tangent to one another, and the lines are entirely inside the spheres. Shown in the picture are geometrical agglomerations of spheres, many of which correspond to the linearly-emphasized topological systems shown in the preceding chart. Fuller assumed that fundamental geometric patterns, which appeared successively as spheres were methodically compounded in all directions around one sphere, must have generalized constancy with respect to any nuclear patterning of the universe. He assumed that knowledge of the atomic nucleus could be discovered through such exploration in pure principle. Frequently, in recent years, nuclear principles discovered in mathematical geometry by Fuller, emerged in the integrated information acquired by nuclear physicists in their "particle" accelerator bombarding ventures, and their subsequent statistical accountings of the ballistic rubble.*

230 *Fuller and research students, with closest-packing agglomerations of spheres in fundamental geometry, and a model of 25-great-circle sphere in process of assembly. (1948)*

231 *When systems are rotated on the axes defined by their vertexes, or the center of their faces, or their mid-edges, then great circle trajectories occur as "equators" of the respective axes of spin. These can be regarded as extensions of the interior planes of the system in respect to its nuclear center. The 25-great-circle pattern, shown in the largest sphere in the picture, results from the spinning of the Vector Equilibrium on all of its axes of symmetry. When the first direct photographs of atoms (taken through the Field Emission Microscope) were published in the early 1950s, the 25-great-circle whirling trails were to be seen, representing all the most economic degrees of freedom of action around a nuclear point. (This picture is also shown on facing page of chapter on Energetic-Synergetic Geometry.)*

232 *Fuller with his Energetic geometry models, Dymaxion map, Geodesic dome, Tensegrity, and Octet Truss structures derived directly from Energetic-Synergetic geometry co-ordinations (Forest Hills, New York, 1951).*

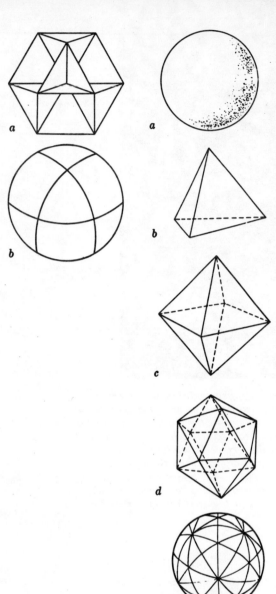

233 *Shown here are: (a) Fuller's model of the Vector Equilibrium showing internal planes formed by edges and radii (radial lines joining external vertexes to central vertex); (b) projection of the Vector Equilibrium on the surface of a sphere. Fuller calls the Vector Equilibrium the "Grand Central Station" of "the co-ordinate mathematical-physical system that is apparently the co-ordinate system employed by Nature to account most economically for its myriad transactions."*

234 *Fuller defines the sphere (a) as "a multiplicity of discrete events, approximately equidistant in all directions from a nuclear center." The discrete points of such a system can be inter-triangulated. The tetrahedron (b), the octahedron (c), and the icosahedron (d) are the only possible cases of omni-equilateral, omni-triangulated finite systems. Pictured at (e) are the 15 great circles developing from rotation of the icosahedron in respect to the 15 axes interconnecting opposite midpoints of the icosahedron's 30 edges. The 120 resulting right spherical triangles represent the maximum unitary subdivision of a one-radius system. This fact was long known in mathematics. Since 120 is 10 times 12, Fuller thinks that this geometric relationship may underlie both the decimal and duodecimal systems of modular accounting; and may have been derived by subdividing a finite system into its lowest common denominator. He believes that we inherited the combined decimal and duodecimal systems from this fundamental thinking in early Babylonian science and in the mathematical invention of the Sino-Indian navigators.*

235 *Fuller's chart of "constants of relative abundance" of the fundamental characteristics of topological systems when subjected to "omni-triangulation and omni-consideration of the additive and multiplicative twonesses of all finite systems." Fuller's basic theorem:* **The difference between the sum of the angles around all the vertexes of any finite system and the number of vertexes of the system times 360 degrees, is always 2 x 360 degrees.** *This is to say that* **the difference between finite systems and infinity is the sum of the planar angles around two points, each of which lies in its separate plane, parallel to the other.** *When angles around points add up to more or less than 360 degrees, convexity and concavity result. In short, Fuller shows that the difference between finiteness and infinity is 2.*

The inherent disparity of convexity and concavity introduces an inherent multiplicative twoness. As the chart shows, Fuller found that the "additive twoness" is that of the two polar points. The "multiplicative twoness" is that of the inherent disparity of convexity and concavity. When the additive twoness and the multiplicative twoness are extracted from any symmetrical and omni-triangulated system, the numbers of vertexes will always be a rational product of one or more of the first four prime numbers: 1, 2, 3, and 5. The number of faces will always be twice that of the vertexes minus 2; the number of edges will always be three times the number of vertexes, minus 2.

SYNERGETICALLY SYMMETRIC

System	True Rational Volume (tetrahedron = unity)	Area : Volume Ratio	Space Fillers	Complementary Space Fillers	Euler Formula (V + F = E + 2)	Fuller synergetic treatment extracts 2 vertices for neutral axis (V − θ, θ − 2, V + F = E)	Fuller synergetic treatment divides by fundamental
VECTOR EDGE TETRA	—	1 : 1		•	4 + 4 = 6 + 2	2 + 4 = 6	2
VECTOR EDGE OCTA	4	1 : 2	•	•	6 + 8 = 12 + 2	4 + 8 = 12	3
ALTERNATING + TO − TETRA VECTOR DIAGONAL	3				8 + 12 = 18 + 2	6 + 12 = 18	5
VECTOR EQUILIBRIUM	20		•		12 + 20 = 30 + 2	10 + 20 = 30	5
VECTOR EDGE ICOSAHEDRON	18.510	1 : 4.63			12 + 20 = 30 + 2	10 + 20 = 30	3 · 5
VECTOR EDGE CUBE	20				14 + 24 = 36 + 2	θ + 12 + 24 = 36	3 · 2
VECTOR DIAGONAL RHOMBIC DODECAHEDRON	18.510				14 + 24 = 36 + 2	12 + 24 = 36	3 · 5
VECTOR EDGE RHOMBIC DODECAHEDRON	8.490		•		14 + 24 = 36 + 2	12 + 24 = 36	3 · 5
VECTOR EDGE DODECAHEDRON	6		•		32 + 60 = 90 + 2	30 + 60 = 90	3 · 5
VECTOR EDGE TETRAXIDECAHEDRON	25.996		•		32 + 60 = 90 + 2	30 + 60 = 90	3 · 5
VECTOR EDGE TRIACONTAHEDRON	65.018				32 + 60 = 90 + 2	30 + 60 = 90	3 · 5
VECTOR EDGE ENENICONTAHEDRON	96		•		92 + 180 = 270 + 2	90 + 180 = 270	3² · 5

Braced volume sums: { 65.018 + 25.996 = 91.004 } and { 8.490 + 18.510 = 27.000 }

Locally Symmetrical, Omni-Triangulated; Locally Mixed Sym-Asym, Omni-Triangulated; Locally Asymmetrical, Omni-Triangulated.

$(1 + 2 = 3)\sqrt{\phi^2}\;\phi + \theta$

TOPOLOGICAL ABUNDANCE CONSTANT

FREQUENCY OF MODULAR SUBDIVISION OF EXTERIOR EDGES OF SYSTEM

2 FACES OR 3 EDGES OR 1 VERTEX

FULLER SYNERGETIC TREATMENT DIVIDES BY FUNDAMENTAL. WITHINNESS & WITHOUTNESS, CONVEX − CONCAVE, TWONESS + 2 ÷ Φ

COPYRIGHT 1955 — R. BUCKMINSTER FULLER

MAPS
AND
CHARTS

236 *Fuller's 1927 mimeographed picture of the "one-town" Air Ocean World. His working assumption of air delivery of his 10-deck buildings to the world's remotest and environmentally most hostile places implemented his program for a world integrated by air traffic between stepping-stone maintenance points and over previously non-feasible routes. Note the airplanes flying the Northwest Orient flight between the U. S. and China; the Dakar-Natal, the trans-African-trans-Siberian, and the Inter-American flights. No such operated air routes existed at the time of Fuller's drawing — which was the year of the Lindbergh flight. This world picture (shown previously as 20) was the start of Fuller's comprehensive design thinking in relation to the resources and world peoples.*

TIME LOCK

26% OF EARTH'S SURFACE IS DRY LAND
85% OF ALL EARTH'S DRY LAND IS HERE SHOWN
86% OF ALL DRY LAND SHOWN IS ABOVE EQUATOR
THE WHOLE OF THE HUMAN FAMILY COULD STAND ON BERMUDA
ALL CROWDED INTO ENGLAND THEY WOULD HAVE 750 SQ FEET EACH
"UNITED WE STAND, DIVIDED WE FALL" IS CORRECT MENTALLY AND SPIRITUALLY
BUT FALACIOUS PHYSICALY OR MATERIALY.
2,000,000,000. NEW HOMES WILL BE REQUIRED IN NEXT 80 YEARS

RBF
1937

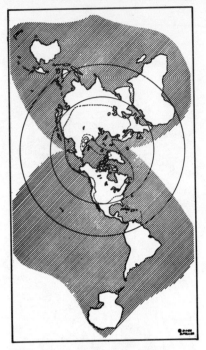

237 *World map roughed out by Fuller from globe as a test of his "intuitive realization" that this patterning arrangement could be derived from exact mathematical processes (1936). The map was reproduced as end papers in Fuller's book,* Nine Chains to the Moon.

238 *Model of Fuller's "one-world island in one-world ocean," constructed for him by his friend, puppeteer Bill Baird in 1937 to illustrate* Nine Chains to the Moon.

Patented Jan. 29, 1946   2,393,676

UNITED STATES PATENT OFFICE

2,393,676

CARTOGRAPHY

Richard Buckminster Fuller, Washington, D. C.

Application February 25, 1944, Serial No. 523,942

3 Claims. (Cl. 35—46)

The invention relates to cartography.

As the earth is a spherical body, so the only true cartographic representation of its surface must be spherical. All flat surface maps are compromises with truth. For example, Mercator's projection is true to scale only along the equator, and azimuthal projection is limited to convergence of the meridians at one pole at a time. Other known systems of projection can be made to give uniform scale along parallels, or to give equal areas albeit with exaggerated shape distortions.

Another expedient has been to resolve the earth's surface into a polyhedron, projecting gnomonically to the facets of the polyhedron, the idea being that the sections of the polyhedron can be assembled on a flat surface to give a truer picture of the earth's surface and of directions and distances. Such a system is fettered to the limitations and gross radial distortions which characterize gnomonic projection.

It is an object of my invention to provide a sectional map of the world, or of a portion of its surface, which is so constructed that its parts can be assembled to give a truer over-all picture of areas, boundaries, directions and distances than is attainable with any type of plane surface map heretofore known.

Another object has been to provide a subdivision of the earth's surface for cartographic purposes which will result in sections that can be assembled with fewer annexes in land areas than is possible with sectional maps heretofore known. Other objects and advantages will appear as the description proceeds.

I have found that by resolving the earth's surface into sections which are entirely bounded by straight line projections of great circles, and constructing a map on great circle grids, it is possible to maintain uniform scale peripheral cartographic delineations and to distribute all subsidence distortion from the periphery toward the center. I have discovered further that this system brings the subsidence distortion to an irreducible minimum which, without correction of any kind, is very considerably less than with any system of projection heretofore devised.

Another discovery which I have made is that if the earth's surface is resolved into six equilateral square sections and eight equilateral triangular sections whose edges match throughout, there is formed a polyhedron all of the vertexes of which lie in great circles of a sphere. This figure I call a "dymaxion." As a consequence, all of the sides of all of the sections are true projections of great circles, and uniform scale peripheral cartographic delineations can be constructed.

With reference to the accompanying drawings, I shall now describe a preferred form of my improved map and the method of constructing it.

Fig. 1 is a perspective view of a "dymaxion," in which the earth's surface is resolved into that form of polyhedron which has six equilateral square sections and eight equilateral triangular sections whose edges match throughout and all of the vertexes of which lie in great circles of a sphere.

Fig. 2 is a map of the world made up of a plurality of square and triangular sections, the cartographic delineations being constructed on great circle grids. In this embodiment of the invention the location of the pole and the orientation of the map relative to the "dymaxion" are such that the land areas can be joined without land sinuses.

Fig. 3 is a view similar to Fig. 2, and shows an arrangement of the sections of the polyhedron of Fig. 1. In this embodiment of the invention the poles are located arbitrarily at the centers of two of the square sections or facets of the polyhedron. The sections are laid in a pattern that approximates the familiar appearance of the Mercator projection. The equator is a continuous line, orienting the world east to west.

Fig. 4 is an elevational view of a cartographic device having a spherical grid composed of intersecting great circles. This is the form of device which I prefer to use in transferring cartographic delineations from a spherical to a plane surface.

Fig. 5 is a plan view of the cartographic device.

Figs. 6 and 7 depict two arrangements of selected map sections illustrating the relationship of sinus to arc. The sections shown have the great circle grids which I will describe, but for the sake of simplicity the cartographic delineations have been omitted in these views.

Fig. 8 is a detail view of one of the triangular sections showing a three-way great circle grid and, superimposed thereon, meridians and parallels.

An essential feature of my invention resides in constructing the map on great circle grids. In the case of the square section, a two-way grid is employed. In the case of the triangular sections, a three-way great circle grid is employed. This will be understood in part from Figs. 4 and 5 which show one form of cartographic device used in constructing my polyhedral map from a globe.

Construction of the cartographic device

The invention, and its distinguishing attributes and advantages, may best be understood by considering first my preferred method of translating true spherical cartographic delineations to the

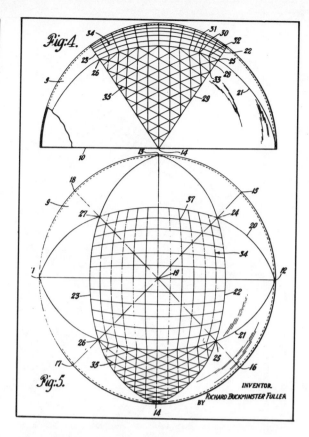

Fig. 4.

Fig. 5.

INVENTOR.

RICHARD BUCKMINSTER FULLER
BY

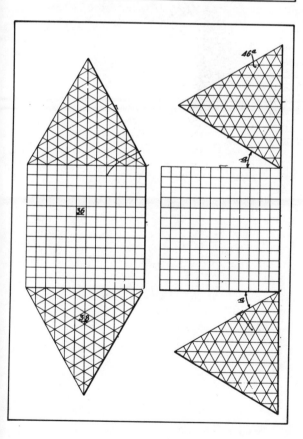

Jan. 29, 1946.   R. B. FULLER   2,393,676

CARTOGRAPHY

Filed Feb. 25, 1944   5 Sheets—Sheet 1

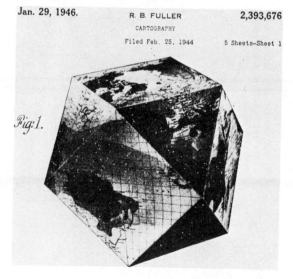

Fig. 1.

239–242 *Pages from Fuller's U. S. patent covering the Dymaxion map.* Science *referred to this as "the first cartographic patent to issue from the U. S. Patent Office." (Top right is also shown on facing page of chapter on Cartography.)*

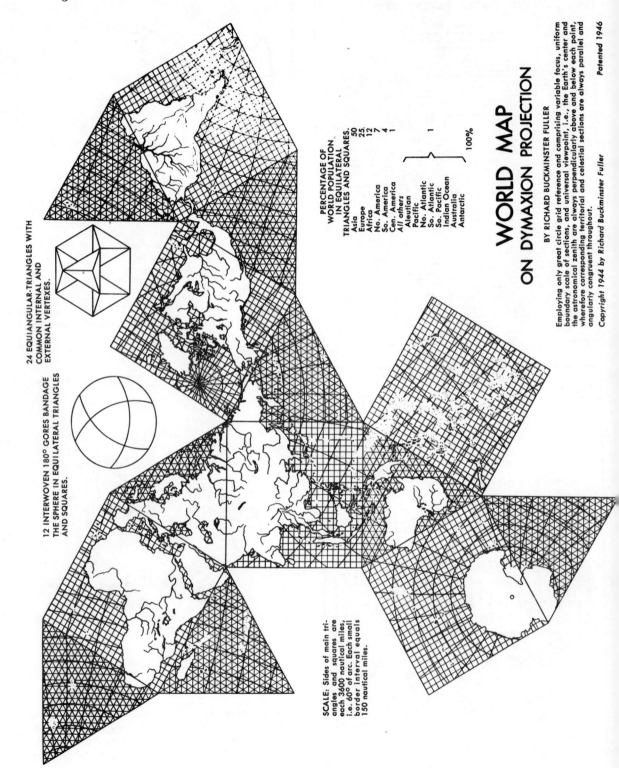

24 EQUIANGULAR-TRIANGLES WITH COMMON INTERNAL AND EXTERNAL VERTEXES.

12 INTERWOVEN 180° GORES BANDAGE THE SPHERE IN EQUILATERAL TRIANGLES AND SQUARES.

SCALE: Sides of main triangles and squares are each 3600 nautical miles, i.e. 60° of arc. Each small border interval equals 150 nautical miles.

PERCENTAGE OF
WORLD POPULATION,
IN EQUILATERAL
TRIANGLES AND SQUARES.

Asia	50
Europe	25.
Africa	12
No. America	7
So. America	4
Cen. America	1
All others	
Aleutian	
Pacific	
No. Atlantic	1
So. Atlantic	
So. Pacific	
Indian Ocean	
Australia	
Antarctic	
	100%

WORLD MAP
ON DYMAXION PROJECTION

BY RICHARD BUCKMINSTER FULLER

Employing only great circle grid reference and comprising variable focus, uniform boundary scale of sections, and universal viewpoint, i.e., the Earth's center and the astronomical zenith are always perpendicularly above and below each point, wherefore corresponding territorial and celestial sections are always parallel and angularly congruent throughout.

Patented 1946

Copyright 1944 by Richard Buckminster Fuller

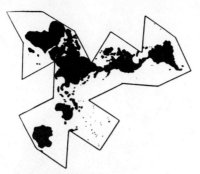

ONE CONTINENT
Bottom of the Areonautical Ocean

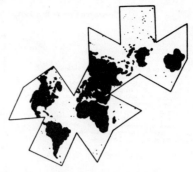

EAST BY STEAM TO THE ORIENT VIA SUEZ

ONE OCEAN
Admiral Mahan named it.
The British discovered and used it.

244–249 *Closeups of special sectional arrangements of the Air Ocean World Map.*

EAST BY SAIL—TO THE ORIENT VIA GOOD HOPE
From the Spanish Main via the Piratical Indian Waters.
12,000-mile great circle route from New York to Australia.

NORTHWARD TO THE ORIENT AND NORTHWARD TO EUROPE
Old and new worlds on either hand.
Russia overhead and McKinder's World Island trisected.

243 OPPOSITE PAGE: *the 1944 edition of Fuller's Air Ocean World Map which displayed for the first time on one surface all the world's geographical data without visible distortion of the relative shapes or sizes, and without any breaks in any continental contours. The pieces could be mounted together as a Vector Equilibrium, or assembled in a variety of ways, each emphasizing unique world geographic relationships.*

STRATOSPHERE STRATEGIC
European triangle controls the altitude merry-go-round.

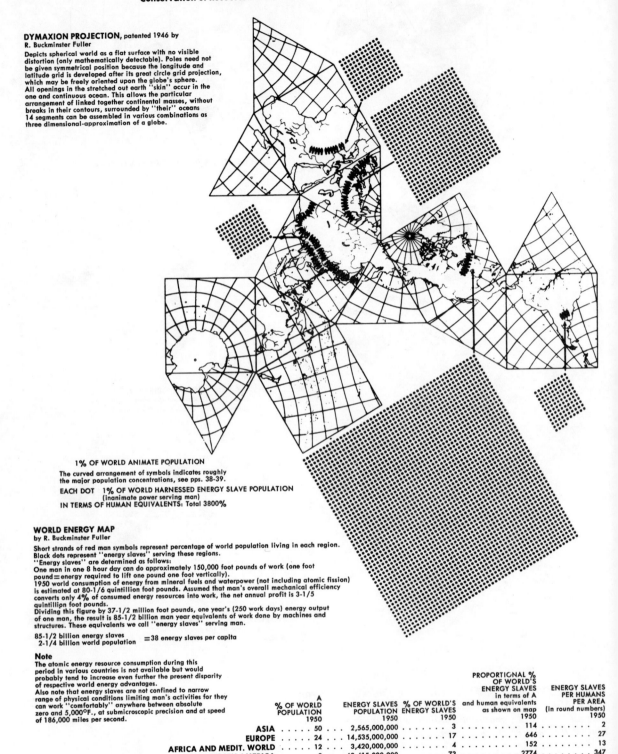

DYMAXION PROJECTION, patented 1946 by
R. Buckminster Fuller
Depicts spherical world as a flat surface with no visible
distortion (only mathematically detectable). Poles need not
be given symmetrical position because the longitude and
latitude grid is developed after its great circle grid projection,
which may be freely oriented upon the globe's sphere.
All openings in the stretched out earth "skin" occur in the
one and continuous ocean. This allows the particular
arrangement of linked together continental masses, without
breaks in their contours, surrounded by "their" oceans
14 segments can be assembled in various combinations as
three dimensional-approximation of a globe.

1% OF WORLD ANIMATE POPULATION
The curved arrangement of symbols indicates roughly
the major population concentrations, see pps. 38-39.
EACH DOT   1% OF WORLD HARNESSED ENERGY SLAVE POPULATION
(inanimate power serving man)
IN TERMS OF HUMAN EQUIVALENTS: Total 3800%

WORLD ENERGY MAP
by R. Buckminster Fuller
Short strands of red man symbols represent percentage of world population living in each region.
Black dots represent "energy slaves" serving these regions.
"Energy slaves" are determined as follows:
One man in one 8 hour day can do approximately 150,000 foot pounds of work (one foot
pound = energy required to lift one pound one foot vertically).
1950 world consumption of energy from mineral fuels and waterpower (not including atomic fission)
is estimated at 80-1/6 quintillion foot pounds. Assumed that man's overall mechanical efficiency
converts only 4% of consumed energy resources into work, the net annual profit is 3-1/5
quintillion foot pounds.
Dividing this figure by 37-1/2 million foot pounds, one year's (250 work days) energy output
of one man, the result is 85-1/2 billion man year equivalents of work done by machines and
structures. These equivalents we call "energy slaves" serving man.

85-1/2 billion energy slaves
2-1/4 billion world population   = 38 energy slaves per capita

Note
The atomic energy resource consumption during this
period in various countries is not available but would
probably tend to increase even further the present disparity
of respective world energy advantages.
Also note that energy slaves are not confined to narrow
range of physical conditions limiting man's activities for they
can work "comfortably" anywhere between absolute
zero and 5,000°F., at submicroscopic precision and at speed
of 186,000 miles per second.

	A % OF WORLD POPULATION 1950	ENERGY SLAVES POPULATION 1950	% OF WORLD'S ENERGY SLAVES 1950	PROPORTIONAL % OF WORLD'S ENERGY SLAVES in terms of A and human equivalents as shown on map 1950	ENERGY SLAVES PER HUMANS PER AREA (in round numbers) 1950
ASIA	50	2,565,000,000	3	114	2
EUROPE	24	14,535,000,000	17	646	27
AFRICA AND MEDIT. WORLD	12	3,420,000,000	4	152	13
NORTH AMERICA	8	62,415,000,000	73	2774	347
SOUTH AMERICA	4	2,565,000,000	3	114	28
CENTRAL AMERICA	1	0	0	0	0
ALL OTHERS	1	0	0	0	0
	100%	85,500,000,000	100%	3800%	

250   *The World Energy Map pictured on a Dymaxion Projection, first published by
Fortune, February, 1940. The man symbols represent the percentage of world population in each region. The black dots represent the percentage of "energy slaves" serving
the regions.*

NAME OF MAP PIECES	POPULATION 1940	POPULATION 1950	% OF WORLD POPULATION 1940	% OF WORLD POPULATION 1950	ENERGY SLAVES POPULATION 1940	ENERGY SLAVES POPULATION 1950	% OF WORLD'S ENERGY SLAVES 1940	% OF WORLD'S ENERGY SLAVES 1950	% OF WORLD'S ENERGY SLAVES In Terms of Human Equivalent As Shown On Map 1940	1950	SLAVES PER HUMANS PER AREA In Round Numbers 1940	1950
ASIA	1,062,500,000	1,125,000,000	50	50	2,211,000,000	2,565,000,000	6	3	102	114	2	2
EUROPE	531,250,000	540,000,000	25	24	8,475,500,000	14,535,000,000	23	17	391	646	16	27
AFRICA AND MEDIT. WORLD	255,000,000	270,000,000	12	12	2,579,500,000	3,420,000,000	7	4	119	152	10	13
NORTH AMERICA	148,750,000	180,000,000	7	8	22,110,000,000	62,415,000,000	60	73	1020	2774	148	347
SOUTH AMERICA	85,000,000	90,000,000	4	4	1,474,000,000	2,565,000,000	4	3	68	114	17	28
CENTRAL AMERICA	21,250,000	22,500,000	1	1	0	0	0	0	0	0	0	0
ALL OTHERS	21,250,000	22,500,000	1	1	0	0	0	0	0	0	0	0
	2,125,000,000	2,250,000,000	100%	100%	36,850,000,000	85,500,000,000	100%	100%	1700%	3800%		

251 *World Energy Chart.*

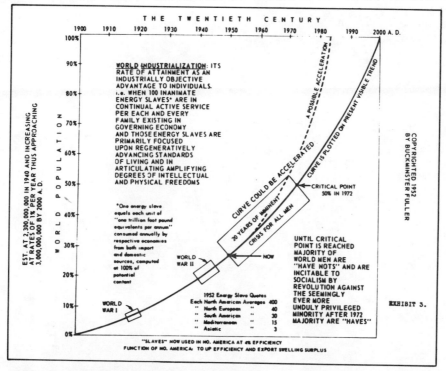

· **252** *Graph showing the rate of attainment of world industrialization to 1952 and the projected rate to the year 2000.*

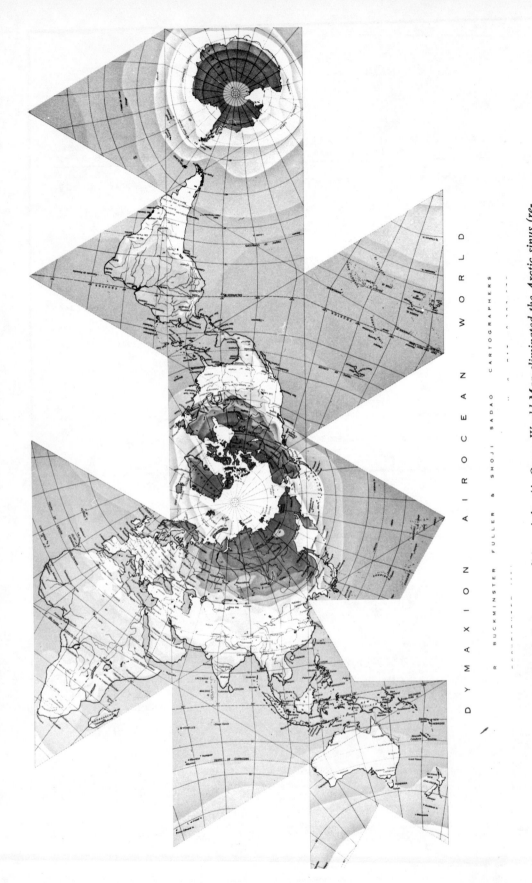

253 *Fuller's 1954 edition of the Air Ocean World Map eliminated the Arctic sinus (re-tained in the 1944 edition) and employed the icosahedronal triangular symmetry instead of that of the Vector Equilibrium.*

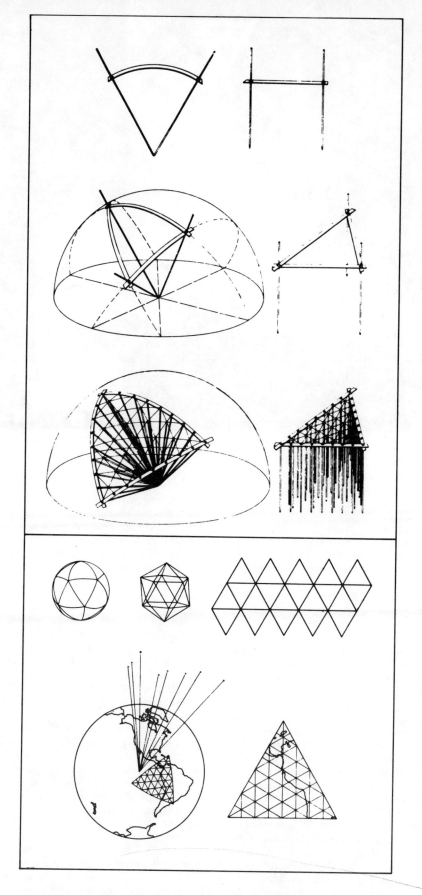

254–255 *Drawings showing method of Fuller's topological cartographic transformation from spherical to planar surfaces.*

256 *World arrangement of Dymaxion Map showing "World One — Water Ocean." The original caption read as follows:*

This is the fundamental pattern of inherently divided lands, and their respective peoples' energies, economics, mores, dreams and volitions. This pattern dominates all pre-World-War-One history. Water routes represented the shortest distances between the otherwise remote lands and peoples. Water routes represented the most economical lines of communication. Long distance communication consisted alone of written or face to face transmission — most swiftly completed by water.

The tonnage commerce of inorganic and organic world resources could only be accomplished in water borne vessels. Only token commerce and slow messages could be accomplished via the backs of men or animals traveling the long way — via the plains and mountains around the headwaters. The divided peoples thought and spoke of their own uniquely predominant oceans as constituting separate oceans — Atlantic, Pacific, Indian. The great one Waterocean world pattern was unseen by world people. It was and is, in fact, one ocean with one central island — Antarctica — clockwise around which ever races west-to-eastward the winds and waters. This gigantic merry-go-round — called the "roaring forties" (entered into at 40 degrees south latitude) — is now known as the southern hemisphere's jet stream area. Ships out of the Atlantic, Indian or Pacific Oceans were swiftly borne west-east by the merry-go-round to choose their re-entries into those oceans and their local lands. Whoever commanded the unsinkable ships (islands) commanding the mouths of the local bays, harbors,

estuaries, channels and passages, and commanded the islands and capes which governed entrance upon the merry-go-round — then they governed the world. It is only now discernible by world peoples that centuries ago the masters of the unsinkable British Isles had discovered, held secret and commanded until World War One this Waterocean World. With only the unpeopled Antarctica at their back, and holding fortified bases at the southern extremities off South America, South Africa and Austral-Asia, they came from the south upon the "soft bellies" of the essentially northern hemisphere dwelling people. Only one-quarter of the earth's surface is land; approximately 85% of the land and 85% of the people are situated north of the equator. The entire pattern of the world's cities and their positionings grew out of the commerce and communication flows of the Waterocean World. Because the key to World One's dominance lay in the water reaches invisibly remote from public sight and ken, the battles for its dominance were remote and often unknown to world peoples. Its masters were inherently invisible. The high priority technologies and resources were usurped by the invisible masters for their invisible struggles for Waterocean World dominance. This was a struggle not only of men against men, but also of men against the sea — its daily sea-quakes and avalanche-magnitude shock impacts, etc.

The glories of technology and wealth went to the sea and much of it eventually to the sea's bottom. The unwanted, inferior technologies and resources were left to "make do" with the inferior magnitude physical problems of the remotely pre-occupied struggling humanity upon their respective separate lands. The theoretical interlinkage of the peoples over the North

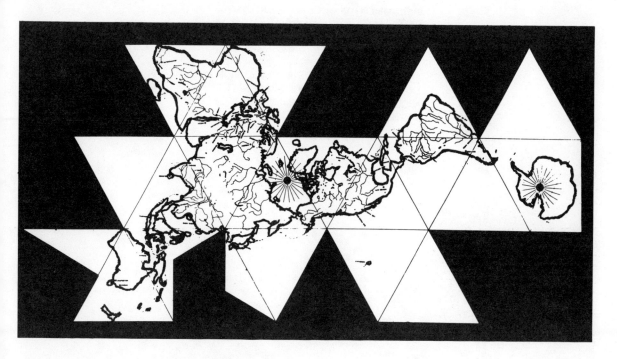

Pole was utterly hidden in that approximately infinite direction of impenetrability. In the polar "infinity" lay the seemingly inherent insurance of the success of the grand strategy of the one invisible ocean world and its secretly known, most favorable dynamic routings. R. Buckminster Fuller, June, 1956.

257 *Rearrangement of same Dymaxion Map showing "World Two — Air Ocean." The original caption read as follows:*

This is the fundamental pattern of inherently integrated lands and their respective peoples' energies, economics, mores, dreams and volitions. This pattern dominates all post-World-War-Two history. It centers about the North Pole, around which, counter-clockwise west-to-eastward, races the northern hemisphere's jet stream at 200 to 400 miles per hour. 88% of the world's people dwell in the Asia-Europe-Africa quadrangle on one side of the Pole. The remaining 12% dwell in the Americas on the other side of the Pole. Approximately all shortest routes between the people in North America to the 88% on the other side of the Pole lie over the Arctic. The Atlantic and Pacific Oceans on either side of North America are routes to nowhere. Shortest distance from North America to South America is over Central America and the West Indies — not over the Atlantic or Pacific.

Voice to ear communication between all peoples anywhere around the world is approximately 186,000 miles per second. In terms of mores, languages, politics, they are as yet months, years and generations apart. In the terms of human needs and longings for understanding, they are as one.

In the swiftly accelerating range and frequency of world peoples' comings and goings, the inherent barriers of mores, politics and languages will swiftly dwindle and disappear. All of the pattern of world affairs will become visible to all its people. Ambitions of individuals or of minorities to seize dominance of the Airocean World are inherently visible "spot news." Democratic mastery of the whole pattern by all the people is inherent and inevitable. The intellectual and technological integration accelerates the constant trend to serve more needs of more people with higher standards with ever more efficient investment of overall resources per given function. This process of doing more with less may be capsuled as "ephemeralization." The more ephemeralization advances the more flyable becomes any one cargo. The trend of the Airocean World is toward an entirely airborne technology. Cities and towns will tend to become Airocean bottom cloverleafs integrating highways and airways. The highways and airways will become a unitary world network. Sea and waterport cities will trend to diminishing cargo interchange significance and increasing recreational and abstract process significance.

SAILING SHIP

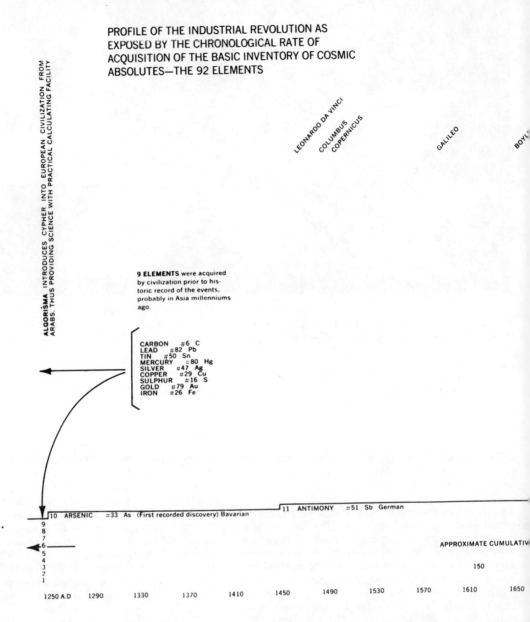

EARTH ORBIT IN MAN MADE ENVIRONMENT CONTROL:
PRODUCT OF SUCCESSFUL APPLICATION OF HIGH PERFORM-
ANCE PER UNIT OF INVESTED RESOURCES

PROFILE OF THE INDUSTRIAL REVOLUTION AS
EXPOSED BY THE CHRONOLOGICAL RATE OF
ACQUISITION OF THE BASIC INVENTORY OF COSMIC
ABSOLUTES—THE 92 ELEMENTS

LEONARDO DA VINCI
COLUMBUS
COPERNICUS
GALILEO
BOYL

ALGORISMA INTRODUCES CYPHER INTO EUROPEAN CIVILIZATION FROM
ARABS. THUS PROVIDING SCIENCE WITH PRACTICAL CALCULATING FACILITY

9 ELEMENTS were acquired
by civilization prior to historic record of the events,
probably in Asia millenniums
ago.

CARBON   #6 C
LEAD   #82 Pb
TIN   #50 Sn
MERCURY   #80 Hg
SILVER   #47 Ag
COPPER   #29 Cu
SULPHUR   #16 S
GOLD   #79 Au
IRON   #26 Fe

10 ARSENIC   #33 As (First recorded discovery) Bavarian   11 ANTIMONY   #51 Sb German

9
8
7
6
5
4
3
2
1

APPROXIMATE CUMULATIV

150

1250 A.D 1290 1330 1370 1410 1450 1490 1530 1570 1610 1650

258 *Dymaxion profile of Industrial Revolution, first presented by Fuller in 1943, at a
meeting of the Chalkley Thursday Science Luncheon Club, a group of leading U. S. and
English scientists who met weekly at the Cosmos Club, Washington, D.C., during World
War II. This is the curve of initial acceleration of pure science events. Fuller holds that
pure science paces applied science, applied science paces technology, technology paces
industry, industry paces economics, and economics paces the social, political, everyday
catch-up. Fuller maintains that this curve is reliable as a fundamental shape of world
history's evolutionary speed-up, because it consists of a controlled family or set of events.
It is the finite set of all isolations by man of all the "regenerative" chemical elements up
to and including uranium. The trans-uraniums are non-regenerative. All the regenerative
elements replace their pattern in nature:*

1690   1730   1770   1810   1850   1890   1930   1970   2010 A.D

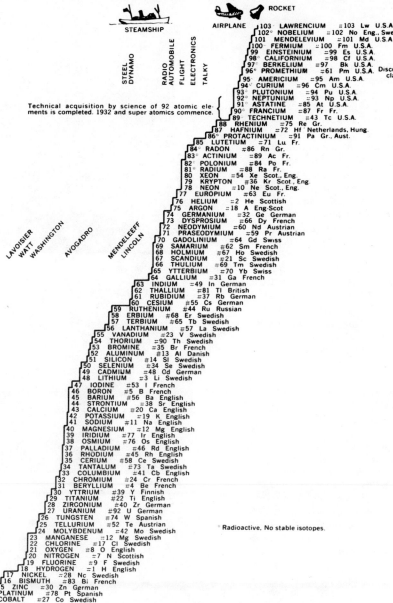

STEAMSHIP   AIRPLANE   ROCKET

STEEL DYNAMO
RADIO AUTOMOBILE FLIGHT ELECTRONICS TALKY

Technical acquisition by science of 92 atomic elements is completed. 1932 and super atomics commence.

LAVOISIER
WATT
WASHINGTON
AVOGADRO
MENDELEEFF
LINCOLN

103   LAWRENCIUM   =103 Lw U.S.A.
102° NOBELIUM   =102 No Eng., Swed., U.S.A.
101   MENDELEVIUM   =101 Md U.S.A.
100   FERMIUM   =100 Fm U.S.A.
99   EINSTEINIUM   =99 Es U.S.A.
98° CALIFORNIUM   =98 Cf U.S.A.
97° BERKELIUM   =97 Bk U.S.A.
96° PROMETHIUM   =61 Pm U.S.A.   Discovery disputed; claims to 1914
95   AMERICIUM   =95 Am U.S.A.
94° CURIUM   =96 Cm U.S.A.
93° PLUTONIUM   =94 Pu U.S.A.
92° NEPTUNIUM   =93 Np U.S.A.
91° ASTATINE   =85 At U.S.A.
90° FRANCIUM   =87 Fr Fr.
89° TECHNETIUM   =43 Tc U.S.A.
88   RHENIUM   =75 Re Gr.
87   HAFNIUM   =72 Hf Netherlands, Hung.
86° PROTACTINIUM   =91 Pa Gr., Aust.
85   LUTETIUM   =71 Lu Fr.
84° RADON   =86 Rn Gr.
83° ACTINIUM   =89 Ac Fr.
82° POLONIUM   =84 Po Fr.
81° RADIUM   =88 Ra Fr.
80   XEON   =54 Xe Scot., Eng.
79   KRYPTON   =36 Kr Scot., Eng.
78   NEON   =10 Ne Scot., Eng.
77   EUROPIUM   =63 Eu Fr.
76   HELIUM   =2 He Scottish
75   ARGON   =18 A Eng-Scot
74   GERMANIUM   =32 Ge German
73   DYSPROSIUM   =66 Dy French
72   NEODYMIUM   =60 Nd Austrian
71   PRASEODYMIUM   =59 Pr Austrian
70   GADOLINIUM   =64 Gd Swiss
69   SAMARIUM   =62 Sm French
68   HOLMIUM   =67 Ho Swedish
67   SCANDIUM   =21 Sc Swedish
66   THULIUM   =69 Tm Swedish
65   YTTERBIUM   =70 Yb Swiss
64   GALLIUM   =31 Ga French
63   INDIUM   =49 In German
62   THALLIUM   =81 Tl British
61   RUBIDIUM   =37 Rb German
60   CESIUM   =55 Cs German
59   RUTHENIUM   =44 Ru Russian
58   ERBIUM   =68 Er Swedish
57   TERBIUM   =65 Tb Swedish
56   LANTHANIUM   =57 La Swedish
55   VANADIUM   =23 V Swedish
54   THORIUM   =90 Th Swedish
53   BROMINE   =35 Br French
52   ALUMINUM   =13 Al Danish
51   SILICON   =14 Si Swedish
50   SELENIUM   =34 Se Swedish
49   CADMIUM   =48 Cd German
48   LITHIUM   =3 Li Swedish
47   IODINE   =53 I French
46   BORON   =5 B French
45   BARIUM   =56 Ba English
44   STRONTIUM   =38 Sr English
43   CALCIUM   =20 Ca English
42   POTASSIUM   =19 K English
41   SODIUM   =11 Na English
40   MAGNESIUM   =12 Mg English
39   IRIDIUM   =77 Ir English
38   OSMIUM   =76 Os English
37   PALLADIUM   =46 Rd English
36   RHODIUM   =45 Rh English
35   CERIUM   =58 Ce Swedish
34   TANTALUM   =73 Ta Swedish
33   COLUMBIUM   =41 Cb English
32   CHROMIUM   =24 Cr French
31   BERYLLIUM   =4 Be French
30   YTTRIUM   =39 Y Finnish
29   TITANIUM   =22 Ti English
28   ZIRCONIUM   =40 Zr German
27   URANIUM   =92 U German
26   TUNGSTEN   =74 W Spanish
25   TELLURIUM   =52 Te Austrian
24   MOLYBDENUM   =42 Mo Swedish
23   MANGANESE   =12 Mg Swedish
22   CHLORINE   =17 Cl Swedish
21   OXYGEN   =8 O English
20   NITROGEN   =7 N Scottish
19   FLUORINE   =9 F Swedish
18   HYDROGEN   =1 H English
17   NICKEL   =28 Nc Swedish
16   BISMUTH   =83 Bi French
15   ZINC   =30 Zn German
14   PLATINUM   =78 Pt Spanish
13   COBALT   =27 Co Swedish
► PHOSPHORUS   =15 P German

° Radioactive, No stable isotopes.

NOTE: NUMBER BEFORE NAME OF ELEMENT INDICATES ORDER OF DISCOVERY. NUMBER FOLLOWING NAME IS THE ATOMIC NUMBER. LETTERS FOLLOWING ATOMIC NUMBER ARE THEIR SYMBOLS. NATIONALITY LISTING IS THAT OF DISCOVERER.

TOTAL OF KEY INVENTIONS OF SCIENCE AND TECHNOLOGY

450   1,450 10,000

1690   1730   1770   1810   1850   1890   1930   1970   2010 A.D

"Unlike an open-ended set of scientific events selected for the individual excitement but having no inherent beginning or end whose chronological patterning has therefore no clearly readable significance, this set of the first regenerative 92 chemical elements which — as far as man knows — has been present in nature forever, and its arrangement chronologically by the dates of the respective isolations by man, represents a true, finite, complete set predicated upon the mathematical regularity of their electron-proton counts from 1 to 92. The visibly quickening chronologicality has therefore valid significance. This radially accelerated curve may have been caused by factors as yet undiscovered. But in itself, its consistent acceleration takes place without man's consciousness of its shaping."

259 *Ecological geometry of Man on Earth. The original caption read as follows:*

Shown here are the three most distinct pictures of the history of man's years on earth. Picture one may be called. "The first half million years were the hardest." Ignorant and isolated, man was unaware of other men and of the potentials of friendship, integrated resources, and mutual survival. The first picture is of a micro-bespeckled, enormous sphere, an arithmetical isolation, a physical impasse, escapable only through intellect, instrumented — through science.

Picture two shows man linking up resource and survival by lines of transport and communication. Wealth is generated astronomically. Standards go up. Health and life expectancy tend to double. But in 5000 years the velocity of integration and increased energy flow leads to an arterial cloggage and explosive high pressure. The two-dimensional picture is a neat linear equation, fulfilled — and again occurs an impasse escapable only by intellect.

Picture three shows the intellectual answer — a new volumetric and dynamic dimension — wireless, trackless, omnidirectional. It is a high-frequency interaction of time synchronized, relaying from resource to logically dispersed processing centers for physical separation, reintegration, and unimpeded direct flow to next function. It bypasses all constrictions, yet in every way facilitates man's range and frequency of voluntary assembly and separation in a continuity of ever higher standards of environment and process control. Picture three is a moving picture. Everywhere its physical facilities move with ever- increasing velocity and synchronized knowledge, allowing man to choose when and how and where he wishes to move. He specifically controls his own accelerations and decelerations. Picture three's scientific key is: to serve an ever-increasing number of functions of more people more of the time, with an ever-decreasing investment of energy, matter, and numbers of parts per unit of function, by ever greater intellectual re-investment of man's unique capital asset, "hours of time of his life."

Picture one is very long, as it was "against forces." Picture two is very short, as it was "transitional." Picture three will again be very long, as it is truly "natural." It synchronizes with the dynamic universe. The evolution of its "transport species" is multiplying. Here we go . . . but you need not hold your hat . . . it won't blow off. Buckminster Fuller, 1950.

500,000 BC–1850

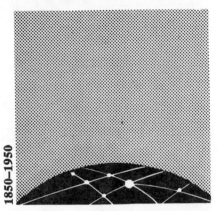

1850–1950

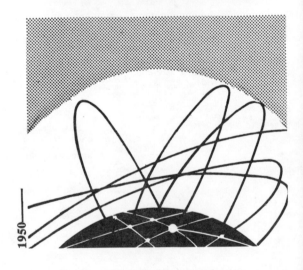

1950—

260 *Miniature Earth, 20 feet in diameter, installed by Fuller and Cornell University students on roof of university building in Ithaca, New York, May, 1952. The patterns of the continents were developed by bronze fly screen overlays. The North-South pole axis, when installed, paralleled the axis of the earth. When the observer sighted through the South Pole, the North Pole lay neatly on Polaris (in the actual sky). Ithaca was in zenith. The center of the Miniature Earth was only 4,000 miles from the center of the actual earth. The star nearest to the earth (the sun) is some 92,000,000 miles away. The displacement between the real earth's and the Miniature Earth's centers was observationally negligible. With the eye of observer at center of the Miniature Earth, the view through the dimly outlined continental screens, was not measurably different from the "view" from the center of the real earth through a transparent crust of the real earth. From this position, all the real stars in the heavens, seen by a Cornell Miniature Earth central observer, appeared in true zenith over points around the Miniature Earth, exactly as they appeared over points around the real earth. A star seen in zenith outward of London, England, Miniature Earth, was actually at zenith over the British Isles. The Cornell Miniature Earth was a psychologically effective planetarium. "From its center," Fuller said, "you began to see, and feel, the earth to be revolving in the presence of the stars, in contrast to the everyday mis-sensing of this phenomenon."*

Fuller, in 1955, developed, with University of Minnesota students, the mathematical calculations for a 400-foot-diameter Miniature Earth, to be mounted on Blackwell's Ledge, in New York City's East River. This project, if completed, would confront the United Nations' Building with a Miniature Earth so large that on it individual, proportionally scaled houses around the earth could be directly visible.

The industrial revolution's railroads and trucks were the beginning of the disappearance of the age-long dominance of the water borne traffic. Railroads and trucks represented shiploads "sailing" over a new Landocean. With man's penetration to the North Pole, discovery of wireless communication and invention of trackless, omni-directional, heavier-than-air air flights at the beginning of the Twentieth Century, the swift obsolescence of World One's Waterocean was certified. World War One and World War Two and their twenty-two-year interim represent the transitional period from a predominantly Waterocean World to an Airocean World.

All the pain of this fundamental historic transition is inherent in the momentum of ignorance of man in general concerning the inexorableness of the fundamental reorientation of his life experience. The operational principles of physical universe persist throughout man's approximately ignorant endurance of the transition. But as men learn more of the persistent verities and integrities of universe, they discover the fundamental necessity of reorientation of knowledge in respect to those verities.

Einstein's Relativity, born at Twentieth Century's opening, and its security in comprehended dynamic equilibrium becomes the newly acquired norm of the Airocean World, replacing the no longer tenable static norm of "at rest" and "death" and its invalidated securities of mass and inertia.

Lincoln's industrially catalyzed awareness that "right" had come to ascendency over "might" is of the essence despite all ignorantly detoured chaos of transition. There are no invisible masters of World Two. Visible masters are anathema in World Two. World Two is inherently governable only by the complementary integrities of initiative of the individuals of democracy. By R. Buckminster Fuller, June, 1956.

TENSEGRITY

261 *Fuller and his first 1927 Tensegrity structure, a mast and double wire-wheel system as seen through the keyhole of a Greenwich Village studio, 1929.*

262–263 *Fuller, with an experimental Tensegrity structure, Wichita, Kansas, 1944.*

264 *Fuller's first Tensegrity Mast, Black Mountain, North Carolina, 1949.*

265 *Fuller with Tensegrity Mast made by Kenneth Snelson, 1949.*

266 *Tensegrity Mast, North Carolina State College, 1950.*

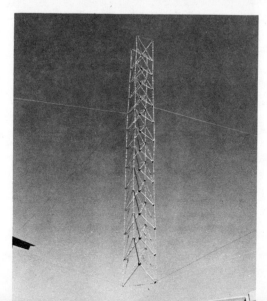

267 *University of Oregon Tensegrity Mast, 1953.*

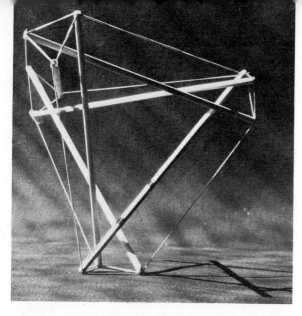

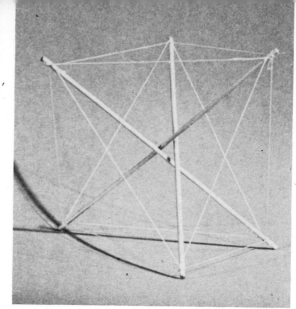

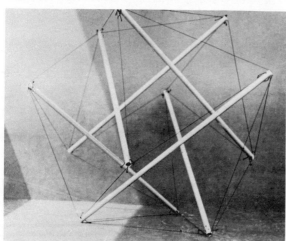

268   *Tensegrity tetrahedron, developed by Fuller's associate, Francesco della Sala, University of Michigan, 1952.*

269   *Tensegrity octahedron, developed by Fuller's associate, Ted Pope, Toronto, 1957.*

270   *Tensegrity icosahedron developed by Fuller, Black Mountain College, 1949.*

271   *Tensegrity Vector Equilibrium, developed by John Moelman, North Carolina State University, 1951.*

272   *Tensegrity tricontahedron (30-sided figure), developed by Lee Hogden, North Carolina State College, 1953.*

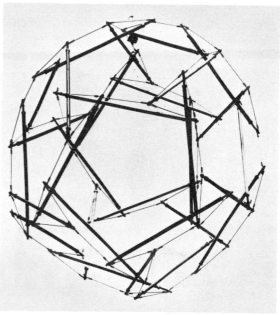

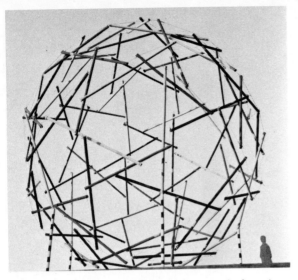

273 *Ninety-strut Tensegrity enenticontahedron (90-sided figure), Princeton University, 1953.*

274 *Forty-foot-diameter, 90-strut Tensegrity, Princeton, 1953.*

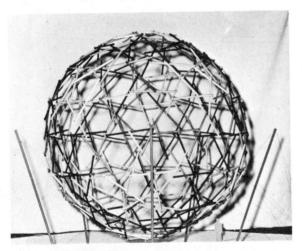

275 *Ekatonogdoicontahedron, 270-strut Tensegrity, University of Minnesota, 1953.*

276 *Forty-foot-diameter, 270-strut Tensegrity hemisphere, University of Minnesota, 1953.*

277 *Closeup of University of Minnesota, 40-foot-diameter Tensegrity, during assembly, showing the discontinuous compression, continuous tension nature of the structure. The struts were 9 feet long, 6 inches in diameter, weighing 6 pounds each, and were fabricated of polyester-fiberglass. Each strut was capable of supporting a 1-ton load when used as a column. If completed, the total weight of this 40-foot Tensegrity would be so small that the buoyancy developed in the hollow struts would be sufficient to float the structure in air. It would have the lift of a balloon despite the fact that the sphere itself was "full of holes."*

278 *Fuller with Tensegrity complex, at Southern Illinois University, 1958. In his right hand is a Tensegrity tetrahedron with interior tensional octahedron in which the struts lead between interior and exterior tensional system, providing a rigid truss.*

279 *University of Oregon students, 1959, with 270-strut Tensegrity, in which every component is identical. In this system, Fuller has broken through to spheroidal systems of* unitary *modular denominators in frequency magnitudes of infinite series. (Each of the earlier Tensegrity systems required components of several modular dimensions.)*

280 *Unitary component Tensegrity hemisphere of 75 S.T. aluminum alloy struts and Monel wires, Metropolitan Museum of Art, New York, 1959. Fuller has calculated the load factors in Tensegrity structures of up to 2 miles in diameter, and found such structures practical for present day aircraft industry fabrication. These hemispheres could be assembled in large segments on the ground, the segments then being flown into position by helicopter. A fleet of 16 of the large Sikorsky helicopters could fly all the pieces into position in a mile-high, 2-mile-wide dome, in three months. A dome of this size would cover New York City, east and west, from the East River to the Hudson, at 42nd Street, and north and south, from 62nd Street to 22nd Street — an area which includes all of the upper Manhattan skyscraper city of 1959. A dome of this kind would prevent snow and rain from falling on the protected area. Since all the New York Steam Company and Edison Company plants which supply this area are outside the circle, the dome would exclude the primary fumes which now pollute the area. Only electrically-powered motor vehicles would be permitted to operate under the dome; thus the fumes now generated by gasoline and diesel cars, trucks and buses would be eliminated.*

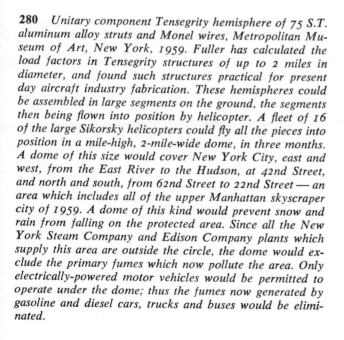

OCTET TRUSS

281   *A section of the aluminum dome over the Ford Rotunda building showing the triangular grid Octet Truss system. (1953)*

282 *Octahedron-tetrahedron ("Octet") truss consisting entirely of struts. No hubs are required. X-shaped terminals of struts unite in such a manner as to weave around the hub nuclei, forming the four planes of the Vector Equilibrium. The truss has phenomenal three-way "finite" strength. In conventional beam structure systems, the supporting units are parallel to one another; their ends are infinite (that is, do not curve back into the system), and therefore do not help one another. In Fuller's three-way-grid Octet Truss system, loads applied to any one point are distributed radially outward in six directions, and are immediately frustrated by the finite hexagonal circles entirely enclosing the six-way-distributed load. Each circle distributes the load 18 ways to the next circle, which "finitely" inhibits the radially distributed load. Thus the system joins together "synergetically" to distribute and inhibit the loads. The total loads are finally distributed three ways to the three point support. An Octet Truss, 100 feet long, 35 feet wide, and 4 feet deep, by Fuller, was exhibited by the Museum of Modern Art in September, 1959, along with one of his Geodesic Radomes, and a Tensegrity mast.*

283–285 *The Octet Truss can be fashioned from flat ribbons by spot welding or other high speed cohering processes.*

  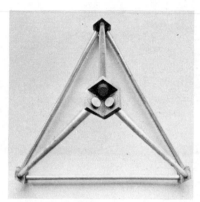

286–287 *The Octet Truss can be fashioned from hubs enploying the 12 faces of the rhombic dodecahedron. These two pictures show inside and outside of 12-way clevis cluster which holds the ends of struts.*

288 *The Octet Truss can be assembled of tubes and rhombic dodecahedron hubs having face-mounted studs to slip into and fasten to tubes.*

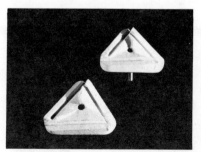 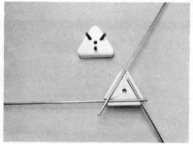 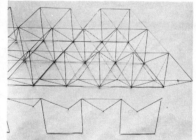

289–290 *The Octet Truss can be woven together with continuous rods and wires, seized together by male and female turbining hubs.*

291 *The Octet Truss can be woven continuously from wire-like fencing structures.*

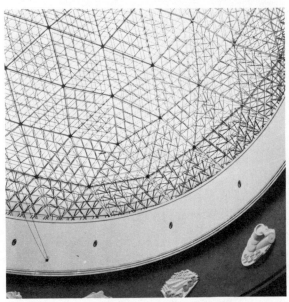

292–297 *Four-pound octahedra associated in Octet Truss complex were joined together to form the Ford Motor Company's 93-foot-diameter Rotunda dome, weighing a total of 8½ tons.*

MINOR INVENTIONS

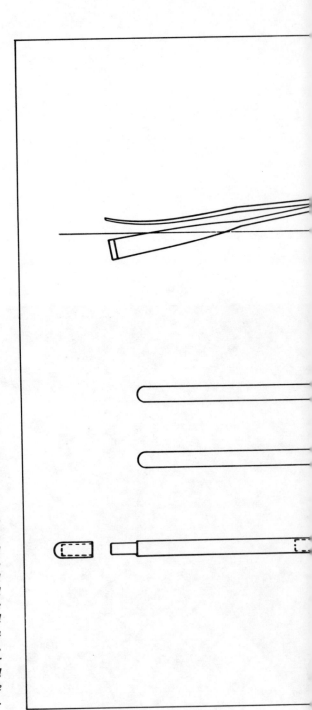

298 *Tubular catamaran rowing shell invented by Fuller in 1947. The shell's tubular bow and stern ends were demountable, as were the old-fashioned socket-assembled fishing rods. The craft's over-all length was 22 feet; when sectioned in three fractions, it could be readily mounted on a car top ski rack. The width could be adjusted for slimness and speed. Light plastic nacelle contained the seat slide and foot tie-downs. Capsized oarsmen tumbled from single shells, cannot re-board and bail out. The catamaran rowing shell, by contrast, provided parallel-bar stability; the rower could easily remount between the bars.*

DYMAXION
TUBULAR ROWING SHELL
OF AIRCRAFT ALUMINUM, STEEL, PLASTIC.
PORTABLE, SOCKET ASSEMBLY.
SWEAT PROPULSION

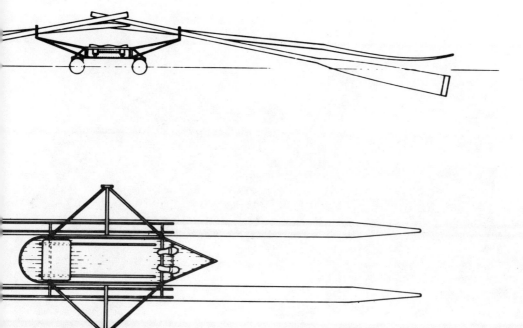

DIMENSIONS AND DISPLACEMENT
DIAMETER OF TUBES : 6".   O.A LENGTH : 22'-0"
PNEUMATIC VOLUME : 8 CU.FT. (@ 62.38 LBS-CU.FT.) · 500 LBS.
DISPLACEMENT AT WATERLINE (½ DIAM.) · 250
WEIGHT OF SHELL · 50 LBS
∴ SAFE WT. OARS & MAN · 200 LBS.

PATENT APPLIED FOR

299 *Fuller installed an overhead-trolleyed, tensionally supported telephone in Wichita when war restrictions permitted only one telephone for an entire project. Fuller's Wichita associates, Herman Wolf and Cynthia Lacey, are shown passing the phone.*

300 *Criss-cross, tensionally supported tables employed by Fuller in the Beech Aircraft Dymaxion Dwelling Machine project, Wichita, Kansas, 1944–45. These tables were first demonstrated by Fuller in the 1928 4D house.*

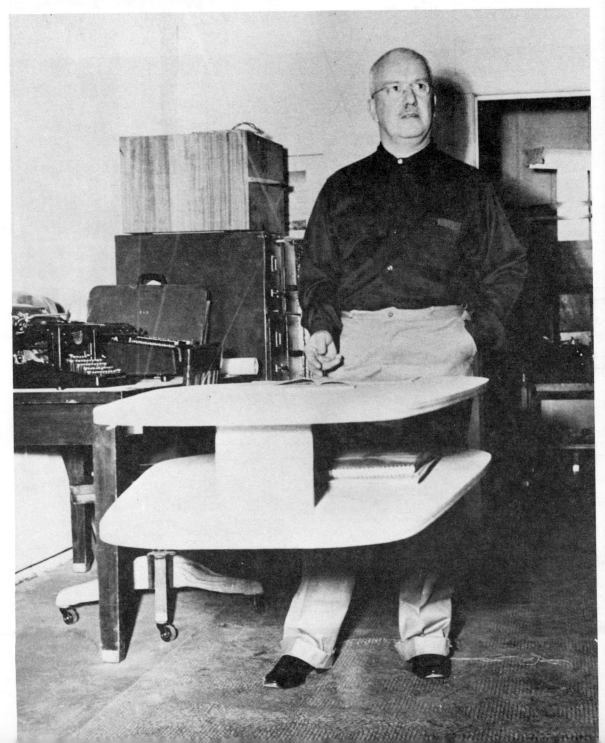

S I D E

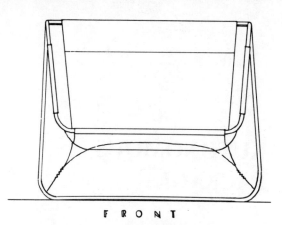

F R O N T

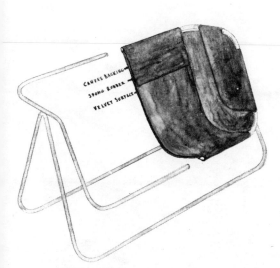

CANVAS BACKING
STRONG RUBBER
VELVET SURFACE

S E C T I O N A L   V I E W

"LOVE SEAT" CHROME STEEL TUBING
WATERPROOFED VELVET

R BUCKMINSTER FULLER DESIGNER

SCALE 1" = 1'-0"   12·30·31   M.L.

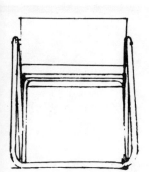

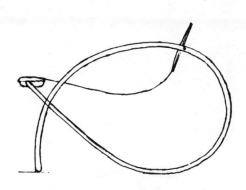

301·302 *Love seat and spring seat designed by Fuller in 1931. Both are tensionally seated.*

AUTONOMOUS PACKAGE

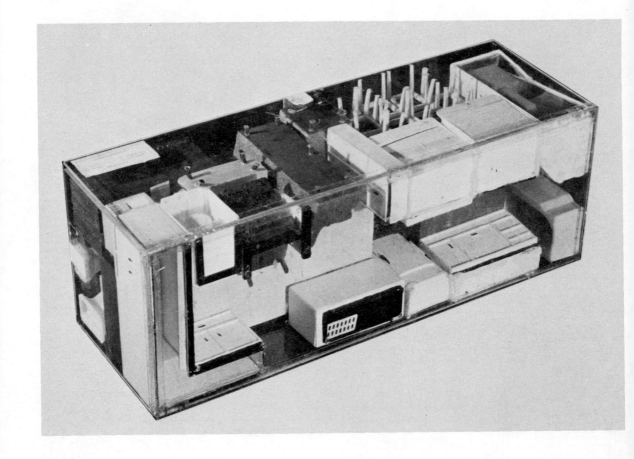

303–307 *Model of 25-foot long, 8-foot high, 8-foot wide, legally-permitted road trailer package, developed by Fuller's students at Chicago's old Dearborn Street Institute of Design in 1948. The unit was formed by six panels which were hinge-mounted together. Each of the four 8 × 25 foot panels, and each of the two 8 × 8 foot panels functioned as a chassis for furniture and utilities. Various items were to be attached as they progressed down the line. A complete inventory of furniture and household apparatus for a family of six, including luxury accessories, could be so grouped and fastened to the six panels that when the panels were hinged out in a T-shaped pattern, they provided the facilities of a bedroom, living room, kitchen, and two baths, with all utilities mani-folded and electrically harnessed together, ready for use. The total working and living area was 928 square feet of floor space. U. S. guaranteed mortgage standards permit first class five-room dwelling loans to 1000 square foot units. The students found an*

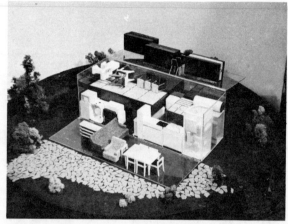

arrangement of these temporarily fastened components on the panels which would permit the panels to be hinged together to form the trailer box package. The items that jutted out from any one panel were positioned to register with spaces in the other panels. This rigid alignment of shipped components — called "jig shipping" — had been developed for the motor deliveries of delicate aircraft parts in World War II. The "Autonomous Package" experiment was not significant in its superficial results. However, it proved that mass assembly and delivery of complete household high standard equipment was possible and economically feasible. Consequences of such mass fabrication, purchase, assembly, and distribution would reduce radically the over-all costs and weights of individual shipping containers. It was found that a family of six could have all the sanitary, metabolic, hobby, and self-development facilities on chattel mortgage terms, for a total of $1500. The same package, with items separately acquired, would cost $18,000.

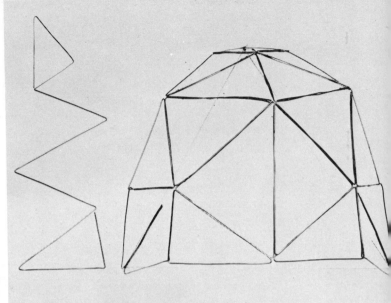

GEODESIC INVENTION AND DEVELOPMENT

308 *Unit of wire shown at left joins with identical components to form a triangulated finite convexity.*

309–310 *Fuller taught Chicago Institute of Design students, 1948, to make 31-great-circle structures of prefabricated triangles, pentagons and hexagons, using struts, hubs, and cables for pan, separate skin and strut components.*

311 *In July, 1948, Fuller, with Black Mountain College students, assembled a 48-foot-diameter hemispheric dome, of 31 great circles, the model of which is shown here. Fuller constructed the dome from 2-inch wide Venetian blind ribbon. He intentionally designed this structure so that its delicate system gently collapsed as it neared completion. He then fortified the individual chords of the triangular system with prismatically arranged additions of two more Venetian blind strips. Gradually the structure reassumed its domical configuration. The purpose of the demonstration was to show students — and through them the public — that so-called "failure" of structures is not necessarily hazardous. The conventional strategy is to overbuild structures to make them safe, using materials so heavy that failures would bring fatalities; consequently the critical limit capabilities of complex structures are never known. Instead, Fuller here arranged to bring structure up to critical capability by the gradual addition of discrete increments. The result was that the safe structure of the 48-foot dome was accomplished with one-hundredth of the weight of material customarily employed.*

312–316 *Thirty-one-great-circle necklace structure of tubular beads and continuous internal cable net, folds up in tight package and unfolds to be tightened finally at its equator into hemispheric dome. The latter is shown in Pentagon Garden, Washington, D.C., February, 1949.*

317–318 *Same necklace structure erected at Black Mountain College, North Carolina, 1949, demonstrated great strength. When covered with double heat-sealed, pneumatic, transparent skin, the structure maintained, in the sun, an interior temperature 10% below that of the outside air.*

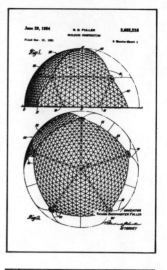

319–325 *Fuller's basic Geodesic dome patent.*

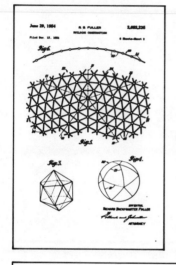

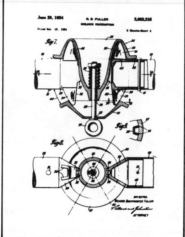

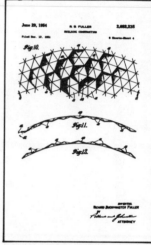

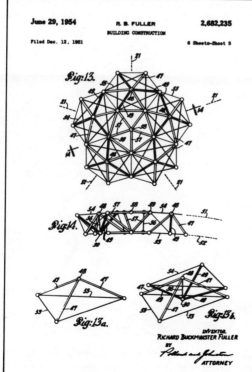

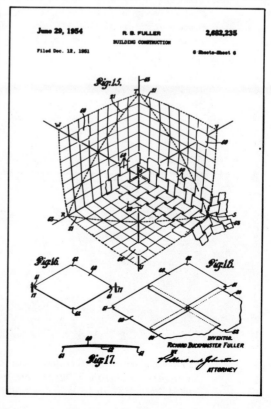

326–328 *First large-size (50 feet in diameter) tube and skin structure, erected by the Fuller Research Foundation, Canadian Division, directed and calculated by Fuller's former Institute of Design students, Jeffrey Lindsay and Don Richter, aided by Ted Pope, in Montreal, December, 1950.*

329 *Two-frequency Geodesic for Arctic Institute, which went to Baffin's Land in Labrador in 1951, shows hyperbolic parabola (positive-negative curvature) of outwardly tensed "Hypercat" skins which inhibit all flutter.*

330 *Three-quarter-sphere, 16-frequency, welded steel wire Geodesic, 20 feet in diameter, by Fuller and Don Richter, Lawrence, Long Island, 1951.*

331 *First wood strut Geodesic, by Zane Yost, Massachusetts Institute of Technology, 1951.*

332 *First wood and plastic Geodesic, by Jeffrey Lindsay, Montreal, 1951.*

333 *Model of Geodesic-covered, automated cotton mill with Octet Truss floors, by Fuller and students, North Carolina State College, 1951.*

334 *Fuller's University of Minnesota students produced 36-foot Geodesic and assembled it in an hour and a half, at Aspen, Colorado, 1952.*

335 *Close-up of University of Minnesota dome, Aspen, Colorado.*

336 *University of Minnesota Geodesic, covered with plastic skin, Aspen, Colorado, June, 1953.*

337–339 *University of Minnesota Geodesic, trailered to Woods Hole, Massachusetts, and assembled, July, 1953.*

340 *Fifty-five-foot, wood and Mylar, hyperbolic parabola Geodesic restaurant owned by architect Gunnar Peterson, Woods Hole, Massachusetts, 1953–54. (This picture is also shown on facing page of chapter on Geodesic Structures.)*

341 *Thirty-six-foot, wood and Mylar hemisphere, University of Oregon, March, 1953. It was fabricated by 40 students working three shifts for eight days. This was the first structure to be covered by Mylar.*

342–343 *Thirty-six-foot, transparent Geodesic "Growth House," fabricated by North Carolina State architecture and agricultural science students, 1953. The double-skin dome slid upwardly from its foundation to increase base ventilation through screened accordion opening 18 inches in height.*

344 *University of Michigan, Architectural Department Geodesic dome, 1954.*

345 *Washington University, St. Louis, Architectural Department Geodesic, 1954.*

346–347 *"Dynamic Dome," designed in a 1954 University of Michigan research and development project, as a centrifuge umbrella to admit air while warding off rain.*

348 *Virginia Polytechnic Institute, Architectural Department research project for U. S. Marine Corps, 1954.*

349 *Laminated wood strut, polyester Fiberglass skin dome, 85 feet in diameter, built by Jeffrey Lindsay to be used as a barn, Montreal, 1954.*

350–351 *Magnesium, five-eights-sphere Geodesic, 42 feet in diameter, erected to cover a naturally-heated swimming pool, Aspen, Colorado, 1954.*

352 *Model of 167-foot Geodesic for Southern Illinois University, 1955.*

353 *U. S. Air Force Academy's acoustically-skinned, aluminum, planetarium dome, test-erected at Geodesic "dome farm," Raleigh, North Carolina, before delivery to Academy's Colorado Springs site, 1957. This Spitz Planetarium Company's dome and its Flint, Michigan, counterpart were prototypes for planetariums later produced by the Spitz Company. Specifications for the prototypes required 1/32-inch tolerance between the horizontal and vertical radii dimensions when domes were assembled because of the delicate astronomical instrument functions to be served by these planetariums.*

354 *Giraffe crane speeded erection of 114-foot Geodesic pavilion at Winthrop Rockefeller's Winrock estate, Hot Springs, Arkansas, 1956.*

355 *One-hundred-foot Geodesic pavilion was built for the mid-continent jubilee, St. Louis, Missouri, on the old fair grounds on the Mississippi River, 1956. This dome now covers the skating rink at Detroit's Northland Shopping Center.*

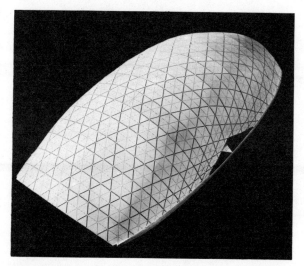

356 *Model of ovaloid Geodesic hockey rink enclosure proposed for Andover Academy, Andover, Massachusetts, 1955.*

357 *Geodesic "Playdome," which went into mass production in 1957, supports group of Harvard students.*

SKYBREAK DWELLINGS

358–363 *Studies by Fuller and students of the "Skybreak Dwelling" potentials of Fuller's domes. With complete grounds enclosed by a dome, eliminating rain, wind, snow and insects, houses themselves can be eliminated. Families can dwell in secondary pavilions within their gardens. The first picture shown here is an exterior view of a model developed for the U. S. Air Force in 1949. The second shows the interior of the same "dwelling." The third is of a model constructed at Black Mountain College, North Carolina, in 1949. The fourth shows a model made by Fuller's students at the Massachusetts Institute of Technology for the Museum of Modern Art where it was shown in 1952. The last two studies were developed by M.I.T. students in Fuller's 1952 research project. The drawings are by John Rauma.*

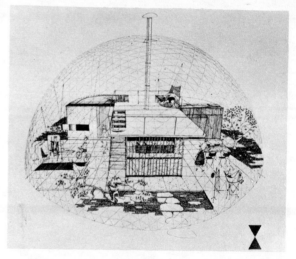

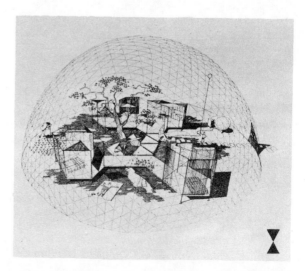

FORD DOME

364 *The famous Ford River Rouge plant. Shown at right foreground is the Rotunda building before the dome was constructed. In 1952, young Henry Ford wanted to dome over the Rotunda court — in respect for his grandfather's wish — as a major feature of the company's fiftieth anniversary in June, 1953. After he had been convinced by engineers that conventional domes were unobtainable within the limited time, and that such domes could not be supported by the lightly-built Rotunda building, Ford resorted to a Geodesic dome. Fuller designed, produced, tested, and installed the structure in four months using Ford Company facilities.*

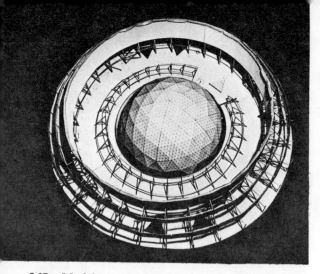

365 *Model of assembly operation on Rotunda roof.*

366 *Fuller with model of the dome and its octa-hedral components.*

367 *Model of Ford Rotunda dome in polarized plastic, by University of Michigan students, disclosing the strain patterns of the structure.*

368 *Dome was assembled from the top down as a rotating, hydrauli-cally-elevated umbrella. The workmen stood on a wide bridge installed above the Rotunda court.*

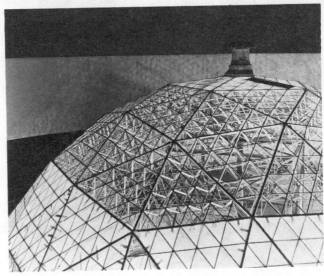

369　*Workmen on the bridge, assembling components.*

370　*Ford Rotunda completed in April, 1953, two days before deadline.*

371　*View from beneath the completed dome, after installation of polyester Fiberglass. Two workmen can be seen climbing the structure. Note many concentric rings of the finite tension-inhibiting pattern, characteristic of the Octet Geodesic structure.*

372　*Life magazine's 180-degree wide-angle lens looks upwardly at Ford Rotunda dome, under which the Ford Motor Company held its first and subsequent stockholder meetings. Ford Motor Company officials were as enthusiastic about the dome after its completion as they had been "gravely and most visibly skeptical before." This first industrial use of Fuller's on-the-shelf capabilities initiated the fast growing acceptance of Geodesic domes by government and industry. By 1959, approximately 1,000 domes had been built.*

373 *Foldable components of Cornell 20-foot Geo-*
desic sphere, 1952.

SEEDPOD FOLDABLE GEODESICS

374 *Foldable Geodesic, University of Michigan,*
Architectural Department, 1953.

375 *Foldable Geodesic, Oberlin College, 1953.*

376–379 *Foldable Geodesic "Flying Seedpod" project, Washington University, St. Louis, Missouri, 1954–55. Magnesium ball-jointed tripods, ball-jointed at their feet, were tensionally opened by piston-elevated masts, driven by 200-pound gas pressure in cylinders located at each vertex of the structure. As the wing-flyable bundle stood upright, a pulling lanyard permitted the 42-foot dome to open and erect itself in 45 seconds. This experiment initiated Fuller's subsequent development of air-droppable and rocketable, remotely installable, controlled environments.*

380–383 *Tensegrity marriage of tripod components eliminates the need for ball joints; permits parallel bundling of total components of large Geodesic structures suitable for moon installations.*

384 *Parallel foldable Geodesic sphere, installed in the Metropolitan Museum of Art, New York, summer of 1959.*

385 *Fifty-five-foot, pneumatic, quilted double-skin Geodesic dome, developed and manufactured by Berger Brothers, New Haven, Connecticut, for the U. S. Air Force. A smaller unit by Berger Brothers floated on an ice island to the North Pole as a well insulated personnel shelter.*

386 *A man climbing on the pneumatically firm skin of the Air Force structure. The pressured air is held only within the skin structure, and not inside the dome which opens to the outside through regular doors and windows.*

U.S. MARINE GEODESICS CORPS

387–388   *Fuller witnesses Marine Corps helilift of his 30-foot, wood and plastic Geodesic, at Orphan's Hill, North Carolina, February 1, 1954. Marines flew dome at 50 knots without yaw, and returned to original spot without damage. This event inaugurated the Marine Corps' rigorous investigation and eventual adoption of Geodesic structures.*

389–390   *Three-helicopter magnesium hangar is being evacuated and lifted by its own helicopter.*

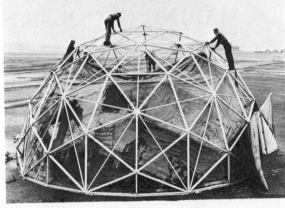

391–393 *A year of daily test assembly of Geodesic domes demonstrated that the structures could be assembled by green crews of Marines in an average of 135 minutes.*

394 *At the last assembly of the year, the dome is anchored firmly to the ground. Two 3,000 h.p. driven propellors of an anchored airplane provided day-long slam loads on the dome of 120 m.p.h. winds. The dome never fluttered.*

395 *Components for standard Marine Corps personnel and hangar structures, manufactured by Magnesium Products of Milwaukee.*

396–400 *Geodesic shown first
on carrier's flight deck,
where helicopter lifts and
flies it away at 60 knots to
effect beachhead maintenance
cover for aircraft.*

401–403 *U. S. Marine Corps encampment, at National Air Show, Philadelphia, Labor Day, 1956, demonstrated mock beachhead landing under simulated atomic bombing conditions. Twin helilift brought Geodesics in ahead of Marines, who came by helicopter from aircraft carrier* Ticonderoga, *moored in the Delaware River.*

404 *Clean-up model of Marine Corps Geodesic personnel shelter.*

405 *One of five Marine Corps Geodesic units, installed at Wilkes Land, Antarctica, in U. S. Geophysical Year base.*

RADOMES

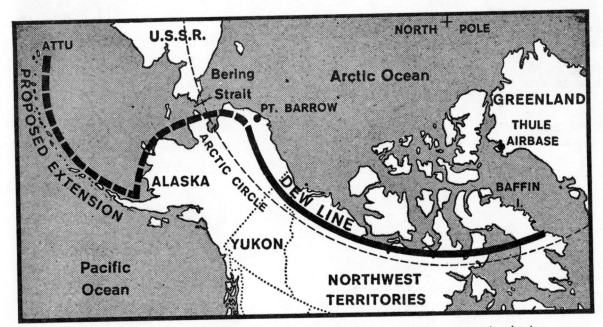

406 *Schematic map of the DEW line, the Defense Early Warning system of radar installations comprising America's first line of defense against surprise attack. Geodesic domes of polyester Fiberglass enclose the radar equipment of the entire system.*

407 *First test segment of polyester Fiberglass Geodesic, furnished by Fuller on request of Lincoln Laboratory, U. S. Air Force DEW line development organization. After two years' testing, sample encouraged physicists to believe Geodesics might successfully replace inadequately performing pneumatic enclosures.*

408 *First Geodesic radome, 30 feet in diameter, furnished by Fuller's Geodesic company, withstood 182 m.p.h. wind, and refused to ice up in 2-year top-of-Mt.-Washington test.*

409 *Intermediary phase of hex-pent, 31-foot Geodesic dome, is lifted to top of Lincoln Laboratories.*

410 *Basic diamond component of Geodesic pan-type polyester Fiberglass radome.*

411–413 *Fully assembled 55-foot radome, ready for final testing which ended in its selection for the production unit.*

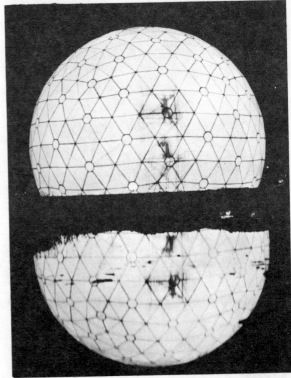

414 *First production model radome to be delivered. It was installed at the Bell Laboratories, Whippany, New Jersey, 1956.*

415 *Geodesic radome installed at DEW line station by Western Electric, prime contractor for the DEW line.*

416 *Model of parabolic mirrored Sky Eye Geodesic sphere produced in response to U. S. government inquiry preliminary to the development of a radio telescope, 600 feet in diameter.*

PAPERBOARD DOMES

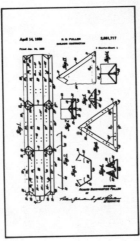
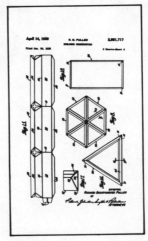
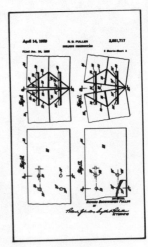

417–420 *Fuller's paperboard Geodesic dome patent.*

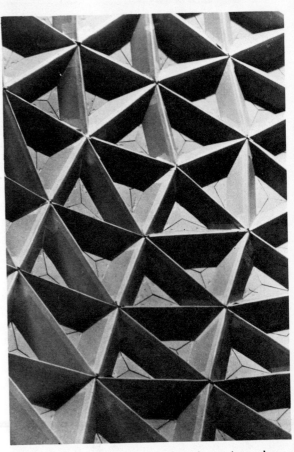

421 *Interior of first paperboard, 30-foot dome, installed by Fuller and students, Yale University Architectural School, 1951.*

422 *Paperboard, foldable, diamond honeycomb Geodesic dome, 1952.*

423 *Paperboard Geodesic dome, coated with polyester resin, Tulane University, 1954.*

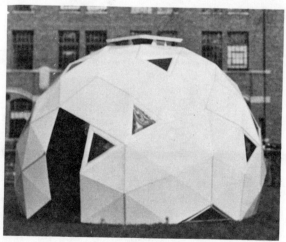

424 *Polyester-resin paperboard Geodesic dome, North Carolina State College, 1954.*

425 *Three-quarter sphere, polyester-resin paperboard Geodesic dome, 14 feet in diameter, developed for U. S. Marine Corps, by University of Michigan students, 1954.*

426–430 *Printed, scored, and cut blanks for 42-foot, double-skin, paperboard Geodesic dome for U. S. Marine Corps and Triennale of Milan, being assembled at Quantico, Virginia, Marine Corps Base, August, 1954.*

431–433 *Forty-two-foot, paperboard Geodesic installed in old Sforza garden, in Milan, where Leonardo da Vinci once worked. The two Geodesic paperboard domes of 1954 (one of which was furnished as a bachelor's apartment) won the Gran Premio of the 1954 Triennale.*

434 *Aluminum-clad paperboard dome erected by architectural students of McGill University with materials donated by Aluminium Company, Ltd., successfully endured Canadian winter, 1957.*

PLYDOMES

435–436 *Two-frequency Geodesic plydomes, Des Moines, Iowa, 1957.*

437 *All the printed and punched ¼-inch Plywood components for a 42-foot dome arrive at site.*

438–439 *Forty-two-foot Plydome is erected.*

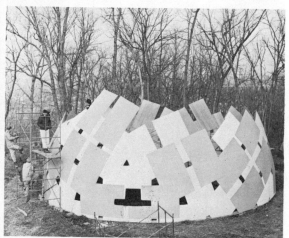

440 *Fuller and associates on top of ¼-inch Plywood dome which has no internal frame. Flat sheets that permit five independent axes of bending, together constitute a spherical system when the necessary mathematics have been computed and the indicated join holes punched into boards.*

441–442 *Geodesic farm shelter, Michigan State University, 1957. The second picture shows it housing a tractor.*

443 *"Pine Cone" 42-foot Plydome Geodesic, installed by Fuller and Cornell University students, Ithaca, 1957.*

444 *Involute Plydome, by T. C. Howard, Synergetics, Inc., 1957.*

445 *Shingled watershed Geodesic Plydome garage; Iowa, 1957.*

446 *Forty-two-foot shingled Geodesic Plydome barn on Iowa farm, 1957.*

447 *Geodesic Plydome chapel of Columbian Fathers adopted by them for leper colonies in the Philippines, Korea, and South Pacific Islands. The chapel has colored plastic windows.*

448–449 *Southern California children show enthusiasm for Plydome "Play-domes."*

WORLD-AROUND
STRUCTURES

450 *Geodesic dome to serve as bachelor officers' quarters, U. S. Air Force, Korea, 1955.*

451–454 *U. S. 100-foot Geodesic pavilion assembled by Afghans, under direction of one American engineer in 48 hours for the Trade Fair at Kabul, Afghanistan, in August, 1956. The Afghans regarded Fuller's Geodesic as a modern Mongolian yurt; consequently a native Afghan type of architecture.*

455–456 *U. S. Geodesic pavilion, installed at Bangkok, Thailand, winter, 1956–1957.*

457–458 *U. S. Geodesic pavilion, first installed at Kabul, was airflown to successive sites; it is shown here at the World Trade Fair in Tokyo, 1957.*

459 *U. S. 114-foot Geodesic pavilion at the 1958 Trade Fair in Poznan, Poland. This was the first trade fair behind the Iron Curtain.*

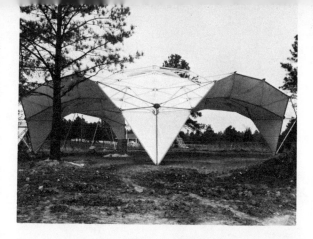

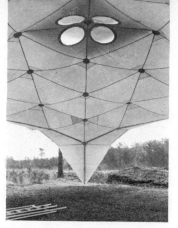

460–461 *Involute-evolute parabolic Geodesic, shown at Geodesic "Dome Farm," Raleigh, North Carolina, prior to installation at Casablanca, Tunisia, and New Delhi.*

462 *Geodesic pavilion of the U. S. Department of Commerce won the Gran Premio at the Triennale in Milan. 1957.*

463 *Corrugated aluminum, 18-foot Geodesic dome, constructed by Fuller and students at University of Natal, at Durban, assisted by architectural students from the University of Capetown, South Africa, May, 1958. It was designed for the Zulus, whose cattle were eating them out of thatching grass required for their woven Indhlus. The corrugated aluminum "Indhlu" (as the dome is called by the Zulus), with plastic windows and Masonite polyethylene floor, complete with anchors, was produced at a materials cost of only $150.*

464 *Inside 100-foot Geodesic pavilion, manufactured and erected in Bombay, India, by the Calico Company, Indian licensees of Fuller, as a theatre for exhibiting textiles. The Calico Company has since erected a larger Geodesic display pavilion in New Delhi which is scheduled to be moved around the world.*

KAISER GEODESICS

465–468 *Kaiser 145-foot Geodesic dome, manufactured in Oakland, California, and erected in 22 hours, in Honolulu, Hawaii, February, 1957. At the 22nd hour, the Hawaiian Symphony Orchestra and audience entered; the concert was completed within 24 hours of Honolulu landing of the dome's components. The orchestra conductor pronounced the acoustics "the best in his experience."*

469–470 *Kaiser 145-foot Geodesic municipal auditorium, Virginia Beach, Virginia, 1957.*

471 *Kaiser 145-foot Geodesic municipal auditorium, Borger, Texas, 1957.*

472–475 *Kaiser 145-foot Geodesic erected over a progressively inflated doughnut balloon, 1958. This structure is used as a grainery-filling equipment-manufacturing plant in Abilene, Kansas.*

476–477 *Casa Mañana Kaiser 145-foot Geodesic theatre-in-the-round, Fort Worth, Texas, 1958.*

478–479 *Kaiser 145-foot Geodesic serves as Citizens State Bank, Oklahoma City, Oklahoma, 1958. Architects: Bailey, Bozalis, Dickenson, and Roloff.*

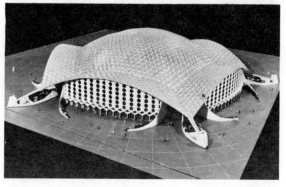

480 *Kaiser 200-foot Geodesic, erected as the U. S. main pavilion at the American exchange exhibit in Moscow, 1959.*

481 *Kaiser 407-foot Geodesic sports palace planned for erection in Oklahoma.*

UNION TANK CAR COMPANY GEODESICS

482–483 *Exterior and interior of all-steel Union Tank Car Company's Geodesic dome, 384 feet in diameter and 116 feet high. It was opened in Baton Rouge, Louisiana, October, 1958, as car rebuilding plant. At that time it was the largest clear-span enclosure ever built anywhere.*

484 *Union Tank Car Company's second Geodesic, 354 feet in diameter, marketed by their Graver Tank Division, as the "Union Dome," under erection by pneumatic cushion lift, at Wood River, Illinois, winter, 1958–59.*

AMERICAN SOCIETY FOR METALS STRUCTURE

485 *Hex-pent, wire-wheel truss, double dome, 250 feet in diameter, erected by the North American Aviation Company over the building and grounds of the new national headquarters of the American Society for Metals, Cleveland, Ohio, spring, 1959. John Kelly: architect. Engineering design: Fuller's Synergetics, Inc.*

LARGE-SCALE PLANS

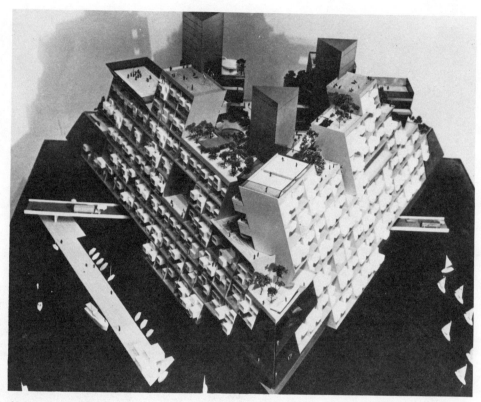

486 *Over 80% of metropolitan areas with a population of one million or more are situated near bodies of water which are sufficient to accommodate floating cities. Most have a depth of water adequate for shipping (25–30 feet) and relatively sheltered harbors. At these depths a maximum average height of twenty stories can be floated.*

With the sea as a highway an entire unit can be built in another location, such as a shipyard or drydock, and then towed to its site in one piece. Thus the economies of shop fabrication can be brought to bear on construction problems which are traditionally soluble only at the final site location.

Triton City provides discrete neighborhood platforms up to four acres in area to house as many as 5,000 people. Its framework superstructure makes possible the flexible distribution of infilling components, such as apartments, classrooms, stores, and offices, with the prefabrication of elements providing assembly-line economies. Additionally, it will be possible to replace outmoded units or rearrange them without disturbing the overall disposition of the city. A whole neighborhood can be treated functionally as a single building with all utilities centrally provided.

Because the megastructure constitutes a neighborhood entity, some new departures in aesthetics and safety can be realized. All parking is within the flotation, so that one major contemporary eyesore, the parking lot, is removed from view. Since wheeled vehicles are not permitted above the entrance level, the streets would be safe for pedestrians. Elevators and stairs in vertical towers, would have glazed sides, so that everyone inside is visible at all times.

Triton City is designed to offer the best of two worlds: the dynamic quality of life in a milieu of urban high density and the view of immediately adjacent open space which is traditionally the province of suburban and rural areas. Since the community is intended as a city complement, it would have all the existing urban amenities, including entertainment, educational, and cultural activities to draw upon as well.

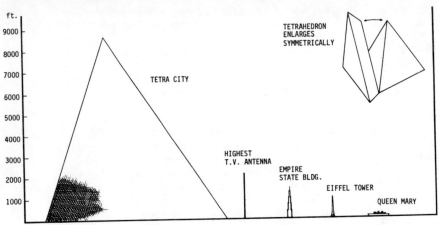

ft.

9000

8000

7000   TETRA CITY

6000

5000

4000

3000   HIGHEST
                     T.V. ANTENNA

2000   EMPIRE
                         STATE BLDG.   EIFFEL TOWER

1000   QUEEN MARY

TETRAHEDRON
ENLARGES
SYMMETRICALLY

487 *We find that a tetrahedronal city, to house a million people, is both technologically and economically feasible. Such a vertical-tetrahedronal-city can be constructed with all of its three hundred thousand families each having balconied "outside" apartments of two thousand square feet floor space. All of the machinery necessary to its operation will be housed inside the tetrahedron. It is found that such a one million passenger tetrahedronal city is so structurally efficient, and therefore so relatively light, that together with its hollow box sectioned reinforced concrete foundations it can float. Such tetrahedronal floating cities would measure two miles to an edge, and can be floated in a triangularly patterned canal. This will make the whole structure earthquake-proof. The whole city can be floated out into the ocean to any point and anchored. The depth of its foundations will go below the turbulence level of the seas so that the floating tetrahedronal island will be, in effect, a floating triangular atoll. Its two mile long "boat" foundations will constitute landing strips for jet airplanes. Its interior two mile harbor will provide refuge for the largest and smallest ocean vessels. The total stuctural and mechanical materials involved in production of a number of such cities are within feasibility magnitude of the already operating metals manufacturing capabilities of any one company of the several major industrial nations around the earth. The tetrahedron city may start with a thousand occupants and grow symmetrically to hold millions without changing overall shape though always providing each family with 200 sq. ft. of floor space. Withdrawal of materials from obsolete buildings on the land will permit the production of enough of these floating cities to support frequently spaced floating cities of various sizes around the oceans of the earth. This will permit mid-ocean cargo transferring and therewith an extraordinary increase of efficiency of the inter-distribution of the world's raw and finished products as well as of the passenger traffic. Three quarters of the earth is covered by water. Man is clearly intent on penetrating those world-around ocean waters in every way to work both their ocean bottoms and their marine life and chemistry resources. Such ocean passage shortening* habitats *of ever transient humanity will permit his individual flying sailing, economic stepping stone travel around the whole Earth in many directions.*

488   BIG GEODESIC DOME OVER MID-MANHATTAN

The way the consumption curves are going in many of our big cities it is clear that we are running out of energy. Therefore it is important for our government to know if there are better ways of enclosing space in terms of material, time, and energy. If there are better ways society needs to know them.

Domed cities can be illuminated by daylight without direct sunlight. That part of the dome through which the sun does not shine directly would be transparent. In summer the dome would be protected by polarized glass; during the sunny hours it would not. hold heat but in winter the sun would penetrate all the dome. The atmosphere will be dust-free.

Controlling the environment through domes offers the enormous advantages of the extraversion of privacy and the introversion of the community.

489   *A one hundred foot diameter geodesic sphere weighing three tons encloses seven tons of air. The air to structural weight ratio is 2/1. When we double the size so that geodesic sphere is 200 feet in diameter the weight of the structure goes up to 7 tons while the weight of the air goes up to 56 tons — the air to structure ratio changes to 8/1. When we double the size again to a 400 feet geodesic sphere — the size of several geodesic domes now operating — the weight of the air inside goes to about 500 tons while the weight of the structure goes up to 15 tons. Air weight to structure weight ratio is now 33/1. When we get to a geodesic sphere one-half mile in diameter, the weight of the air enclosed is so great that the weight of the structure itself becomes of relatively negligible magnitude for the ratio is 1,000/1. When the sun shines on an open frame aluminum geodesic sphere of one-half mile diameter the sun penetrating through the frame and reflected from the concave far side, bounces back into the sphere and gradually heats the interior atmosphere to a mild degree. When the interior temperature of the sphere rises only one degree Fahrenheit, the weight of air pushed out of the sphere is greater than the weight of the spherical frame geodesic structure. This means that the total weight of the interior air, plus the weight of the structure, is much less than the surrounding atmosphere. This means that the total assemblage, of the geodesic sphere and its contained air, will have to float outwardly, into the sky, being displaced by the heavy atmosphere around it. When a great bank of mist lies in a valley in the morning and the sun shines upon it, the sun heats the air inside the bank of mist. The heated air expands and therefore pushes some of itself outside the mist bank. The total assembly of the mist bank weighs less than the atmosphere surrounding it and the mist bank floats aloft into the sky. Thus are clouds manufactured. As geodesic spheres get larger than one-half mile in diameter they become floatable cloud structures. If their surfaces were draped with outwardly hung polyethelene curtains to retard the rate at which air would come back in at night, the sphere and its internal atmosphere would continue to be so light as to remain aloft. Such sky-floating geodesic spheres may be designed to float at preferred altitudes of thousands of feet. The weight of human beings added to such prefabricated "cloud nines" would be relatively negligible. Many thousands of passengers could be housed aboard one mile diameter and larger cloud structures. The passengers could come and go from cloud to cloud, or cloud to ground, as the clouds float around the earth or are anchored to mountain tops. While the building of such floating clouds is several decades hence, we may foresee that along with the floating tetrahedronal cities, air-deliverable skyscrapers, submarine islands, sub-dry surface dwellings, domed-over cities, flyable dwelling machines, rentable, autonomous-living, black boxes, that man may be able to converge and deploy around earth without its depletion.*

INDEX

INDEX

Material in the text section of this volume
is indexed by page number in standard type;
*material in the illustrated sections of this
volume is indexed by illustration number in
italic type.*

ILLUSTRATION CREDITS

The illustrations in this book are from the files of Mr. Fuller and are reproduced with his kind permission. Known credits are listed below. Numbers given are picture numbers.

American Studio, *143*
Architectural Forum, *146, 168, 174*
Baird, Bil, *238*
Beechcraft Photo, *189-192, 208*
Casazza, Donald, G., *269*
Defense Department (Marine Corps), *391*
Freemesser, B. L., *279*
Hoffman, Bernard (Courtesy of *Architectural Forum*), *76, 83, 84*
Interiors (Copyright: 1954, Whitney Publications, Inc.), *433*
International News Photos, Inc., *131*
Jacoby's Photo Service, *481*
Kaufmann & Fabry, *139, 141*
Kravitt, Samuel, *80*
Lewis, Taylor B., Haycox Photoramic, Inc., *469*
Lincoln, F. S., *19, 98-104, 130*
Linney, Arthur H., *117, 120, 122*
Little, *272*
Long Island Press (Courtesy of *Art News*), *232*
McCormick Armstrong Co., *187*
Miller, Wayne F., *230*
Molitor, Joseph W., *266*
Morse, Ralph (Courtesy of *Life,* Copyright: 1955, Time, Inc.), *235*
Namuth, Hans, *280*
Scherschel, Frank (Courtesy of *Life,* Copyright: 1953, Time, Inc.), *295*
Stoy, Werner, Camera Hawaii, *467*
Taylor, Ed, *358*
Weissmann, Ernest (Courtesy of *Architectural Forum*), *164, 169, 170*